NO LONGER AN
AMERICAN LAKE?

RESEARCH SERIES/NUMBER 73

NO LONGER AN AMERICAN LAKE?

Alliance Problems in the South Pacific

JOHN RAVENHILL, Editor

INSTITUTE
OF INTERNATIONAL
STUDIES
University of California, Berkeley

Library of Congress Cataloging-in-Publication Data

No longer an American lake?

(Research series / Institute of International Studies,
University of California, ISSN 0068-6093 ; no. 73)
   Includes index.
   1. Pacific Area—National security. 2. United States—
Military policy. 3. Soviet Union—Military policy.
4. France—Military policy. 5. Australia—Military
policy. 6. New Zealand—Military policy.
I. Ravenhill, John. II. Series: Research series
(University of California, Berkeley. Institute of
International Studies) ; no. 73.
UA875.N6   1989   355′.330182′3   89-7612
ISBN 0-87725-173-8

Printed in the United States of America

CONTENTS

ACKNOWLEDGMENTS

Carl Rosberg, Director of the Institute of International Studies, suggested that a symposium on this theme be prepared for publication after several of the chapters had been presented at the 1987 conference of the International Studies Association in Washington, D.C. Those chapters have since been extensively revised, and others have been added. All have benefitted from the comments of four referees. My thanks to Paul Gilchrist and Bojana Ristich, who have greatly improved the manuscript through their expert and conscientious editing. My thanks also to John Iremonger for his help in arranging co-publication with Allen & Unwin Australia.

As this will be one of the last of the Institute's publications before Carl Rosberg retires as Director, I would like to add a personal note of thanks for all the help he has given me over the years. I am sure that this feeling is shared by hundreds of graduate students and faculty members alike, for whom his door has always been open.

J. R.

Sydney, Australia
April 1989

NOTES ON CONTRIBUTORS

JOHN RAVENHILL is Associate Professor of Government at the University of Sydney.

HENRY S. ALBINSKI is Professor of Political Science and Director, Australia–New Zealand Studies Center, Pennsylvania State University.

ROBERT ALDRICH is Senior Lecturer in Economic History at the University of Sydney.

GRAEME GILL is Associate Professor of Government at the University of Sydney.

RICHARD HIGGOTT is Associate Professor of Politics at Murdoch University and Director, Australian Institute of International Affairs.

ANDREW MACK is Director of the Peace Research Centre, Australian National University.

MICHAEL McKINLEY is Lecturer in Political Science at the Australian National University.

Chapter 1

POLITICAL TURBULENCE IN THE SOUTH PACIFIC

John Ravenhill

> Quite recently the Pentagon regarded the Pacific Ocean as
> a kind of American lake. Now the American nuclear fleet
> is being impeded by none other than one of Washington's
> allies in the ANZUS militarist bloc.*

With the defeat of Japan in 1945, the Pacific Ocean became an
American lake. U.S. dominance was unchallenged. Neither the Soviet
Union nor war-torn China was capable of projecting power into the
Pacific, and European colonial powers were in retreat. Australia and
New Zealand looked to the United States for a guarantee of their
defense—a relationship formalized with the signing of the ANZUS pact
in 1951.

For three-and-a-half decades, ANZUS was the least controversial of
the alliances the United States constructed following World War II. The
benign neglect that the United States was able to accord ANZUS testified
to the success of the partnership with Australia and New Zealand.
ANZUS became the framework for a large number of arrangements
(primarily bilateral) in the defense field, and served as shorthand for the
totality of relations between the three partners. Australia and New
Zealand, governed for most of the postwar period by conservative parties, were not just dependent but also dependable allies who fought
alongside Americans in both Korea and Vietnam.

The refusal by the newly elected Labour government in New
Zealand in 1984 to accept visits by nuclear-armed or nuclear-powered
ships, and the subsequent U.S. suspension of its security obligations
toward New Zealand under the ANZUS alliance, dramatically ruptured

*Moscow Domestic Service, 5 February 1985; quoted in Dibb (1985: 75).

1

this harmonious relationship. In recent years the benefits of the alliance with the United States have increasingly been called into question in Australia. While the security partnership with the United States continues to be valued by the major political parties and the general public, unease at growing American protectionism and dumping of agricultural products has turned into anger. Groups that have traditionally supported the alliance enthusiastically have demanded that the continued presence of U.S. communications facilities in Australia be linked to greater regard for Australia's economic interests in the formulation of U.S. foreign economic policies.

From the U.S. standpoint, the actions of the New Zealand government have been the most obvious manifestation of growing political turbulence in the South Pacific. Elsewhere in the region, several island states have experienced increasing political instability, most vividly illustrated by the military coups which occurred in Fiji in 1987—the first in the South Pacific. Several factors have contributed to the growth of political turbulence in the island states: the replacement of the independence generation by younger leaders less sympathetic to the West, the growth of ethnic conflict (Papua New Guinea) and racial strife (Fiji, New Caledonia), economic frustrations and increasing population pressure on limited supplies of land, and increased intrusion of external actors (the Soviet Union, Indonesia, and Libya) into the region.

Resentment at the slow pace of decolonization in New Caledonia and at French nuclear testing in Mururoa continues to generate anti-French feeling, and the failure of Washington to criticize French policies has caused this resentment to spill over into a general condemnation of the West in some island states. Short-sighted policies by the United States in fishing disputes have opened the way for the Soviet Union to establish a regional toehold by signing fishing agreements with Kiribati and Vanuatu. Perceptions that Australia and New Zealand have acted paternalistically toward the island states have prompted new assertions of independence, which in some countries have taken the form of support for the Non-Aligned Movement.

In short, the political environment of the South Pacific has changed such that the United States can no longer afford to take the fealty of the region for granted. In this book we shall examine the principal changes that are occurring in the economic, political, and strategic realms in the South Pacific region and assess their significance for U.S. interests and their implications for management of the ANZUS alliance.

ANZUS: A CHANGING BALANCE SHEET

The United States was initially a reluctant partner in ANZUS. The treaty had its origins in the search by the Australian government for a new protector after Britain's inability to defend its former colony was exposed in World War II. Australia's concerns were twofold: fear of renewed Japanese militarism should a "soft" peace be negotiated, and growing apprehension about the "Communist threat" from Soviet and/or Chinese expansionism. Although the Australian government initially hoped for an alliance that would link North America, South Asia, and the South Pacific, it was willing to abandon this broad proposal to secure its principal objective: an American guarantee for Australian security. New Zealand, more remote from Asia and thus less concerned about immediate external threats, was less enthusiastic about a trilateral arrangement with Australia and the United States. Wellington proposed a defense agreement which would include Canada, and was reluctant to exclude the United Kingdom from any defense pact.

Of the three future partners, Washington was the most reluctant to negotiate a formal alliance. As early as 1937, President Roosevelt had rebuffed a proposal from the Imperial Conference for a Pacific pact. In the early postwar years, several Australian proposals for defense relationships (essentially involving the United States in underwriting Australian security) were rejected. Secretary of State Acheson in 1949 specifically ruled out a security pact with Australia as a quid pro quo for Australian acceptance of a peace treaty with Japan, and in a National Press Club speech in January 1950 defined the U.S. defense perimeter in the Pacific in a way that excluded not only South Korea but also New Zealand and Australia (Millar 1978: 205).

Two factors contributed to a change of heart in Washington. The first was the extraordinary determination of the Australian Minister for External Affairs, Percy Spender, to negotiate an alliance, despite the lukewarm support of Prime Minister Robert Menzies, who continued to look primarily to Britain for defense cooperation (Barclay 1985: ch. 2).* But Spender's efforts most likely would have come to nought had it not been for the second factor: the outbreak of the Korean War. Australia and New Zealand were quick to dispatch forces in support of the American

---

*Menzies had suggested that, in attempting to construct an alliance with the United States, Spender was "trying to build a castle on a foundation of jelly" (quoted in Bell 1988: 45).

effort, and their reward was the negotiation of the ANZUS pact in February 1951.

The agreement was not, however, the fully elaborated military alliance that Spender had hoped for. In particular, unlike Article 5 of the 1949 North Atlantic Treaty, which specifies that an armed attack on one or more of the parties shall be considered an attack against them all, Article IV of the ANZUS pact states merely that "Each Party recognizes that an armed attack in the Pacific Area on any of the Parties would be dangerous to its own peace and safety and declares that it would act to meet the common danger in accordance with its constitutional processes." Despite the assertions of Secretary of State Dulles that the qualified language was necessary in order to secure Congressional support for the pact, and that it did not render the prospects for U.S. support in the event of conflict any less certain, there were complaints in Australia and New Zealand that they had been given a second-class treaty. One commentator, pointing to Article IV, posed this rhetorical question at the time of the treaty's signing: "Is this not an open proclamation to the world that America regards the Pacific as of secondary importance, and that she is reluctant to commit herself to extreme measures there?" (Sissons 1952: 23).

Perceptions that ANZUS was a second-class treaty were reinforced by the absence (in contrast to the NATO treaty) of provisions for standing forces. Nor were there to be American troops stationed in Australia or New Zealand to act as a tripwire. Dulles specifically reassured Congress that there would be no question of sending U.S. troops to defend Australia or New Zealand. Exactly what sort of support these countries could expect from the United States in the event of armed conflict in the region is a matter that has exercised their governments throughout the life of the treaty.

A strong case can be made that the United States has received most of the tangible benefits from the ANZUS pact. Certainly that is the perception of many commentators, of the current New Zealand prime minister, and of contemporary public opinion in Australia and New Zealand (Millar 1983: 157; Lange 1985: 1014).* ANZUS has imposed few

---

*Public opinion in Australia increasingly perceives the United States to be the main beneficiary of ANZUS: 45 percent of respondents in an October 1986 poll believed this to be the case; 31 percent thought Australia and the United States benefited equally; 18 percent perceived Australia to be the primary beneficiary. This represents a dramatic change from October 1982, when respondents were divided almost equally between perceiving Australia as the principal beneficiary (31 percent) and seeing both Australia and the United States as gaining equally (32 percent); in this poll only 25 percent thought the United States benefited most (USIA 1986: 16).

costs on the United States. American forces have not been called upon to defend Australia or New Zealand. Neither country has received economic or military aid from the United States, but Australia has been one of the most important customers for U.S. military equipment.* The consultation called for by Article III of the pact has at best been perfunctory, suggesting that Australia and New Zealand have not been treated as true allies; certainly they have never been invited to participate in U.S. military planning.† Washington's failure to provide information to its partners has sometimes seriously embarrassed them. Thus the failure to alert Canberra to pending changes in U.S. policies toward Vietnam and toward recognition of the People's Republic of China humiliated conservative governments in Australia that were ardently defending the old line.** Finally, alliance commitments have not prevented American governments from discriminating against primary product exports from Australia and New Zealand.

In contrast, the United States has received significant benefits from the treaty and its associated arrangements. Australia and New Zealand have served as effective intermediaries for the United States in the South Pacific, and their forces made modest but significant contributions (in both political and military terms) in support of U.S. troops in Korea and Vietnam. Both Australia and New Zealand have provided staging facilities for U.S. aircraft and naval vessels, but probably the most important contribution the alliance has made to U.S. security in recent years has

*In the 1960s Australia was the third largest market for U.S. arms sales (Pemberton 1987: 331).

†Opposition from the U.S. Joint Chiefs of Staff to Australian proposals for joint military planning was a principal factor in the Pentagon's reluctance to agree to an ANZUS pact, and led to a watering down of the original draft of the treaty's Article VIII, which had proposed that the ANZUS Council should "co-ordinate its planning so far as possible with that of other regional organisations and associations of States of which one or more of the Parties are members." The Australian government had hoped that a formal pact with the United States would afford it access to NATO military planning (*ibid.*, p. 27).

**From the perspective of the junior partners, consultation procedures appeared not to have improved by the early 1980s. A confidential report prepared by the General Accounting Office for Senator John Glenn in mid-1981 noted that "Australian officials were less than satisfied with the current 'consultations' or notifications, since policies which often have an impact on their country were made with minimal Australian input." ANZUS Council meetings (the report continued), although "designed to develop unified courses of action and policy direction . . . often result in explanations of unilaterally determined foreign policies" (*Sydney Morning Herald*, 27 May 1987).

been through Australia's hosting of command, control, communications, and intelligence (C^3I) installations (the "joint facilities").*

Desmond Ball (1980) estimates that there are more U.S. installations in Australia than in any other country save the United Kingdom, Canada, West Germany, and Japan. Three of these (discussed by Mack in ch. 6 below) are of critical importance: the two U.S. defense satellite ground stations at Pine Gap and Nurrungar, and the U.S. naval communications station at North West Cape. Pine Gap monitors information from satellites that is crucial for the verification of arms control agreements. This function can be performed effectively only if the facility is sited in the unique geographical setting that Australia offers. Nurrungar is a ground station for Defence Support Program satellites that provide early warning of ballistic-missile attacks. North West Cape is an important link in the communications network for U.S. nuclear submarines. Location of these facilities in Australia gives the United States a considerable advantage over the Soviet Union and China, which do not have access to ground stations at an equivalent latitude.

For Australia and New Zealand, the benefits from the ANZUS alliance have been less evident. Conservative governments in office in the two countries through most of the 1950s and 1960s were preoccupied with a perceived Communist threat, and they placed a high value on ANZUS as an ultimate guarantee of their security. This view was expressed by Australian Prime Minister Gorton in 1969 when he asserted that ANZUS was "perhaps the strongest guarantee of Australia's future security against physical attack" (quoted in Barclay 1976: 459)—a sentiment echoed as late as 1978 by New Zealand's *Defence Review*. Anxious to ensure a continued U.S. presence in the region, Australia and New Zealand offered port facilities to the U.S. fleet and encouraged U.S. involvement in Vietnam. They were able to free ride on the U.S. military presence and thereby avoid increases in defense expenditures that would otherwise have been necessary.

Attempts to induce the United States to spell out exactly what is included in the security guarantee (most recently by former Australian Foreign Minister Hayden at the 1983 ANZUS Council meetings) have consistently been rebuffed. The vagueness of the security guarantee—inevitable, given the separation of powers in the U.S. government—has enabled critics to assert that the guarantee is of little value since the United States will always place its global interests before those of its

*For detailed consideration of the intelligence links between the three partners, see Richelson and Ball (1985).

ANZUS partners. U.S. assistance, therefore, cannot be counted upon in the event of armed conflict within the region—especially if it involves another ally of the United States or a country that it considers to have strategic significance. Here critics point to the possibility of conflict between Australia and Indonesia, the country in the region that most worries Australia's strategic planners. To support their argument, they note that on the two occasions in which Australia sought U.S. assistance under ANZUS—both involving Indonesia—Washington refused to make a public commitment that it would honor its ANZUS obligations for fear of offending the Djakarta government.*

Therefore, critics assert, ANZUS guarantees the security of Australia and New Zealand only in circumstances—a threat from a major Communist power—where the United States would provide assistance anyway, whether or not an alliance existed.[†] There is some validity to this argument, but it overlooks the probability that the alliance partners could count on various other types of assistance from the United States, short of the commitment of troops, in the event of regional conflict—as Britain was able to do in the Falklands/Malvinas dispute with Argentina. An alternative perspective to that of the critics has been put forward by Kim Beazley, Australia's current Minister of Defence. He suggests that the proper question to ask is not *whether* the United States will assist Australia under the terms of ANZUS, but rather *what kind* of U.S. assistance Australia *should* rely on if it becomes involved in a regional conflict. It would be unrealistic to base its defense posture on the assumption of automatic assistance involving armed forces, but (he argues) Australia "can rely on intelligence, resupply, and other assistance under virtually any circumstances" (1988; see also Babbage 1980: 13). From this perspective, ANZUS is of continuing value in that it assures Australia of some

*The two instances were the Indonesia-Malaysia "confrontation" which began in 1963, and the dispute over the decolonization of West New Guinea (Irian Jaya). President Kennedy was reportedly so concerned that the United States might be dragged into the "confrontation," which he regarded as primarily a matter for the Commonwealth, that he ordered a review of U.S. obligations under ANZUS. Although Washington was unwilling to give Canberra the public guarantee of support under ANZUS that the Australian government sought, it privately informed the Indonesian government that it would support Australia (Pemberton 1987: 176–90).

†Interestingly, close to 70 percent of respondents to New Zealand polls in 1985 and 1986 believed that the United States would still come to New Zealand's assistance if it was attacked—despite the suspension of alliance obligations under ANZUS (Campbell 1987: 57–58). For critical assessments of ANZUS, see Camilleri (1987) and Suter (1987).

form of support from the United States in the event of regional conflict. It may not provide a guarantee of direct military assistance, but it does increase the uncertainty a potential adversary must face, and thus contributes to deterrence.

Australia and New Zealand have derived other advantages from the alliance, including opportunities for joint military exercises with American forces, sharing of U.S. intelligence, access to high-level decision-makers, and the option to purchase advanced weaponry.* The value of these alleged advantages is increasingly being questioned, however. Other countries not in alliances with the United States have also been able to purchase advanced military equipment, and access to high-level decision-makers in the United States has seldom led to any changes in policy along the lines advocated by Australia or New Zealand, especially in the economic sphere. Even the value of U.S. intelligence has been questioned by critics who maintain that Australian intelligence services are often swamped by largely irrelevant material and receive only the information the United States wants to pass on (Ball 1980: 180).

Perhaps in response to these criticisms, Australian governments in recent years have placed less emphasis on the benefits the alliance brings to the junior partners and more on the contribution that Australia makes to the Western alliance and to global security in general by its hosting of U.S. defense installations. ANZUS has increasingly been portrayed as an obligation Australia undertakes on behalf of the Western community.†

On the other side of the balance sheet, it is now generally recognized, by officials as well as commentators, that membership in ANZUS has entailed a number of significant costs for the junior partners, some self-imposed. During the alliance's first twenty years, when conservative governments dominated political life in both Australia and New Zealand, foreign policy attitudes were marked by sycophancy, particularly in Australia. Liberal/Country Party governments were so preoccupied with maintaining the American presence in the region that they were reluctant to criticize any aspect of U.S. foreign policy in public. Australia's enthusiasm for U.S. policies—epitomized by Prime Minister Harold Holt's use of the slogan "All the Way with LBJ" on a visit to

---

*According to the current leader of the National Party and former Minister of Defence, this may include consultation at the research-and-design stage of new weapons (Sinclair 1984: 142–47).

†As former Australian Defence Minister Gordon Scholes stated it: "The alliance symbolizes our support for the Western Community as a whole" (1984: 140).

Washington—suggested a lack of maturity on the part of Australian leaders and an inability (or unwillingness) to see that Australia's national interests and U.S. interests were not always identical. Even an American ambassador to Canberra described the obsequious attitudes of previous Australian governments as a "downright embarrassment" (Marshall Green; quoted in Meaney 1980: 205).*

The overriding commitment to ensuring the continuation of the U.S. security guarantee dictated a policy of "forward defense" in which Australia would fight alongside the United States in Southeast Asia against the southward spread of "Communism." A clear statement of the intentions behind Australia's policy was made by Alan Renouf (subsequently Head of the Department of Foreign Affairs and Australian ambassador to the United States) in advocating the dispatch of Australian troops to Vietnam in 1964:

> Our objective should be ... to achieve such an habitual closeness of relations with the United States and sense of mutual alliance that in our time of need . . . the United States would have little option but to respond as we would want.... The problem of Vietnam is one, it seems, where we could without a disproportionate expenditure pick up a lot of credit with the United States (quoted in Camilleri 1987: 14).†

The concern to prove oneself to be a good alliance partner also distorted defense policies. Forward defense necessitated organizing military planning around allied operations overseas; as a consequence, no attempt was made to develop independent national defense policies until the late 1960s. Equipment and force structures were tailored to meet the needs of allied operations, which often led to the purchase of equipment that was subsequently regarded as inappropriate for national defense (Babbage 1984: 163; 1980).

Another major cost the alliance imposed on Australia was to make it a certain target in a nuclear confrontation because of its hosting of the major U.S. C^3I facilities. As the U.S. government has acknowledged, and

---

*In Holsti's study of national role conceptions, he found in Australian foreign policy statements during this period of conservative rule "no themes emphasizing Australia's complete freedom of action in foreign policy" (1970: 279).

†Prime Minister Holt asserted that "the USA are there [in South Vietnam] to stay. We will win there and get protection in the South Pacific for a very small insurance premium" (quoted in Pemberton 1987: 316). These arguments echoed earlier statements by Percy Spender, who had described the commitment of Australian troops to the Korean conflict as a move that "will repay us in the future one hundredfold" (quoted in Mack 1986: 450).

Soviet spokesmen have confirmed, Pine Gap, Nurrungar, and North West Cape would be likely early targets in a nuclear exchange between the superpowers. Peace advocates have argued that port facilities in Australia and New Zealand are also likely targets if they admit U.S. vessels, but these arguments are not very persuasive (see McKinley, ch. 2 below). The Australian government maintains that the risks involved in hosting the facilities are justified because of the contribution they make to global nuclear deterrence, and because they afford Australia some "moral standing" in its advocacy of arms control (Hayden 1983: 516).*

Perceptions of the costs and benefits of the ANZUS alliance have changed quite dramatically in recent years in Australia and New Zealand. The Vietnam War and President Nixon's announcement of the "Guam Doctrine" in 1969 were major precipitants of the change. Doubts about U.S. handling of the Vietnam conflict generated a questioning of U.S. judgments, capacities, and ability to manage the alliance relationship. U.S. policy in Vietnam also called into question the will and capability of Washington to guarantee the security of its junior partners in ANZUS. These doubts were reinforced by the proclamation of the Guam Doctrine, which, in the words of Australia's current Minister of Defence (Kim Beazley), "dealt a fatal blow to the premise upon which Australian defence policy had traditionally been based" (quoted in Mediansky 1987: 156). Initially the doctrine was perceived by conservative governments in Australia and New Zealand as a betrayal of America's loyal allies; their first response was to make new efforts to induce the United States to strengthen its commitments under ANZUS (Meaney 1980: 175). When it became clear that the United States would not modify its stance, Australia and New Zealand began to develop defense policies that placed far greater emphasis on national self-reliance.

Revised evaluations of the external threats they faced were important in shaping their new policies. Earlier fears of a southward advance of Communism gave way to more sanguine assessments of their security environments. The Whitlam government, in power in Australia from 1972 to 1975, based its defense posture on the conclusion that no major threat to Australian security could be foreseen for the next 10–15 years. Similar judgments were made by succeeding governments. Similarly, governments in New Zealand now downplayed the possibility of a threat from

---

*Public opinion has endorsed the government's position that "the benefits gained from the joint defence facilities are worth the added risks they may entail." Over 60 percent of poll respondents agreed with this statement in October 1986; only 26 percent disagreed with it (USIA 1986: 19).

China or the Soviet Union.* The threats to security perceived as most likely were low-level types, such as the interdiction of shipping or raids by commando units. For these contingencies, assistance from the United States under ANZUS could not be expected. The 1976 Defence White Paper in Australia emphasized greater self-reliance and higher priority to regional responsibilities in defense; this was echoed in the 1978 *Defence Review* in New Zealand. ANZUS appeared increasingly peripheral to the defense concerns of the two countries.

From the late 1970s, at a time when the benefits from ANZUS were seen as diminishing, the costs of the alliance were perceived to be increasing. Here a growing concern about the nuclear threat in official circles and among the general public became important. A considerable portion of the blame for this concern rests with the Reagan administration. The administration's apparent lack of interest in arms control agreements (during its first term in office), its pursuit of the potentially destabilizing Strategic Defense Initiative, its talk of nuclear war-fighting strategies, and its references to the Soviet Union as an "evil empire"—all undermined confidence in the judgments of the "great and powerful friend" (quoting Sir Robert Menzies).† In both Australia and New Zealand, popular concern over the policies of the Reagan administration fuelled an unprecedented growth of peace movements, which were seen as the only means of protesting against nuclear weapons in general and the Reagan administration policies in particular. Public opinion polls conducted in Australia in 1984 showed that a majority of voters supported peace marches and

*Even public opinion, which has lagged behind official thinking, generally became more optimistic on the external threats issue. In May 1987, 49 percent of those polled thought Australia would not face a military threat during the next ten years, while 37 percent thought it would. Indonesia was perceived as the country most likely to pose a threat (24 percent), followed by Libya (20 percent), the Soviet Union (14 percent), and Japan (7 percent) (*The Australian*, 15 May 1987). In New Zealand in 1985 only 18 percent of respondents to a poll believed that an armed invasion of New Zealand was likely, and only 11 percent considered it a present concern. In both countries, the United States is now viewed as a potential threat, but only by a very small minority (5 percent in Australia and 14 percent in New Zealand). For data on Australia, see Matthews and Ravenhill (1987: 161–72); for data on New Zealand, see New Zealand (1986).

†These doubts persisted into the second Reagan administration. Asked in September 1987 which of the superpowers was making a greater effort to reach a nuclear arms control agreement, 48 percent of a college-educated sample in Australia cited the Soviet Union in contrast to only 15 percent who cited the United States. More than 57 percent of the respondents had "not very much/no confidence in U.S. ability to deal responsibly with world problems" (USIA 1987: 6).

believed the government should do more to promote nuclear disarmament (see Goot and King, n.d.: 9–10). In both Australia and New Zealand, the moderate leadership of the principal parties of the left (Labor in Australia, Labour in New Zealand) was threatened both by radical, anti-ANZUS elements within their own parties and by the growth of third parties that capitalized on anti-nuclear sentiment.*

ANZUS came to be seen by an increasing percentage of the public, especially in New Zealand, as generating insecurity in an environment where there was no significant external threat. In the words of New Zealand's prime minister: "Nuclear weapons are themselves the greatest threat which exists to the future, and . . . far from adding to our security, they only put us more at risk" (Lange 1987: 2). As McKinley notes below, changing perceptions of threats became tied in with anti-nuclear sentiments and environmental concerns in New Zealand in an alternative world-view that emphasized the possibilities of peaceful coexistence and cooperation, and perceived the remnants of the postwar system of alliances as a threat to peace.

NEW ZEALAND AND THE DEMISE OF ANZUS

The decision by the Lange government to ban nuclear-powered and nuclear-armed ships from its ports should have come as no surprise to Washington. New Zealanders in general, and the Labour Party in particular, have a long tradition of antipathy toward matters nuclear. Sixty-five percent of New Zealanders live in municipalities that have declared themselves nuclear-free, and New Zealand has led efforts to ban nuclear testing in the Pacific and to establish a nuclear-free zone in the South Pacific. With Britain's entry into the European Community, New Zealand has sought to redefine its international identity and its foreign policy priorities. Increasingly, New Zealanders have perceived themselves as living in a bicultural South Pacific country whose principal foreign policy concerns are to keep the region free from superpower conflict and from such environmentally damaging activities as French nuclear testing.†

*In the 1984 Australian election, two anti-nuclear parties—the Democrats and the Nuclear Disarmament Party—together polled 15 percent of the vote. The Democrats held the balance of power in the Australian Senate following the election. In New Zealand, two minor parties—Social Credit (which became the Democratic Party) and the New Zealand Party—opposed not only port visits by nuclear-armed or nuclear-powered vessels, but also membership in ANZUS.

†The assertion of New Zealand nationalism coincides with the rise to political power of a younger, better-educated group of political leaders (see Phillips 1988).

The Labour Party has a long-standing commitment to anti-nuclear policies, and by 1978 it had adopted an unequivocal policy of closing New Zealand's ports to nuclear-powered or nuclear-armed vessels.

Public opinion on the issue of visits by nuclear-armed ships shifted dramatically in the early 1980s. Whereas in 1982 and 1983 a plurality of respondents supported such visits, by 1984 a majority opposed them (Campbell 1987: 63). The 1984 election was precipitated when the National Party government, as a consequence of defections from within its own ranks, nearly lost a vote on a private member's bill to ban nuclear vessels from New Zealand's ports. The defense policy on which the Labour Party fought the election was a compromise between radical factions of the party that wanted New Zealand to withdraw from ANZUS, and moderates who favored continued alliance membership but wanted New Zealand to be nuclear-free.

The Reagan administration appeared to misjudge the commitment of the party to an anti-nuclear policy, and the ability of Prime Minister Lange to override the party on the issue. While the Labour Party when in office is not as strictly bound by party conference resolutions as its constitution would suggest, the leadership cannot afford to ignore rank-and-file opinion. Opinion polls showed that a substantial majority of Labour Party supporters favored breaking defense ties with the United States rather than change the party's anti-nuclear policies (McMillan 1987: 85). At a time when the government was pursuing a program of economic liberalization that was unpopular with large sections of the party, an abandonment of the anti-nuclear policy would have split the party and almost certainly have led to the ouster of Lange as prime minister.

Could a compromise acceptable to the United States have been reached? At one stage this seemed possible—if New Zealand could determine from its own intelligence whether or not a vessel was nuclear-armed. This would have allowed the United States to continue its policy to "neither confirm nor deny" (NCND) the presence of nuclear weapons on its vessels. Such a compromise would probably not have been acceptable to the United States, however, since it would have undermined the essential purpose of the NCND policy. New Zealand's decisions on admission of individual vessels would have signalled whether or not they were nuclear-armed.* In the event, any possibility of

*Whether New Zealand had the capability to determine if nuclear arms were carried by U.S. ships is doubtful. General-Secretary Gorbachev recently announced that the Soviet Union has developed technology that enables it to determine if vessels are nuclear-armed, but most experts believe that such detection systems could be fooled by placing emission devices on non-nuclear-armed ships.

compromise was undermined by the mysterious leaking of two pieces of sensitive information: first, that Prime Minister Lange had requested an alternative, non-nuclear vessel to substitute for the proposed visit by the nuclear-capable USS *Buchanan;* second, that a letter from Australian Prime Minister Hawke to his New Zealand counterpart had warned that New Zealand could not expect to remain part of the ANZUS alliance if it did not accept the same obligations as its partners.* The first leak made it impossible for the United States to substitute another vessel without giving the appearance of backing down, and the publication of Hawke's letter made any compromise on Lange's part impossible because he would appear to be bowing to external pressure. Who was responsible for the leaks has never been revealed, but their combined effect was to lock the parties into the stalemate of their publicly stated positions.

New Zealand in itself is of minimal strategic interest to the United States. In the years 1976–84, only forty-one U.S. naval vessels visited its ports (Firth 1987: 123). Washington's concerns about its anti-nuclear policies have always been centered on the possible contagion effect: a failure to respond decisively to New Zealand's actions might encourage other allies to pursue similar policies.† Although Lange has been careful to insist that New Zealand's policy is designed for its unique geopolitical circumstances, other government members have proposed that other countries should follow New Zealand's lead.

New Zealand has attempted to exploit the generality of the ANZUS treaty's language to argue that ANZUS is not a nuclear alliance, that it is a regional pact rather than part of a global alliance system, and that New Zealand therefore has no obligation to contribute to strategic deterrence (see Lange 1985: 1011). There is little logical or legal basis for New

*Hawke was concerned that New Zealand's stance would encourage the anti-nuclear wing of his own party to press for similar action by the Australian government.

†In addressing the House Foreign Affairs Subcommittee on Asia and the Pacific in 1985, U.S. Deputy Assistant Secretary of Defense James Kelly asserted: "Port access in New Zealand by itself is not of critical military importance to the United States. The military posture and basic military strategy of the U.S., however, could be markedly degraded by access denials by other friends and allies. The potential spread of access denials policies to other countries with very active anti-nuclear factions is of serious concern" (quoted in Camilleri 1987: 142). Recent actions by the British Labour Party (in proposing unilateral nuclear disarmament), the Chinese government (in announcing in April 1985 that it would not accept visits from nuclear-armed U.S. ships), and the Canadian New Democratic Party (in proclaiming a new anti-nuclear defense policy in July 1987) lend substance to these concerns.

Zealand's position (see McKinley below). Under Article II of the treaty, the parties agree that they "separately and jointly by means of continuous and effective self-help and mutual aid will maintain and develop their individual and collective capacity to resist armed attack." To deny port facilities to some classes of U.S. naval vessels contradicts the obligation to provide mutual aid. Ironically, under the treaty's Article V, conflict is defined to include not only armed attack on the metropolitan and island territories of the parties, but also on their armed forces, public vessels, or aircraft in the Pacific. If New Zealand maintained its antinuclear stance and remained within the alliance, it could, hypothetically, find itself obligated to come to the aid of a vessel it had banned from its ports. Given their desire to maximize the chances of U.S. assistance in the event of threats to their security, it is in Australia's and New Zealand's interest to give the treaty its broadest possible interpretation. A unilateral redefinition of the treaty that gives a narrow interpretation of the type of vessels eligible to visit ports is inconsistent with this approach (Thakur n.d.).

Argument over the logic or legality of New Zealand's stance is largely beside the point, however. Now that the decision has been made, the policy will be difficult to reverse. Attempts by the United States to pressure the Lange administration to change its stance have rallied public opinion behind the government, as the literature on international sanctions would lead one to expect. A poll conducted in May 1986 for the Defence Committee of Enquiry (established to assess the state of public opinion on defense issues) found that a slim majority (52 percent) preferred to accept visits by nuclear vessels in order to remain in ANZUS, while 44 percent preferred to maintain the port ban and withdraw from ANZUS, but most observers believe that the subsequent U.S. decision to suspend its treaty obligations to New Zealand galvanized public opinion in support of the government's stance. New Zealanders may have preferred to remain in ANZUS, but they were not willing to do so on terms dictated by what they saw as a heavy-handed Washington administration.*

The stance taken by the Lange government, and the international attention it received, stirred feelings of pride and nationalism among New Zealanders. Indirect evidence of public support for the government's

---

*In a poll taken in March 1985, 53 percent of respondents answered "No" to the question "Do you think that New Zealand has been treated fairly by US officials following the NZ ban on nuclear ships?"; 38 percent answered "Yes." Fifty-three percent rejected the assertion that New Zealand had neglected its responsibilities under ANZUS (Campbell 1987: 56–57).

position can be seen in the Opposition's unwillingness to repudiate the nuclear-free stance in its 1987 election platform. (The Lange government was returned to office with a small increase in its majority.) The Opposition proposed that nuclear weapons should continue to be excluded, but that the United States should be relied upon to honor the policy and not required to deny the presence of nuclear weapons. The electorate did not find this credible.* The prospects that a New Zealand government will abandon the nuclear-free policy in the foreseeable future appear slim. Even if a new National Party government changed its policy and supported nuclear ship visits, there would always be the possibility that it would be replaced in a subsequent election by a Labour government that would reinstate the present policy. Clearly this is not a foundation on which an alliance can operate.

Despite the U.S. suspension of its treaty obligations to New Zealand, the Lange government has not repudiated the ANZUS treaty. Indeed it has consistently asserted that it wishes to maintain its cooperative relationship with the United States in conventional (as opposed to nuclear) areas, and it continues to furnish the United States with intelligence on the South Pacific region and to provide support facilities for U.S. military transport planes en route to the Antarctic. Close to 90 percent of the respondents in recent opinion polls would welcome visits by non-nuclear American ships. Public support for ANZUS remains strong in New Zealand, although a majority believe the treaty should be renegotiated (Campbell 1987: 56).

Many New Zealanders were stunned by what they viewed as a totally inappropriate reaction on .the part of Washington to their anti-nuclear stance. The response confirmed widely held perceptions of the Reagan administration as arrogant, aggressive, and unwilling to countenance the possibility that its allies might not completely share its world-view. When the U.S. Army began to exclude New Zealanders from its Staff College at Fort Leavenworth, while continuing to accept officers from non-aligned Third World countries, the United States appeared to reduce New Zealand to the status of less than a friend (Hanson 1987: 137–55). New Zealand's anti-nuclear stance is inconsistent with membership in ANZUS, but it is in the Western interest for Washington to reestablish

---

*With good reason, given the evidence that the U.S. Navy has not honored Japan's non-nuclear constitution (see La Rocque 1974). Indeed a case can be made that New Zealand's stance is the only way of ensuring that allies will not abuse the NCND policy (see White 1988).

a working defense relationship with New Zealand, albeit outside the context of ANZUS (see ch. 8 below).

WILL AUSTRALIA FOLLOW THE NEW ZEALAND PATH?

Part of the concern felt by Washington at the anti-nuclear policies of the Lange government arose from fears that the Australian Labor Party (ALP) might follow the lead of its New Zealand counterpart. Under the previous Labor government, Australia had acquired the reputation of being an unreliable ally because of Prime Minister Whitlam's outspoken criticism of U.S. bombing of Vietnam. Doubts about the ALP were exacerbated by the foreign policy platform adopted by the party while it was in opposition. Australia's Minister of Foreign Affairs from 1983 to 1988, Bill Hayden, flirted with a non-nuclear stance while he held the position of opposition leader. In 1982 he backed the proposal of the Victorian State Premier, John Cain, to ban port visits by nuclear ships. Hayden failed to gain the support of his party, however, and was forced to retreat under pressure from the government of Malcolm Fraser and the United States. This has often been seen as a major factor in Hayden's replacement as party leader by Hawke prior to the 1983 federal election.

The left wing of the ALP has a long tradition of opposition to U.S. foreign policies and to the presence of U.S. transnational corporations in Australia. It has also questioned the utility of the ANZUS alliance and opposed port visits by nuclear-armed or nuclear-powered ships. Despite its high visibility at party conferences, however, the Labor left has few representatives in the leadership, particularly in the most important portfolios of the Cabinet. Even the Whitlam government, certainly more left-wing in its outlook than the three ministries of current Prime Minister Hawke, never questioned the utility of the ANZUS alliance.

Although the current ALP government has sought to establish an independent foreign policy, and has not backed away from criticism of U.S. policies on arms control, SDI, Central America, and Kampuchea/Vietnam, it has given strong support to the ANZUS alliance. Shortly after taking office in 1983, it commissioned a review of the alliance. In a statement to Parliament, Foreign Affairs Minister Hayden summarized its conclusions:

> The review has led us to a firm and unequivocal reaffirmation of the alliance as fundamental to Australia's national security and foreign and defence policies. . . . Although the Treaty was drawn up a generation

ago, and in very different circumstances, we have reached the conclusion that the commitments and obligations that were accepted then
remain as valid and appropriate today. The Treaty has the full support
of this Government; but we recognize that we must still pull our full
weight in our own protection (Hayden 1983: 512–13; see also *ANZUS
Alliance* 1982).

The provisions of the treaty, said Hayden, provide substantial benefits to
both Australia and the United States.

Prime Minister Hawke is more effusive in his friendship toward the
United States than most members of his party. At times this has caused embarrassment. In 1984, for example, a revolt in the party forced Hawke to
back down from his offer to the United States of facilities in Australia to assist with monitoring of MX-missile tests. On the other hand, when Hayden,
in an August 1984 speech to the Conference on Disarmament in Geneva,
appeared to make continued U.S. access to the joint facilities in Australia
conditional on progress in arms control negotiations, Prime Minister
Hawke moved quickly to undermine his remarks by asserting that the
Australian government was happy with the U.S. position on arms control.

Despite differences in emphasis between Hawke and some of his
senior ministers, the value of the American alliance has not been questioned during the life of the current Labor government. Nor has the
question of banning ship visits resurfaced on an agenda dominated by
the ALP right wing. Both Hawke and Hayden have expressed regret at
New Zealand's stance on port visits and have supported the U.S. position, but have made no attempt to mediate between the two parties.

Australia is very different from New Zealand both in its
geostrategic situation and in the prevailing attitudes toward the ANZUS
alliance. Australia is much closer to Asia; its northern coastline is nearer
to Djakarta than to Canberra. Despite the sanguine threat assessments of
the past fifteen years, there is an underlying concern in the general
population—remembering the Japanese bombardment of Darwin and
the penetration of Sydney harbor by Japanese mini-submarines during
World War II—that one or more Asian countries may in the future pursue an aggressive foreign policy toward mineral-rich Australia. New
Zealand, primarily an agricultural country and another 1800 miles from
Asia, has no such concerns about Asian aggression, but is fearful of the
potentially disastrous consequences for its economy of a nuclear accident
in the South Pacific. In contrast to New Zealand, Australia is a middle-
rank power with substantial interest in continuing to purchase advanced
military equipment from the United States and exercising with American

forces, and it perceives itself as making a significant contribution to the Western alliance through its hosting of the joint facilities.

Any move by an Australian government that threatened to rupture the ANZUS alliance would be electoral suicide in a country in which "Communist scares" were used very effectively by conservative parties in the 1950s and 1960s. Opinion on the value of the alliance reflects public concern over Australia's long-term security. Support for ANZUS in public opinion polls has consistently run at over 70 percent and been bipartisan.* Approval of the joint facilities has been over 60 percent (even though few are able to name any of them or identify their functions). Opinion has been more equivocal on the issue of port visits by nuclear-armed or nuclear-powered ships. Anecdotal evidence suggests that opposition to such visits may have waned since reaching a peak in the early 1980s: many more people toured the battleship USS *Missouri* when it was opened to the public on a visit to Sydney in 1986 than were involved in protesting the visit.[†] Opinion among decision-makers also strongly supports the alliance. A survey of two hundred members of the Australian "foreign policy elite" revealed that although only 30 percent of the elite gave an unqualified yes to the question of whether the United States will come to Australia's assistance under the ANZUS treaty in the event of conflict in the region, more than two-thirds considered ANZUS helpful in solving regional problems (Matthews and Ravenhill 1987: 168–71).

Since 1984 the principal threat to the ANZUS relationship has come not from the nuclear ships issue but from Australian resentment at U.S. economic policies, particularly in the agricultural sphere (see Higgott, ch. 5 below). Despite enjoying a substantial trade surplus with Australia, the U.S. government currently imposes restrictions on commodities that constitute one-third of Australia's exports to the United States (Gallagher 1988: 135).

Most Australians understand that the policies of the European Community (and, to a lesser extent, of Japan) are the root of the current problems in international agricultural trade, but they resent American

*There is some evidence, however, that ANZUS is now seen as less important for Australia than in the past. Whereas in October 1983, 72 percent of college-educated Australians polled believed that ANZUS was important for Australia's security, in September 1987 this figure had fallen to 60 percent (USIA 1987: 7).

†Polls conducted in 1986 support this conclusion: the percentages of respondents favoring visits by nuclear-powered or nuclear-armed ships were approximately 6 percent higher than in the previous year's polls. A useful compilation of Australian public opinion polls on defense issues is presented in Campbell (1986).

retaliation against the European policies, especially the Export Enhancement Program, which also threatens Australia's exports to its traditional markets. The growth of bilateralism in trade negotiations as a consequence of trade imbalances, particularly between the United States and Japan, also threatens some of Australia's principal exports, especially coal and beef to Japan.* Australia is a remarkably efficient producer of agricultural products, but it cannot afford to match the subsidies paid by the EEC and the United States to capture overseas markets for their agricultural surpluses.

The growth of U.S. protectionism threatens the ANZUS alliance by eroding public support for ANZUS in Australia. Higgott notes that even staunchly pro-American groups such as the National Farmers Federation have questioned the utility of an alliance with a partner that treats Australia's economic interests so cavalierly. Australia's ambassador to the United States, Rawdon Dalrymple, offers this warning:

> The United States must recognize that the political support which it looks for from the Pacific countries has a price. If that price is not paid, it is not just the economies of friends and allies that will suffer: Western security interests will also suffer. . . . By pursuing policies which cause fundamental damage to Australia's economic welfare, the United States risks eroding the very strong community support in Australia for the alliance with the United States (1987: 143).

If Australia suffers significant losses in export earnings, that must inevitably lead to reduced expenditures on imports and/or capital transfers overseas. Australia is one of the few industrialized countries with which the United States has consistently enjoyed a trade surplus in recent years. This has been due in part to substantial earnings from sales of U.S. military equipment to Australia—especially to the Royal Australian Air Force (RAAF). Currently the RAAF is modernizing its strike force through the purchase of 75 FA-18 fighters. Continuing trade problems may force the postponement or cancellation of some planned military purchases, causing U.S. defense contractors to suffer reduced sales. More important, Australia's capacity to contribute to the security functions of the alliance may be damaged.

Australia's foreign aid program is another victim of its trade problems. Through its economic assistance to South Pacific states,

*In May 1988 a Japanese spokesman admitted that Tokyo had used "administrative guidance" to increase the U.S. share of the Japanese beef market at the expense of Australia (*Australian Financial Review*, 19 May 1988).

Australia makes an important contribution to security in the region, but its ratio of foreign aid to gross domestic product has fallen markedly in recent years. In 1986–87 the total development assistance budget was reduced by 12.8 percent compared to 1985–86. These cutbacks have occurred at a time when growing foreign power involvement in the South Pacific region has given the island states new leverage to demand increased assistance in return for their continuing adhesion to the Western alliance.

When trade tensions between Australia and the United States were at their height in September 1987, members of the Hawke ministry suggested that the joint facilities might be used as leverage in negotiations with Washington.* The prime minister commented that the alliance did not have "infinite elasticity" and, adopting popular terminology, referred in a radio interview to the joint facilities as "bases," which prompted the U.S. embassy in Canberra to seek clarification of the Australian government's position. However, any Australian threat to use the joint facilities as bargaining chips lacks credibility. It contradicts the government's repeated claims that the facilities enable Australia to make a vital contribution to the Western alliance, and indeed plays into the hands of the peace movement, which has long opposed the facilities' presence. The facilities are perceived to be so significant to the alliance that Prime Minister Hawke in March 1984 warned the Labor left wing that he would step down if the party repudiated them.

Australia's frustrations at Washington's policies notwithstanding, the joint facilities cannot be credibly threatened. The facilities may not be part of the ANZUS alliance, but they are, as both Washington and Canberra have agreed, "within the spirit of the provisions of the ANZUS treaty" (Wolfowitz 1984: 151). As New Zealand has discovered, it is impossible to repudiate one element of the security arrangements (even if it is not formally mandated under the treaty) while continuing to benefit from the others.[†]

While economic disputes may not directly threaten the joint facilities, they can have a lasting impact on the climate of opinion.

*This would not be the first attempt by an Australian government to make such linkage. The previous Liberal/National Country Party coalition administration of Malcolm Fraser raised the issue in attempting to increase Australia's beef quota in the United States, as well as during a dispute over compensation for an American company—the Dillingham Corporation—which had been denied an export license for sand mining on Fraser Island (Renouf 1986: 119).

†Less than a quarter of the respondents to a 1986 poll favored the use of the joint facilities as a bargaining chip in trade negotiations (USIA 1987: 23).

Certainly they appear to affect the Australian public's perceptions of which party benefits most from the alliance. They may also explain the erosion in the Australian public's confidence in the U.S. defense commitment to Australia—down from 79 percent in 1982 to 68 percent in 1986. The proportion expressing not much or no confidence in the U.S. commitment rose from 15 to 28 percent in the same period. Australians have also become less supportive of the U.S. position in its dispute with New Zealand. Here both the perception of U.S. bullying of Wellington plus discontent with U.S. economic policies may be at work. Whereas 35 percent of respondents supported the U.S. position in March 1985, only 20 percent did so by October 1986. The proportion supporting the New Zealand position remained constant at 22 percent while those believing that Australia should remain neutral in the dispute rose from 37 to 56 percent (USIA 1987: 15, 21).

Public opinion about the value of the alliance may be affected by the new emphasis on self-reliance in Australia's defense policies. Concern has been expressed in some quarters in Washington about the new direction of Australian policy, in particular the reduced emphasis on ANZUS (Mediansky 1987: 156–60). In response to the Guam Doctrine, and to a reappraisal of the threats Australia faces, successive governments since the mid-1970s have been redirecting policies away from a strategy of forward defense, intended to draw a commitment from allies to assist Australia, toward one in which Australia accepts responsibility for its own defense against most threats. The 1986 *Review of Australia's Defence* and subsequent Defence White Paper provide the most sophisticated statements of the new approach. (They are examined by Mack in ch. 6 below.) The new defense strategy foresees little role for Australian involvement in allied operations overseas, but it assumes that Australia will continue to make a significant contribution to the Western alliance through its hosting of the joint facilities and its self-reliance in deterring local and regional threats. Neither the government nor the public believes that Australia can effectively provide for its own defense outside the context of an alliance with the United States.

Despite differing with New Zealand over its stance on ANZUS, Australia has continued its cooperation in the defense field with its trans-Tasman neighbor under the ANZAC Pact (1944). Although ANZAC came to be overshadowed by ANZUS, the pact remains significant because it provides an independent legal basis for defense cooperation between the two countries. The pact, which had its origins in the concern of the two dominions that they were being excluded from military planning during

World War II, and their determination to play a role in the postwar settlement, commits the parties to (a) establishment of a regional zone of defense comprising the Southwest and South Pacific, (b) a common doctrine for the organization, equipment, training, and exercising of their armed forces, joint planning, and the interchange of staff, (c) coordination of policy on military procurement, and (d) creation of a joint secretariat. The secretariat was never established, but an extensive consultative machinery has been created to oversee the relationship (see Ball 1985: 34–52).

Australia has indicated on several occasions that it has no intention of taking the place of the United States in New Zealand's defense planning, but intensified cooperation between the two countries is a next logical step as both increasingly focus their defense efforts on the immediate region and strive for greater self-reliance. Plans for joint building of naval vessels have been agreed to, and the two countries will share intelligence from the satellite ground stations each plans to build.

INSTABILITY IN THE SOUTH PACIFIC

Besides their hosting of U.S. military installations and participation in allied military operations in Asia, the principal contribution Australia and New Zealand have made to Western security has been the role they have played in the Pacific island states. The United States has been satisfied to leave Western influence in the region primarily in the hands of Australia and New Zealand, and they have been remarkably successful in denying strategic access to the Soviet Union. The Soviets have less influence in the South Pacific than in any other region of the world. This is due in part to Moscow's traditional lack of interest in this remote area, and its limited capabilities to project its power there (discussed in more detail below), but it is also a consequence of the characteristics of the island states and the relationships they have enjoyed with Australia and New Zealand.

The South Pacific was the last region in the world to experience decolonization. With the partial exception of Vanuatu, where there was a minor uprising by settlers, it was a peaceful process. Western Samoa was the first island state to receive its independence (1962); Vanuatu is the latest (1980). These islands are among the smallest and most vulnerable members of the international community. Their populations range from 7,000 in Nauru to 3.5 million in Papua New Guinea; with the exception of Fiji (700,000), the populations of the other islands are under 160,000. Enormous distances separate the islands from one another; in some cases, individual island states are fragmented, with various component islands widely dispersed. The South Pacific islands are roughly twice as far removed from Australia and New Zealand as the Caribbean islands are from the Americas. All of the islands, even those possessing some mineral resources (Papua New Guinea, New Caledonia, and Nauru), depend heavily on foreign aid. The region has the highest per capita aid receipts in the world. For Kiribati and Tuvalu, for instance, aid per capita—currently over $500 per annum—is greater than the recorded per capita GDP ("Fiji Report" 1987: 13). The islands have been characterized as "MIRAB" economies—dependent on migration, remittances, aid, and bureaucracy (Connell 1988: 65).

Fishing figures prominently as a source of livelihood for many islanders. The conclusion of the Law of the Sea Treaty provided a significant windfall with the creation of 200-mile exclusive economic zones (EEZs). At present the principal benefit from the enormous EEZs for many of these states is derived from control of fishing rights. Mining of the seabed may prove lucrative in the future.

Generalization about the South Pacific islands is somewhat hazardous. Besides differing in size and economic structure, they have different colonial traditions, different ethnic and racial mixes, different political systems and ideologies, and different lineage structures and systems of land tenure. Nevertheless, the islands' leaders perceive themselves as belonging to a distinct regional entity and place considerable emphasis on regional cooperation as a means of overcoming their economic vulnerabilities. The most prominent symbol of this is the South Pacific Forum—an annual meeting of senior representatives (usually heads-of-government) of twelve island states and Australia and New Zealand, initiated in 1971.* Compared to most regional groupings, relations between the Forum states have been harmonious; this has given rise to the notion of a "Pacific Way" of settling disputes. Forum meetings are dominated by the two regional "powers"— Australia and New Zealand—whose support is needed if the Forum is to effectively pursue initiatives such as the South Pacific Nuclear Free Zone. Australia and New Zealand must act with great sensitivity, however, to ensure that their efforts are not damaged by perceptions that they are exercising a heavy-handed paternalism.

*The members of the Forum are Australia, Cook Islands, Federated States of Micronesia, Kiribati, Marshall Islands, Nauru, New Zealand, Niue, Papua New Guinea, Solomon Islands, Tonga, Tuvalu, Vanuatu, and Western Samoa. For further details about the South Pacific Forum and other regional organizations, see Herr (1976: 170–82).

Economic vulnerability is the principal preoccupation of the island countries. With the exception of Papua New Guinea, which has troublesome border problems with Indonesia [West Irian], the islands perceive little threat from either intra-regional conflict or from attack by external powers.* In security matters their principal concerns are to keep the region free from superpower competition, and to end its usage as a testing ground for nuclear weapons.

Australia and, to a lesser extent, New Zealand have been major providers of economic support to the South Pacific region over the past fifteen years. In 1986–87 Australia supplied Aus$86 million in economic aid to the smaller island states in addition to Aus$314 million to Papua New Guinea. Most exports from the island states enter Australia and New Zealand duty-free under the South Pacific Regional Trade and Economic Cooperation Agreement (SPARTECA). Economic assistance has been the principal weapon employed by Australia and New Zealand in the pursuit of strategic denial in the South Pacific, aimed solely at the Soviet Union. Facilitated by the general pro-Western sentiment in most of the islands, the policy has worked well. In contrast to China, whose regional role has been perceived as positive by Australia and New Zealand and the island states, the Soviet Union still has no resident missions in the South Pacific outside Australia and New Zealand.

The environment that facilitated the successful pursuit of strategic denial is changing rapidly, however. Disillusionment has set in as anticipated gains from independence have failed to materialize. Throughout the region the generation that brought the South Pacific to independence is being replaced with new leaders who are often less pro-Western than their predecessors, and more prone to place emphasis on racial solidarity. The slow pace of economic development has increasingly been blamed on the colonial legacy and the inherited structure of economic relations. Frustrations have generated demands for greater economic assistance and have also caused political turmoil in Fiji and Papua New Guinea.

Fiji, once widely praised for its multiracial democracy, has the unhappy distinction of being the site of the region's first military coups (in May and September 1987, both led by Colonel Rabuka). The April 1987 election brought to power a radical Labour Coalition government that advocated Fijian membership in the Non-Aligned Movement and, had it

*See the assessment of the former Papua New Guinea Minister for Foreign Affairs and Trade quoted in Herr (1984: 184). A useful discussion of the problems of small states in the international community can be found in Commonwealth Secretariat (1985).

survived, would probably have reinstated a 1982 ban on port visits by nuclear-armed and nuclear-powered ships. (The ban had been lifted in 1983.) The election and subsequent military coups exposed the depth of racial animosity in Fiji between the Melanesian and Indian populations, and revealed emerging class cleavages. The military coups brought into office a conservative, pro-Western government, but may also have ushered in intensified racial conflict, political turmoil, and economic crisis. (Fiji's tourism industry—its principal foreign-exchange earner—has been badly affected by the internal strife.)

The Fiji coups have been widely perceived as setting an unfortunate precedent for extra-constitutional political change, and have underlined the limits to Australian and New Zealand influence within the region. Australia's response to the first coup appeared indecisive and raised questions about the adequacy of its intelligence in Fiji. Both Australia and New Zealand cut off economic assistance to the military regime, and local trade unions briefly imposed economic sanctions, but Canberra and Wellington found that they lacked leverage. Attempts to enlist the support of the South Pacific Forum foundered when other Melanesian nations expressed support for their kinsmen in Fiji; Papua New Guinea broke ranks by recognizing the government of Colonel Rabuka. Other countries attempted to fill the vacuum left by the withdrawal of support by Australia and New Zealand: Indonesia offered to replace Australia as supplier of Fiji's oil imports, and France promised economic and military assistance. The second military government (installed when Colonel Rabuka objected to the new constitution that civilian politicians had negotiated) initially threatened to seek help from the Soviet Union and China. Faced with the prospect of a loss of influence, the Australian government had little option but to recognize the republican government Rabuka appointed in December 1987 and resume its economic aid.

In Papua New Guinea (PNG), the government faces difficulties in managing its border with Indonesia, severe economic problems, high rates of urban unemployment and crime, and growing ethnic tensions. Although PNG's relations with Indonesia are currently good, Indonesian trans-settlement of West Irian and the activities of the Libya- and Vanuatu-backed Free Papua Movement (made up primarily of refugees from Irian Jaya) create a potentially explosive situation. Recently a PNG Forestry Minister was sacked for accepting U.S.$140,000 in campaign contributions from the former head of the Indonesian armed forces, while the commander of the PNG Defence Force was dismissed for allegedly leaking details of the defense agreement between Australia and PNG to the

Indonesian government. Also, in 1987 PNG announced it would apply to join the Non-Aligned Movement.* All of these developments have undermined Australia's influence in its former trust territory.

Vanuatu, a former French/British condominium, plays the maverick in the region. It is a member of the Non-Aligned Movement, and in the short period since independence has been stridently anti-colonial and anti-nuclear.† The current government of Father Walter Lini would like to see strategic denial extended to exclude the United States as well as the Soviet Union from the region. It has connections with Libya, which has created anxiety in other states in the region, but Libyan influence to date has been minimal (Hegarty 1987). Barak Sope, a challenger in the competition to succeed ailing Premier Lini, is a staunch supporter of Colonel Ghaddafi. Violent demonstrations in Vila in May 1988 by Sope's supporters over access to land underlined the fragility of the current political situation.

Australia's and New Zealand's response to the growing instability in the region has been to increase their economic assistance and embark on new programs of defense cooperation. Except for a 1987 "joint declaration" by Papua New Guinea and Australia, neither Australia nor New Zealand has defense pacts with any of the island states. Defense cooperation is limited to the provision by Australia and New Zealand of some equipment (mainly patrol boats) and troop training, air and sea patrols to help the islands enforce their 200-mile EEZs, and intelligence-sharing. In February 1987 Australia's Minister of Defence announced a new defense initiative for the region which will include the supply of twelve patrol boats and additional aerial surveillance. Because of increased concern about Libyan activities in the region, the South Pacific Forum agreed to establish new intelligence-sharing arrangements.**

*Acting Foreign Minister Aruru Matiabe insisted it was time for PNG to be seen in its "true colours. So far other people have seen us to be in the Western mould led by Australia and New Zealand in this region. I do not believe PNG should be seen in this light any more—not in this day and age" (*Sydney Morning Herald*, 5 September 1987).

†Premdas and Howard argue that Vanuatu's non-alignment is primarily symbolic given its continued dependence on economic assistance from the West (1985: 177–86).

**In May 1987, Australian concern at reported Libyan activities in the region reached its peak. Foreign Minister Hayden took an early morning flight to New Zealand to consult Prime Minister Lange on the matter, prompting statements in Wellington that Australia had overreacted to the "Libyan threat." Prime Minister Hawke ordered the Libyan People's Bureau in Canberra closed, asserting

Australian and New Zealand attempts to maintain their policy of strategic denial face two principal constraints. The first is the budgetary problems both countries are experiencing, which severely limit expansion of their economic and defense cooperation programs. The second is the growing interest of outside actors in the region, especially Indonesia and the Soviet Union. While the possibility of playing potential donors off against one another has given the island states new leverage in their demands for assistance, their dependence on foreign aid makes them particularly vulnerable to external interference.

To a considerable extent the West—especially the United States and France—has itself to blame for enabling the Soviet Union to gain a toehold in the region. Western insensitivity to island interests led their governments to turn elsewhere for assistance. Their most recent concerns have been the slow pace of decolonization in New Caledonia, French nuclear testing in the Pacific, and exploitation of their fishing resources by the U.S. tuna industry.

Of these, by far the most damaging in the short term (and one that could easily have been avoided) was a drawn-out conflict between the island governments and the U.S. tuna industry. As alternative stocks were exhausted, U.S. tuna fishermen turned their attention to the South Pacific in the early 1980s. By 1984 over fifty American vessels were fishing regularly in South Pacific waters and refusing to respect the islanders' claims to 200-mile exclusive economic zones. U.S. tuna vessels were seized for illegally fishing in island waters by Papua New Guinea (1982), the Federated States of Micronesia (1984 and 1986), Kiribati (1984 and 1987), and the Solomon Islands (1984). When the U.S. government in retaliation applied the punitive provisions of the Magnuson Fishery Conservation and Management Act and imposed trade sanctions against the Solomon Islands, it did enormous damage to the American image in the region.

The Reagan administration's support for the U.S. tuna industry (during its first term) led to stalemate in negotiations with the islands over fishing rights, which the Soviet Union exploited by offering

---

that "there is no plausible explanation in terms of geography or legitimate national interest for Libyan activity in this region" (*Australian Foreign Affairs Review*, May 1987, 283). The Hawke government committed a diplomatic faux pas by publicly criticizing Libyan activities in the island states before consulting the islands themselves. This reinforced resentment at what has increasingly been seen as Australian–New Zealand paternalism.

generous fishing agreements to both Kiribati and Vanuatu. These agreements enabled the Soviet Union to establish a presence in the islands for the first time. Meanwhile, lengthy negotiations between the islands and the U.S. government over a very modest sum for the fishing license fees caused a further loss of goodwill toward the United States (Allen 1987: 50–56).

SOVIET INTERESTS IN THE PACIFIC

Despite signing fishing agreements with Kiribati and Vanuatu, and the non-resident accreditation it enjoys in Fiji, Tonga, Vanuatu, and Western Samoa, the Soviet Union has negligible influence in the South Pacific region. In part this is a result of the distance from Soviet territory to the South Pacific. The closest point—Vladivostok—is more than 6000 kilometers (3500 miles) away. The USSR has no regular military presence in the South Pacific; although it undoubtedly is transited by submarines, there have been no reports of Soviet military aircraft or surface warships in the region.

Moscow apparently intends to increase its presence in the South Pacific. Gorbachev's Vladivostok speech, the establishment of a Pacific Ocean Countries branch in the Foreign Ministry in 1986, and the greater attention that has recently been given to the Pacific region in Soviet academic institutions attest to a new interest. In March 1987 Foreign Minister Shevardnadze expressed a belief that Soviet political influence would follow the development of commercial ties with the South Pacific islands (Hegarty 1987: 1), but despite these developments, the South Pacific remains on the periphery of Soviet interests (see Gill, ch. 4 below).

There are two principal views on Soviet activity in the South Pacific, reflecting the globalist and regionalist perspectives often found among U.S. foreign policymakers. The first—very much the traditional Cold Warrior approach—views all Soviet actions in the region as subversive. Commercial activities, especially fishing agreements, are seen as a front for espionage and a means of creating economic vulnerabilities in the island states that can later be exploited (Tanham 1988: 85–94). Soviet Pacific military forces, especially those deployed at Camranh Bay in Vietnam, are viewed as a significant threat to the stability of the South Pacific. The second approach, while wary of Soviet actions and acknowledging that a principal Soviet objective is to diminish U.S. influence in the region, has a more sanguine view of Soviet activities. It explicitly acknowledges that the Soviet Union is a Pacific superpower with legitimate diplomatic and commercial interests in the region. While these "regionalists" recognize that the Soviet Pacific fleet has been significantly expanded in recent years, they regard it as still inferior to the U.S. fleet, and see it as no threat to the South Pacific states.

The first of these perspectives has been popular in the Reagan administration (especially in the Pentagon, and to a lesser extent in the State Department), but the Hawke and Lange governments have adopted the second viewpoint. The Australian government has placed itself at odds with the United States in encouraging an increased Soviet presence in the region. En route to Moscow in November 1987, Prime Minister Hawke stated that he "would welcome a constructive involvement by the USSR in political and economic developments in the Asia-Pacific region."* The Australian government has been far more sanguine than the United States on the buildup of the Soviet Pacific fleet. Defence Minister Beazley, comparing data on the Soviet and American Pacific fleets, concluded that "The United States has over the last six years considerably increased its maritime power and . . . effectively checkmated any position that the Soviet Union had effectively developed in the Pacific." He dismissed the concerns of the conservative press in Australia over Soviet use of Camranh Bay, arguing that it does not have "front-line craft" there.† This assessment accords with that of most strategic analysts, who emphasize the deficiencies of the Soviet Pacific fleet (see Dibb 1984).**

*Following domestic criticism of these remarks, Hawke argued that Australia needed to respond to the opportunities offered by *perestroika* and *glasnost*, which "were likely to lead to a more subtle and imaginative diplomacy by the Soviet Union. . . . The Soviet Union is of course a Pacific nation and it therefore has a legitimate interest in the Pacific. We recognize the fact that the Soviet Union is entitled to economic relations with Pacific countries. . . . I told the Soviet leadership that we would judge the Soviet's intentions in our region not by their words but by their actions in, for example, Indo-China and Afghanistan. That is in part what I mean when I say that we would welcome a constructive involvement by the Soviet Union in our region. We do not want any fishing agreement signed by the Soviet Union with an island state to be anything other than just that—a fishing agreement" (Hawke 1987: 642–43). Foreign Minister Hayden similarly insisted that the Soviet Union's presence in the region must be limited to non-strategic relations.

†*Australian Foreign Affairs Record* 58, 2 (February 1987): 88. Australia has consistently argued that the Soviet presence in Vietnam is more a political than a military problem.

**A detailed review of the Soviet Pacific fleet concluded that the overwhelming preponderance of Soviet naval forces deployed there were not equipped for high-seas surface engagements but only for close-in shore defense (Da Cunha 1988).

Neither Hawke nor Lange is a Soviet dupe. Hawke is profoundly suspicious of the Soviet Union, in part as a consequence of his experience on a visit to Moscow as head of Australia's trade union movement when the Soviets reneged on a commitment to permit some "refuseniks" to emigrate. Lange has publicly warned the Soviet Union on several occasions against attempting to exploit the rift between New Zealand and the United States. That they are generally more sanguine about the Soviet threat in the South Pacific than Washington is does not mean that they are any less opposed to the Soviet Union's establishing a military presence in the region. There is, however, a considerable difference in emphasis between the Pacific policies of the current governments in Australia and New Zealand and those of the Reagan administration. The globalist emphasis in the Reagan administration's policy has been seen by Australia and New Zealand as counter-productive to Western interests in the Pacific.*

Undoubtedly the Western alliance would prefer that the policy of strategic denial be successfully maintained, but this is unrealistic given the desire of Soviet leaders to be accorded the recognition they feel they deserve as a superpower. Moscow will attempt to establish a presence in all regions—no matter how remote or tangential to Soviet interests. As Gill observes, the Soviet Union has legitimate interests in the South Pacific: diplomatic relations, transit for submarines (and perhaps surface vessels and aircraft en route to Antarctica), oceanographic information-gathering, and economic relations (especially fishing rights).

Increased Soviet influence in the South Pacific is inevitable given its total exclusion in the past, but such influence is likely to remain at a low level. The Soviet refusal to renew fishing agreements with Kiribati and Vanuatu when they would not agree to lower license fees suggests that Moscow is not pursuing a policy of expanding its influence regardless of cost. One component of their cost calculations would be the likely response of Australia, New Zealand, and the United States to any attempt to establish military facilities in the region—a response likely to be

*Australian Ambassador to the United States Rawdon Dalrymple argues that it would be desirable "if a special office for the South Pacific were set up in the State Department, an office which would have its own voice and interests in the bureaucracy. . . . Another thing that is important is that you get into the habit of sending to [the South Pacific] representatives and emissaries of the United States who see the world not just in terms of the overall ideological conflict between the West and the East and in terms of the power struggle between the Soviet Union and the United States" (quoted in Burnett 1988: 182).

disproportionate to any benefit they might hope to derive. The opportunities the Soviet Union has exploited so far are largely of Western making—currently primarily the effects of French policies.

FRENCH INTERESTS IN THE PACIFIC

France has a legitimate interest in maintaining a presence in the South Pacific, but its current policies are the most important source of political instability in the region (see Aldrich, ch. 3 below). Its attitudes on nuclear testing and decolonization for New Caledonia, and its sinking of the Greenpeace vessel *Rainbow Warrior* in Auckland harbor, have consistently displayed arrogance and insensitivity toward the South Pacific states.

Nuclear testing is a particularly sensitive issue for countries in the South Pacific because of the exploitation of the region as a "nuclear playground" (Firth 1987). Fears of contamination from the testing may be exaggerated given the enormous distances that separate the French site at Mururoa atoll from other Pacific islands, but the resolve of the South Pacific Forum on this issue should not be taken lightly. It not only colors attitudes toward France but spills over into antipathy toward the United States as a supporter of the French. Washington's position was argued by the Defense Department Director for East Asia and the Pacific in testimony to the House of Representatives Subcommittee on Asia and the Pacific:

> The Free World and all those nations that wish to deter the expansionist policies of the Soviet Union benefit from the fact that there is a French testing program. . . . Because French testing contributes an additional level of deterrence against Soviet nuclear capabilities, the United States cannot in good conscience sign a protocol against it (quoted in Mack 1987: 3).

American decision-makers appear to discount the damage this stance does to U.S. standing in the region. The Australian ambassador to the United States has argued that continued French testing at Mururoa would be "absolutely certain to prejudice the South Pacific people against the West, against that is to say United States and Australian interests in a way that will quite possibly prove very costly." He noted that French testing has been a "major influence in the formation of the climate of opinion in New Zealand which is now causing such anxiety to both the United States and the Australian governments in relation to the future of

ANZUS" (quoted in Firth 1987: 130).* The South Pacific Forum argues that if testing is as safe as the French claim, then it should be conducted on Corsica or in the Jura, where geological formations similar to those of Mururoa are found. If Washington does not distance itself from France on this issue, it will be providing a golden opportunity to the Soviet Union to expand its influence in the region.

French policy in New Caledonia is another source of anger and frustration within the South Pacific Forum. Decolonization in countries with large settler populations has always been a thorny issue; in New Caledonia it is particularly complex because the settlers include not only Europeans, who constitute 37 percent of the population, but also Wallisians (8 percent) and assorted other "foreigners" (mainly Tahitians, Indonesians, Vietnamese, and Ni-Vanuatu), who comprise 12 percent of the total. Together these immigrants outnumber the native Melanesians (Spencer 1985). Not only the Europeans, but also the other immigrants oppose independence under Melanesian rule, fearing that they will sooner or later be driven out.

The French have a substantial interest in maintaining their influence in New Caledonia (see Aldrich below). The island is a major producer of nickel, and it is the only significant Western source of cobalt outside Zaire. New Caledonia also has a potentially valuable exclusive economic zone. France has substantially modernized the port facilities in Nouméa and is reportedly planning a new military base on the island. (*Le Monde* has described New Caledonia as "an aircraft carrier anchored in the center of the Pacific.") Aldrich notes that some influential members of the French defense community perceive ANZUS as too fragile a vessel to be entrusted with safeguarding Western interests in the Pacific.

The intransigence of the Chirac government over granting greater autonomy to the Melanesian population created the potential for violent conflict between the Melanesian nationalists and French authorities. If escalating violence is to be avoided, a new formula which grants some form of independence to the Melanesians yet guarantees the rights of settlers will be necessary. The September 1987 referendum staged by the Chirac government, without the presence of UN observers and boycotted by most of the Melanesian population, was greeted with widespread scepticism even by the French president (Mitterrand). The South Pacific Forum "completely rejected" it, and renewed its efforts in the UN to press

*Similarly, Richard Falk has observed that "French nuclear testing was a decisive source of disenchantment with United States leadership in the southern Pacific" (Foreword to Camilleri 1987: vii).

for decolonization. The recent defeat of the Chirac government was greeted with relief by all independent South Pacific states, and the early moves by its socialist successor toward a constitutional formula that accommodates both Melanesian and Kaldoche aspirations were widely welcomed.

Australia and New Zealand believe that French intransigence, besides leading to an increase in violence within New Caledonia, has opened the way for increased Libyan and Soviet influence in the region. There have been reports of Libyan training of members of the pro-independence Kanak Socialist National Liberation Front (Hegarty 1987). There is also the possibility that Melanesian nationalism will become radicalized. Any fragmentation of the South Pacific Forum along racial lines would reduce the influence of Australia and New Zealand within the region, and partly for this reason they have championed the cause of New Caledonia in the UN and its reinstatement on the UN list of territories to be decolonized.

Relations between France and Australia and New Zealand have been strained in recent years. Ministerial contacts between France and Australia were broken off for most of 1987, and the Australian representative in New Caledonia was expelled amid accusations that Australia was fomenting violence in New Caledonia. New Zealand's relations with France were complicated by the *Rainbow Warrior* affair, and the refusal of the French government to show any contrition for this act of "state terrorism." However, neither Australia nor New Zealand enjoys any leverage over France. The Australian government's embargo on uranium sales to France in protest of French nuclear testing had to be lifted when the country faced balance-of-payments problems, and the New Zealand prime minister was forced to strike a deal favorable to the two French agents convicted in the *Rainbow Warrior* bombing when Paris threatened to block New Zealand's access to the European market. Canberra and Wellington have the power only to antagonize and perhaps embarrass the French. Both governments emphasize that they are not attempting to exclude French influence from the region; rather they fear that current French policies will damage not only France's long-term interests, but also those of the Western alliance as a whole.

THE SOUTH PACIFIC NUCLEAR FREE ZONE

A nuclear free zone in the South Pacific was first proposed by the 1972–75 Labour government in New Zealand. The proposal gained the backing of the South Pacific Forum and the UN General Assembly, but it was shelved with the return of conservative parties to government in Australia and New Zealand in 1975.* When the Labor Party was returned to office in Australia in 1983, it revived the proposal. Its revival was intended to serve five major purposes:

(a) It would underline the government's commitment to arms control;

(b) It was a way of protesting against nuclear weapons in general and French nuclear testing in particular;

(c) It would forestall domestic criticism by Australia's anti-nuclear parties and possible losses of votes to them;

(d) It would symbolize Australia's sincerity and leadership on nuclear issues to the Pacific island states;†

(e) It would avert more radical proposals that might adversely affect U.S. interests in the region.

Australia's proposal was carefully crafted with U.S. interests in mind—so much so that the peace movement asserted that it and the subsequent nuclear free zone treaty are meaningless. In particular, the Hawke government was concerned that the treaty not affect visits by nuclear-armed or nuclear-powered vessels or aircraft. It prohibits the testing, storage, acquisition, and deployment of nuclear weapons in the South Pacific, but it does not ban the sale of uranium, the hosting of communications and surveillance facilities associated with nuclear weapons, or the testing of missiles within the region.

After carefully tailoring the treaty to accommodate U.S. concerns, the Australian government was dismayed at the Reagan administration's refusal to sign it.** This allowed the Soviet Union to score a propaganda

---

*The United States had expressed concern at the implications of the New Zealand proposal for the transit of its vessels and aircraft in the region and the use of port facilities. These had been echoed by the Whitlam government in Australia (see Fry 1985: 101–2).

†Foreign Minister Hayden asserted that the success of the treaty "was critical to regional comity in which Australia played an important part, and in particular to Australia's credibility in that region" (*Australian Foreign Affairs Record* 58, 6 [June 1987]: 304).

**The treaty appears to meet all except one of the criteria that the State Department has specified as necessary if nuclear free zones are to gain the support of the United States:

(1) The initiative for the creation of the zone should come from the states in the region concerned;

(2) All states whose participation is deemed important should participate in the zone;

coup at the expense of the West. Moscow signed the second and third protocols of the treaty in 1986, pledging (a) not to test any nuclear explosive device in the South Pacific and (b) not to use or threaten to use nuclear weapons against countries in the Pacific. At the time the Soviet government issued a qualifying statement stipulating that there should be no transit of nuclear weapons through the treaty zone, and expressing concern about "aggressive actions" by Pacific countries in conjunction with a nuclear power. These reservations were withdrawn following representations from the Australian government, and in February 1988 the Soviet Union became the first nuclear power to ratify the Treaty of Rarotonga.* By refusing to sign the treaty, the United States again appears to have placed its standing with France ahead of its relations with the countries in the South Pacific Forum. It should not be surprised if anti-French feeling within the region spills over into anti-Americanism.

---

(3) The zone arrangement should provide for adequate verification of compliance with its provisions;

(4) The establishment of the zone should not disturb existing security arrangements to the detriment of regional and international security;

(5) The zone arrangement should effectively prohibit its parties from developing or otherwise possessing any nuclear explosive device for whatever reasons;

(6) The establishment of a zone should not affect the existing rights of its parties under international law to grant or deny to other states transit privileges within international waters, including port calls, and overflights; and

(7) The zone arrangement should not seek to impose restrictions on the exercise of rights recognized under international law, particularly the principle of freedom of navigation of the high seas, in international waters, and through straits used for international navigation, and the right of innocent passage through territorial waters.

The one condition that the treaty fails to satisfy is that requiring participation by all states deemed important to its success. France, against whom the treaty is primarily aimed, is clearly not going to participate. Britain has also refused to sign, but may do so if pressured by the United States.

*China has also signed the treaty and is expected to ratify it without reservation. The treaty entered into force 11 December 1986. Besides the Soviet Union, ten other states have ratified it: Australia, Cook Islands, Fiji, Kiribati, Nauru, New Zealand, Niue, Papua New Guinea, Tuvalu, and Western Samoa. The Solomon Islands signed, but as of November 1987 had not ratified the treaty. Tonga currently opposes the treaty because it fears that it will adversely affect U.S. interests, but Vanuatu is now reportedly considering signing it after previously criticizing it for not banning nuclear-powered and nuclear-armed vessels from the region. For a discussion of the negotiations from the perspective of an Australian participant, see Sadleir (1987: 489–500).

* * *

The South Pacific has entered a new era of turbulence. The days when it was an American lake which could be treated with benign neglect by the United States have ended. New forces of nationalism are rife—not only in the island states but also in Australia and New Zealand, which are striving to forge their own national identities and redefine their roles in the world now that their long-standing ties with Britain have largely been terminated. U.S. relations with the Pacific require more careful management in the future to avoid further damage to Western interests. In the remaining chapters of this book, the major issues that currently confront the United States in the region are discussed, along with their implications for U.S. foreign policy.

REFERENCES

Allen, Scott [Lt. Commander]. 1987. "The South Pacific: Setting Priorities." *Proceedings of the U.S. Naval Academy.* July.

ANZUS Alliance. 1982. Parliament of the Commonwealth of Australia, Joint Committee on Foreign Affairs and Defense. Canberra: Australian Government Publishing Service.

Babbage, Ross. 1980. *Rethinking Australia's Defence.* St. Lucia: University of Queensland Press.

———. 1984. "Australian Defence Planning, Force Structure and Equipment: The American Effect." *Australian Outlook* 38, 3 (December).

Ball, Desmond. 1980. *A Suitable Piece of Real Estate.* Sydney: Hale and Iremonger.

———, ed. 1985a. *The ANZAC Connection.* Sydney: George Allen & Unwin.

———. 1985b. "The Security Relationship between Australia and New Zealand." In Ball 1985a.

Barclay, Glen St. J. 1976. "The Future of Australian-American Relations." *Australian Outlook* 30, 3 (December).

———. 1985. *Friends in High Places.* Melbourne: Oxford University Press.

Beazley, Kim. 1988. "Thinking Defence: Key Concepts in Australian Defence Planning." *Australian Outlook* 42, 2 (October).

Bell, Coral. 1988. *Dependent Ally.* Melbourne: Oxford University Press.

Burnett, Alan. 1988. *The A-NZ-US Triangle.* Canberra: Strategic and Defence Studies Centre, Australian National University.

Camilleri, Joseph A. 1987. *ANZUS: Australia's Predicament in the Nuclear Age.* Melbourne: Macmillan.

Campbell, David. 1986. *Australian Public Opinion on National Security Issues.* Canberra: Peace Research Centre, Australian National University, Working Paper No. 1.

————. 1987. *The Domestic Sources of New Zealand Security Policy in Comparative Perspective.* Canberra: Peace Research Centre, Australian National University, Working Paper No. 16.

Commonwealth Secretariat. 1985. *Vulnerability: Small States in the Global Society.* London.

Connell, John. 1988. "New Caledonia: A Crisis of Decolonization in the South Pacific." *The Round Table* 305 (January).

Da Cunha, Derek. 1988. "Soviet Naval Capabilities in the Pacific in the 1990s." Paper presented at conference on the Soviets in the Pacific in the 1990s, Australian National University, Canberra, May.

Dalrymple, Rawdon. 1987. "The Pacific Basin: Alliance, Trade and Bases." *Australian Foreign Affairs Record* 58, 3 (March).

Dibb, Paul. 1984. "The Soviet Union as a Pacific Military Power." *Pacific Defence Reporter* 11, 5 (November).

————. 1985. "Soviet Strategy Towards Australia, New Zealand, and the South West Pacific." *Australian Outlook* 39, 2 (August).

"Fiji Report." 1987. In *Australian Development Studies Network Newsletter* 8 (July).

Firth, Stewart. 1987. *Nuclear Playground.* Sydney: Allen & Unwin.

Fry, Greg. 1985. "Australia, New Zealand and Arms Control in the Pacific Region." In Ball 1985a.

Gallagher, Peter. 1988. "The Economic Objectives." In *In Pursuit of National Interests: Australian Foreign Policy in the 1990s,* eds. F. A. Mediansky and A. C. Palfreeman. Sydney: Pergamon.

Goot, Murray, and King, Peter. N.d. "ANZUS Reconsidered: The Domestic Politics of an Alliance." University of Sydney; mimeo.

Hanson, Allan F. 1987. "Trouble in the Family: New Zealand's Anti-Nuclear Policy." *SAIS Review* 7, 1 (Winter/Spring).

Hawke, Robert. 1987. "Visit by Prime Minister to Singapore, the Soviet Union, and Japan." *Australian Foreign Affairs Record* 58, 10 (November-December).

Hayden, Bill. 1983. "Review of ANZUS." *Australian Foreign Affairs Record,* September.

Hegarty, David. 1987. *Libya and the South Pacific.* Canberra: Strategic and Defence Studies Centre, Australian National University, Working Paper No. 127.

Herr, Richard A. 1976. "Regionalism, Strategic Denial and South Pacific Security." *Journal of Pacific History* 21, 4.

————. 1985. "The American Impact on Australian Defence Relations with the South Pacific Islands." *Australian Outlook* 38, 3 (December).

Holsti, K. J. 1970. "National Role Conceptions in the Study of Foreign Policy." *International Studies Quarterly* 14, 3 (September).

Hoyle, J. H. A. 1985. "The Security of Small Island States." In Ball 1985a.

Lange, David. 1985. "New Zealand's Security Policy." *Foreign Affairs* 63, 5 (Summer).

————. 1987. "Facing Critical Choices." *New Zealand International Review* 12, 4 (July/August).

La Rocque, Gene [Rear Admiral]. 1974. "Proliferation of Nuclear Weapons." Testimony to Subcommittee on Military Applications, Joint Committee on Atomic Energy, U.S. Congress; 10 September.

Mack, Andrew. 1987. "The French Nuclear Test Program and 'SPINFIZZ.'" *Peace Research Centre Newsletter* 2, 3 (December).

Matthews, Trevor, and Ravenhill, John. 1987. "ANZUS, the American Alliance and External Threats: Australian Elite Attitudes." *Australian Outlook* 41, 3 (December).

McMillan, Stuart. 1987. *Neither Confirm Nor Deny*. New York: Praeger.

Meaney, Neville. 1980. "The United States." In *Australia in World Affairs 1971–1975*, ed. W. J. Hudson. Sydney: George Allen & Unwin.

Mediansky, F. A. 1986. "Nuclear Weapons and Security in the South Pacific." *Washington Quarterly*, Winter.

————. 1987. "The Defence of Australia and the American Alliance." *Australian Outlook* 41, 3 (December).

Millar, T. B. 1978. *Australia in Peace and War*. Canberra: Australian National University Press.

————. 1983. "Australia and the United States." In *Australia's External Relations in the 1980s*, ed. Paul Dibb. Canberra: Croom Helm.

New Zealand. 1986. *Defence and Security: What New Zealanders Want*. Report of the Defence Committee of Enquiry. Wellington: Government Printer.

Pemberton, Gregory. 1987. *All the Way: Australia's Road to Vietnam*. Sydney: Allen & Unwin.

Phillips, Jock. 1988. "New Zealand and the ANZUS Alliance—Changing National Self-Perceptions." Paper presented to conference on Socio-Political Change and National Images, East-West Center, Honolulu, August.

Premdas, Ralph, and Howard, Michael C. 1985. "Vanuatu's Foreign Policy: Contradictions and Constraints." *Australian Outlook* 39, 3 (December).

Renouf, Alan. 1986. *Malcolm Fraser and Australian Foreign Policy*. Sydney: Australian Professional Publications.

Richelson, Jeffrey T., and Ball, Desmond. 1985. *The Ties That Bind*. Boston: Allen & Unwin.

Scholes, Gordon. 1984. "Australia's Strategic Outlook and Defence Policy." *Australian Outlook* 38, 3 (December).

Sinclair, Ian. 1984. "Australia's National Security—The Region and the United States." *Australian Outlook* 38, 3 (December).

Sissons, David C. S. 1952. "The Pacific Pact." *Australian Outlook* 6, 1 (March).

Sadleir, David. 1987. "Rarotonga: In the Footsteps of Tlatelolco." *Australian Foreign Affairs Record* 58, 9 (September/October).

Spencer, Michael C. 1985. *New Caledonia in Crisis*. Canberra: Australian Institute of International Affairs, Occasional Paper No. 1.

Suter, Keith. 1987. *Is There Life after ANZUS?* Sydney: Pluto Press.

Tanham, George K. 1988. "Subverting the South Pacific." *The National Interest*, Spring.

Thakur, Ramesh. N.d. "New Zealand and the ANZUS Alliance: Security Guarantee or Nuclear Pollutant?" University of Otago; mimeo.

USIA [United States Information Agency]. 1986. "Australian Public Opinion on the U.S. Alliance: 1986." East Asia and Pacific Branch, Office of Research, Washington, D.C. December; mimeo.

———. 1987. "Australian 'Successor Generation' Attitudes Toward the U.S. and ANZUS." Washington, D.C. December; mimeo.

White, Robert E. 1988. *The New Zealand Nuclear Ship Ban: Is Compromise Possible?* Canberra: Peace Research Centre, Australian National University, Working Paper No. 30.

Wolfowitz, Paul D. 1984. "The ANZUS Relationship: Alliance Management." *Australian Outlook* 38, 3 (December).

Chapter 2

THE NEW ZEALAND PERSPECTIVE ON ANZUS AND NUCLEAR WEAPONS

Michael McKinley

ANZUS IN HISTORICAL PERSPECTIVE

ANZUS is a treaty embodying anxiety. When the negotiations which led to its establishment commenced in early 1951, it was an anxiety about the sort of arrangement which would guarantee Australian and New Zealand security in an age of British incapability. That this was felt more keenly in Australia than in New Zealand was not at the time significant; both countries had perceived, over several years, a need for the United States to be the successor guarantor of their vital interests. The pressure, therefore, for an arrangement came from Australia and New Zealand—not from the United States.

In the 1940s and early 1950s the United States steadfastly took the position that no formal treaty was necessary, but this in no way signified indifference or a lack of commitment. Indeed in Washington the prevailing attitude was expressed by Admiral Ernest J. King to President Franklin Roosevelt in 1942, when Australia and New Zealand were threatened by Japanese attack: "We cannot in honour let Australia and New Zealand down. They are our brothers" (quoted in "ANZUS Expert Sets Record Straight" 1985). The U.S. position against any sort of formal agreement persisted until the end of 1950, when several developments induced a change in Washington.

The first of these developments was a U.S. sense of solidarity and appreciation with Australia and New Zealand after the latter two sent ground forces to Korea during the Korean War. The second was a shared concern about Asian security caused by the entry of the People's Republic of China into this war. The third was the consequent stimulus to the American desire for a "soft" peace with Japan and hence a need to obtain the support of U.S. allies who still feared a revival of Japan. Although this development was a prime reason for the ANZUS treaty, it might sometimes have been overemphasized by Australian and New Zealand negotiators for tactical purposes and might thus have obscured the fourth development, which itself loomed large in contemporary perceptions. In effect, this was the second development writ large—i.e., a concern about worldwide Communist imperialism in general and regional Communist expansionism on the Asian mainland in particular. Overall there is no doubt that the ANZUS treaty was seen as an appropriate vehicle by which to promote solidarity and to withstand aggression. Moreover, there was at that time a sense of shared values, similar history, and common purposes which made a high level of close cooperation seem perfectly natural.

For all that, Australia and New Zealand differed. As noted, Australia wanted a formal arrangement more than New Zealand; in addition, the *nature* of the arrangement was perceived differently. New Zealand wanted—and for several years had been trying to interest the Americans in—a unilateral declaration by the United States that it would protect New Zealand, like that given to Canada in 1938. This had an obvious attraction to Wellington because, if effected, it would not involve New Zealand's giving anything in return. It would also allow New Zealand to both avoid making extra commitments and continue its emotional involvement with Britain. It must be realized that New Zealand had not yet developed a serious interest in the Pacific, and the overseas defense plans it viewed as most important remained those in association with Britain for action in the Middle East and Europe.

In the event, however, Australia's preferences for a formal treaty, with provisions for consultation, won out. The terms of the treaty were seen as providing a potential for gradually securing a share of American policymaking power, similar to that which the "old" (white) Commonwealth countries had achieved with Britain. While this outcome involved New Zealand's accepting a formal treaty with reciprocal obligations, the experience of annual ministerial and other kinds of official consultations in what was seen as an intimate and effective diplomatic liaison was both reassuring and comforting. Indeed according to Frank Corner, former secretary of the New Zealand Department of Foreign Affairs, the easy access of Australian and New Zealand officials to their counterparts throughout various U.S. administrations was a cause of envy among representatives of other countries in Washington ("ANZUS Expert Sets

Record Straight" 1985).* Moreover, the experience of the lesser powers in ANZUS was confirmation of the findings by Holsti, Hopmann, and Sullivan (1985), who derived six formal propositions from a study of alliances, one of which stated that small powers have disproportionate influence over their larger allies. According to the authors, this influence derived from the former being able to commit the latter.

Insofar as the fundamental interest of New Zealand's defense was concerned, the benefits ANZUS was claimed to provide expanded with the passage of time and certainly reflected the Holsti et al. thesis almost as an entrenched article of received wisdom. As *Defence Review* (1978) stated, "ANZUS has been accepted by successive New Zealand Governments as the ultimate guarantee of security in the region." What bothered and still bothers many critics and commentators is that this interpretation transcended a strict construction of the treaty. According to such an approach, a much more prudent and skeptical assessment of ANZUS is that it is in reality a useless piece of paper because each party is bound only to "consult" and to "act to meet the common danger according to its constitutional processes." Indeed as Desmond Ball stated in an address to the Foreign Policy School at the University of Otago,

> The ANZUS Treaty itself . . . is neither an absolute nor watertight guarantee, and nor is it the primary determinant of United States military assistance to Australia and New Zealand. Whether or not the United States would come to the assistance of Australia and/or New Zealand in any particular situation, the nature of that assistance, and the conditions on which it would be forthcoming would depend essentially on the calculation of interests made by the United States Government at the time (1983: 79).

Ball was alluding to the essentially equivocal nature of the U.S. guarantee under ANZUS in certain circumstances. In support of this argument Ball was able to cite not only two historical examples of U.S. equivocation, but also to present scenarios in which the United States, its willingness notwithstanding, would be unable to provide other than incidental help (1983: 79–82). Central to ANZUS, therefore, is an element of uncertainty caused by what the demands of Australia and/or New Zealand at a particular time might be, on the one hand, and the need for both the U.S. President and the Congress to insist upon their respective rights on the other.

*At various stages in his career, Frank Corner was also New Zealand's ambassador to Washington and his country's permanent representative to the United Nations. He took part in the ANZUS negotiations and was present at the treaty's signing.

Attempts to reconcile such competing demands are necessarily fruitless because the exigencies of a particular situation will be the determinants, not the prevailing articles of faith. As the aforementioned *Defence Review* statement indicates, this did not prevent New Zealand governments until 1984 from weaving a garment of faith (abetted by hope and inference) they called the "ultimate guarantee" of ANZUS. Having so designed it, great care was taken to make it as comfortable as possible. Down the years, loose threads and ragged edges were eliminated so as to make it so snug and warm that when it was worn, the wearer could imagine himself to be immune to the ordinary dictates of national sovereignty—constructive self-criticism and maximum independence. No matter that it bred an uncritical reliance beyond what could be rationally and reasonably expected. In official quarters the opinion abounded that it was a superb article and well worth the price.

For New Zealand, the price seems seldom to have been in evidence. The benefits extracted from the alliance were significant to a high degree while the costs were seen either as inevitable—in which case they were beyond argument—or hidden—in which case they were also beyond argument. As the following assessment indicates, New Zealand defense came to be viewed, almost as reflex, in an ANZUS framework. Given this referent, it flourished beyond the capabilities which could otherwise have been expected of it.

NEW ZEALAND AND ANZUS:
A CONTEMPORARY ASSESSMENT OF BENEFITS

The existence of a defense policy in any society is predicated on the existence of potential danger, if not of immediate conflict.* In this regard New Zealand follows the rule. It also subscribes to the concept of a defense policy whose ultimate aim is the maintenance of peace, or—should peace break down—the containment of violence and the restoration of peace with minimal force. To achieve this aim New Zealand is currently committed to have forces of all three armed services trained and able to operate in defensive roles involving the following: (1) surveillance of the South Pacific region; (2) deterrence of attack should

*The general source for the material in this section is *Briefing Papers Prepared for the Minister of Defence*, a series of papers supplied to the Minister of Defence, the Hon. F. D. O'Flynn, on taking up his appointment and released by him on 19 October 1984. The particular source is Brief 2 of these papers, pp. 9–14, which I have only slightly abridged.

this region be threatened; and (3) the defense of national interests by use of arms. With forces established for these core purposes, the country also developed its capacities in civil defense, disaster relief in the Pacific, Antarctic support, military training assistance, and the like in peacetime. Furthermore, with forces so equipped and trained, the potential existed for military expansion to meet higher levels of conflict as they arose. All of this was meant to be achieved within the greatest possible degree of self-reliance.

While these objectives are laudable, New Zealand lacks the capacity to look after the interests it has defined for itself. For a start, it is abundantly clear that New Zealand cannot cover all modern defense options. The list of military specializations in which it has no present capacity at all is long. For example, it lacks air defense for airfields and ground forces, heavy artillery, satellite communication systems, and over-the-horizon radar. In addition, there is no effective interceptor/fighter capacity in the air and no surface-to-surface or air-to-surface guided missiles for any of the three armed services. The army has no main battle tanks; the navy lacks submarines—or even an oil tanker to extend the range of its ships—as well as vessels able to provide logistic support for operations in the Pacific or Antarctic; the air force, like the navy, is faced with limited reach because it lacks an aerial refueling system. And this is but a partial catalogue of deficiencies.

Of these deficiencies only a few were programmed to be partially overcome during the implementation of the 1983 defense review with the inclusion of logistic support vessels, aerial refueling, heavy artillery, and air defense. Other additions, such as satellite communications, were being examined. Yet it must be noted that some of these deficiencies were beyond New Zealand's resources to remedy. Moreover, defense planners regarded them as unnecessary because in the high-intensity conflict in which they would be required, the capability would be supplied by one or another of New Zealand's alliance partners. In view of this assumption, New Zealand adopted the practice of determining its equipment needs in terms of the limited area in which its forces would act independently—i.e., New Zealand and its immediate vicinity in the South Pacific, within which the scale of warfare would most likely be of low intensity. New Zealand's forces were therefore to be seen in such a regional and operational context.

Of recent times, the possibility of independent military operations beyond the South Pacific was discounted, although limited contributions to peacekeeping operations or in support of alliance partners further afield were not thought impossible. In the latter context New Zealand saw the need for its forces to be prepared to integrate with partners—and this would also have applied if the scale of warfare in the South Pacific was beyond the country's capacity. Thus vital components of New Zealand's defense policy have been the following:

Maintain professional military skills within a core of regular servicemen who can meet any limited conflict which might occur at short notice and provide the base for expansion in the event of greater need;

Be able to operate with the forces of partners and allies as necessary; and

Have developed the necessary procedures and practices for collaboration in intelligence, communications, defense logistics, defense science, and so on as to ensure that experience be pooled and there is maximum economy and efficiency of effort.

Under the aegis of the ANZUS treaty New Zealand developed a network of defense cooperation arrangements toward achieving the above objectives, as the following will indicate.

INTELLIGENCE

Not only are New Zealand's independent defense intelligence collection facilities limited, but also the Directorate of Defence Intelligence is almost totally dependent upon data and information supplied by the intelligence agencies of allied countries, including Australia and the United States. Nevertheless, through its own limited input New Zealand has been able to participate in intelligence assessment and evaluation drawing on a huge range of source material. Conclusions so drawn have therefore reflected a much more knowledgeable and realistic perception of the world than otherwise would have been possible.

Cooperation in this field has included consultation between defense intelligence agencies to produce projections of the security situation in the areas of concern to the three ANZUS partners; an exchange of intelligence officers with Washington and Canberra which has provided on-the-job training in intelligence research work (*experience which cannot be gained in New Zealand*); and a very close liaison among intelligence staffs, which has made possible consultation with the two large intelligence staffs in times of crisis. It has been the view of the New Zealand Ministry of Defence that although all material obtained was subjected to independent (national) analysis, without such material and the cooperation involved, it would have been impossible for the defense and foreign policymaking organs to have obtained the range and character of information relevant to their needs.

MILITARY STAFF

In the absence of a permanent military headquarters or central staff, military matters affecting ANZUS were dealt with by existing national defense staffs in Canberra, Honolulu, and Wellington. This resulted in formal ANZUS staff meetings at brigadier level twice a year. Their main purpose was to ensure a satisfactory degree of interoperability among national forces in time of conflict. These meetings and supporting ANZUS seminars dealt with basic logistic and equipment issues, operational procedures, laws of war tactics, and training. In essence, they developed into useful forums for the exchange of ideas and the subsequent promulgation of documents setting out policy guidelines and planning ANZUS activities.

Beyond this primary function the staff meetings became a useful link among the military planning staffs of the three partners and permitted the coordination of national activities, particularly military exercises, so that advantage could be taken of the experience and facilities provided by the others. As a result, New Zealand's scale of defense activities was extended, as was the professional military experience available to the armed forces. Again, these benefits were well beyond the country's peacetime capability.

LOGISTIC SUPPORT

New Zealand obviously depended heavily upon the United States as a source of major military equipment and the ongoing support necessary to keep that equipment working. The 1982 New Zealand/United States Memorandum of Understanding (MOU) on Logistic Support was accordingly used as a basis for the continuation of support through the U.S. Foreign Military Sales (FMS) of such defense equipment as the A4 Skyhawk, P3 Orion, Iroquois utility helicopter, M113 armored personnel carrier, communications equipment (including cryptographic items), artillery, and small arms.

The MOU also gave a very practical basis for establishing special arrangements within the huge U.S. logistics system to meet particular

New Zealand purchasing problems. FMS "cases" (money packages) were established from which to buy new U.S. Department of Defense–sourced equipment. It was understood by New Zealand, however, that should the MOU be terminated or the ANZUS treaty be altered or allowed to lapse, its "favored nation" treatment would be severely curtailed or even withdrawn. Then a deterioration in the readiness and capability of the New Zealand armed forces could be expected, and/or a substantial increase in the costs of procurement and maintenance. In this circumstance the pre–1985 U.S. interest in fostering an offset capacity in New Zealand's currently limited industrial sector would also be a casualty.

OPERATIONAL ACTIVITIES AND EXERCISES

After the signing of the ANZUS pact, the New Zealand armed forces turned increasingly away from Britain and toward the United States for information across the whole spectrum of military activity. While Australia contributed much to New Zealand in the form of training, access to the sophisticated capabilities of the United States, provided under the auspices of ANZUS, proved invaluable.

Under the aegis of the treaty local New Zealand exercises were designated ANZUS exercises, thus lending them a broader scope. As they involved international effort, Australia and the United States were able to give them a high priority in their own programs. Once more, for New Zealand the benefits were clear and considerable, with the presence in the exercises of submarines and aircraft that would not otherwise be available. Indeed all three armed services came to depend heavily on participation in ANZUS maneuvers to build up operational standards and to ensure the compatibility of procedures and interoperability of equipment. The Royal New Zealand Navy, for example, was by any estimate too small to maintain effective operational procedures without operating in an exercise environment with larger forces. Similarly, without ANZUS exercises New Zealand senior officers would simply never obtain the necessary experience of command and control for the direction of major formations. Nor did the Royal New Zealand Air Force have alternative means of exercising in large combined or joint settings. While all air force roles are affected by the cancellation of ANZUS exercise programs, the major impact will be felt in the maritime and strike roles, to which the air force, in accordance with the policy direction in the 1983 *Defence Review*, was to assign a greater emphasis. As the air force's exchange program with the United States included strike and air transport pilots, a maritime operations officer, and helicopter crews, its cessation is bound to have serious consequences. While the numbers involved are small, they have in the past been significant in terms of the development of role and operational expertise, and it will most likely be difficult to locate suitable substitutes. This of course applies to the other two services in similar fashion.

DEFENSE SCIENCE

New Zealand does not have an indigenous defense industry capable of providing modern high-technology defense equipment. The country's armed forces are therefore almost totally dependent on overseas suppliers for such equipment. To substantially change this situation—by developing a domestic defense industry infrastructure—would without any doubt require adherence to a concept that could never be cost-effective.

The ANZUS relationship provided many advantages. Under Phase 1 of the P3 Orion update program for the New Zealand air force, technology was acquired which brought New Zealand up to a state-of-the-art level. Spinoffs from it enabled the fledgling aerospace industry to tender for overseas contracts, provide additional employment, and earn overseas funds. Meanwhile, the navy was granted a long-term lease from the United States of the oceanographic research ship HMNZS *Tui.*

More generally, New Zealand was an enthusiastic supporter of scientific and technical exchange programs, not all of which were directly connected to ANZUS, but which resulted from agreements which fell within the general umbrella of mutual cooperation and understanding provided by the treaty. In this way a large proportion of New Zealand scientific work was undertaken in cooperation with the two alliance partners.

The most important defense-related agreement in this respect was the Technical Cooperation Program, within which there existed a number of subgroups covering such important subjects as undersea warfare, communications, infrared technology, radar, aeronautics technology, and materials. In addition, New Zealand was party to a number of bilateral data-exchange agreements with Australia, Britain, Canada, and the United States known as the ABCA and AFCC agreements. These agreements provided for the exchange of classified information up to secret level and were designed to ensure the protection of the information from disclosure to potential enemies.

In short, the ANZUS connection gave a dimension and depth to mutual defense exchanges among the services of the three nations which went beyond those provided by other bilateral or multinational arrangements. It fostered a high degree of understanding and confidence which would have been difficult if not impossible to achieve by other means. This in turn encouraged the New Zealand armed forces to derive a sense of purpose and commitment in significant part from the alliance. Moreover, while much emphasis in New Zealand was placed on the traditional bilateral link with Australia, there existed a realization that given the weight the latter placed on ANZUS, a sound relationship between New Zealand and Australia had to be founded on the trilateral treaty. In any case, this permitted New Zealand an independent and sovereign influence in relation to matters far beyond the individual or collective competence of the South Pacific partners.

CHALLENGES, ALTERNATIVE VIEWS, AND AMBIGUITIES

The development of New Zealand's defense capability inside ANZUS, as outlined, proceeded without serious challenge after 1951. It was facilitated by the fact that for over twenty-six of the years between 1951 and 1988 the National Party, which regarded ANZUS as the essential foundation of New Zealand's security, was in government. Ironically, if a radical challenge to ANZUS existed, it came not from the New Zealand Labour Party as a whole, but from third parties—such as the Values Party, Social Credit, the New Zealand Party, Manu Motuhake, and least of all from a *section* of the Labour Party. Moreover, challenges date only from the founding of the Values Party in 1972—i.e., some two decades after the treaty had been in force.

The essence of the views of those opposed to ANZUS is that the treaty and its associated arrangements are a hindrance rather than a benefit to New Zealand security. Whereas traditional views of the treaty reflected assumptions of an uncertain and threatening world which could be controlled or prevailed over by a strong alliance system to which New Zealand contributed, the alternative view assumed a less hostile environment which could be maintained by mutual cooperation and extended by the dismantling of aggressive political structures such as treaties. Similarly, where the traditionalists saw active alliance membership as both contributing to New Zealand's influence in the decision-making processes of much larger alliance partners and assisting in furthering the nation's economic goals, the opposition proclaimed that intra-alliance influence was unnecessary since the best recourse lay in national initiatives in time of crisis or, failing that, nonviolent resistance; in economic matters self-interest was held to prevail—in which case noneconomic considerations would be irrelevant. Overall, alliance membership was thought to create more problems than it solved, and superpower protection to involve more costs than benefits. (For a fuller discussion of the competing sets of assumptions on which the traditional and alternative defense strategies are based, see Kennaway 1984: 2–5.)

The alternative views were of course not original to New Zealand. As New Zealand suffers the "tyranny of distance" every bit as much as Australia, such views owed their conception to places and influences far away. It must be added that traditionally the New Zealand Labour Party adopted opposing views only in a mutant or modified form. In effect, Labour chose a compromise path and adopted elements of both the traditional and alternative views, as Richard Kennaway writes:

> It has wished to maintain ANZUS but to broaden it and place greater emphasis on economic and development aspects. It has wished to ban nuclear ship visits and to promote actively the concept of the South Pacific Nuclear-Weapons-Free-Zone—to which the National Party has also paid lip service—but it has also wished to continue to rely in the last instance on the United States for protection against conventional attack (1984: 2).

Three characteristics of intellectual life in New Zealand are relevant to the current imbroglio. The first is that the initial challenge to ANZUS was part of a wider transnational movement of the late 1960s and early 1970s concerned with what was popularly known as "the quality of life" and ultimately, as the New Zealand experience indicates, a preoccupation with the deeper, nonmaterial needs of people in society. The second is that there is a relative paucity of debate, both qualitatively and quantitatively, inside New Zealand on matters affecting the country's security. Noticeably, when there was debate, it was largely reactive, a response to the assertions of a party which was rightly categorized by its founder as "[n]on-existent before June and unknown to most New Zealanders until a television programme five weeks before the election [in 1972]" (Brunt 1983: 79). The third has to do with the self-confidence, or lack thereof, with which New Zealand approaches issues; it is perhaps best illustrated by historian Keith Sinclair's judgment:

Here [in New Zealand] we find, not the original though primitive, but the fairly sophisticated and second-hand. The New Zealanders were never obliged, in isolation, to cultivate their own mental or spiritual resource, to contemplate their souls (cited in McIntyre 1967: 337).

Sinclair is not alone in his assessment. Another historian, W. David McIntyre, reached a similar conclusion in 1967 and noted that the country's foreign policy was made up of "three fascinatingly inter-woven strands: the traditional strand, the idealistic strand, and the strand of hard-headed pragmatism" (McIntyre 1967: 327). Taken together, Sinclair and McIntyre point to a likely conjunction in New Zealand of modes of thought—such as utopianism and realism—which are not only borrowed without sufficient care as to their suitability for the circumstances, but which are also ambiguous (where they are not downright contradictory) in their application.

For some observers of Australia and New Zealand this conjunction of borrowed modes of thought no doubt injures the image of the close relationship between the two countries which was born during the Great War and nurtured in peace and during subsequent wars. Certainly this author does not deny the existence of a close relationship, yet it must be emphasized that Australia and New Zealand are different countries with different interests, and their differences have had an effect in the policy arena. Significantly, the differences have been well appreciated by the United States down the years; the divergent approaches of Australia and New Zealand to the founding of ANZUS itself were surely an indication of how the differences operated and what they might portend. (For a fuller and very well-researched discussion of the historical differences between Australia and New Zealand over the nuclear issue, see Campbell.) New Zealand's involvement in the Vietnam War realized such possibilities. Even under a committed, pro-alliance National Party government, its responses to U.S. requests were slow, its troop commitment minimal, its support for U.S. initiatives perfunctory, and its preference clear for alternative strategies to those pursued by the United States. Thus the New Zealand stand on Vietnam was distinct from the relative congruency which existed between Canberra and Washington (Jackson 1980: 58–59).*

*In the Australia–New Zealand dyad, attraction and aversion work simultaneously, the one challenging the other continuously because neither geographical proximity, common historical experience, nor mutual affinity can overcome essential differences in identity. Thus there are times when New Zealand's view of its defense needs is shaped less according to the centripetal

If defense debate had been healthy in New Zealand, the chances are that many of the ambiguities noted above and disparities between thought and action would have been addressed for what they were and are—i.e., insults to rational government and atavistic practices inimical to national security. Even since the advent of the Labour government of David Lange in July 1984 and its ANZUS-related policies, debate is still uneven and attenuated.*

Prior to the Lange government's Defence Committee of Inquiry, established in 1985, there was only one contemporary work of any note which attempted to define New Zealand's strategic choices in a comprehensive manner; interestingly, it was authored by an Indian academic teaching at the University of Otago (Thakur 1986; see also *Defence and Security*).† For the most part, this state of affairs reflects the general disinterest of the academic community in defense and strategic issues and the absence of a research-based catalyst—such as Australia has in the Strategic and Defence Studies Centre and the Peace Research Centre, both at the Australian National University.** Defense reviews, when they appear—which is on average every six years—only gently disturb the general torpor. The fact that the Defence Committee of Inquiry was ordered only after considerable acrimony and tension had appeared in the ANZUS relationship also indicates the extent to which diligence is exercised in security issues.

---

forces of being close by Australia in the vastness of the Indian and Pacific oceans and more by the defining dissimilarities afforded by the intervening Tasman Sea.

*I readily concede that this account is impressionistic, although it is based on a close reading of the very few periodicals which cover defense issues in New Zealand, a survey of the offerings of the seven New Zealand universities, and attendance at various academic conferences on politics. Interestingly, at the 1985 annual conference of the New Zealand Political Studies Association, of the seven papers whose subject was ANZUS or strategic issues (broadly defined), only one had New Zealand authorship; the other six were by Australian academics.

†Consistent with my claims regarding the defense debate in New Zealand, the Defence Committee of Inquiry was established only *after* the Labour government had undertaken its ANZUS/non-nuclear *démarche*; in other words, it has the taint of appearing to be a post hoc rationalization for such policies rather than the more desirable basis for them.

**Perhaps the clearest indication of academic disinterest is the fact that in the 1980s the country's sole journal of politics, *Political Science*, has published but one article on a topic which could be broadly defined as strategic. Even then it dealt with U.S. policy in South Asia. Again it was by Ramesh Thakur.

The besetting consequence of this general disinterest is that defense debate takes place almost entirely in quasi-academic periodicals and in a truncated fashion since it is the business of such publications to feature short articles on topical issues, not to provide a forum for detailed analysis.* This type of debate is unlikely to redress the deficiencies noted because it is essentially an integral part of them. Observers should therefore note the origins of and structural influences upon New Zealand defense policy.

THE POLICY ON WEAPONS AND CRAFT

New Zealand's non-nuclear policy is to be seen from three perspectives: first, a revulsion against nuclear arms in general; second, a desire to insulate New Zealand's immediate region, the South Pacific, from both nuclear weapons and superpower competition and confrontation; and third, a desire by New Zealand to effect security by distancing itself as far as possible from any association with nuclear weapons which might cause it to be a target should war break out (see *New Zealand Foreign Affairs Review* 1985).

Within these views, practicalities are also a necessary consideration for a country whose economic well-being is defined by its ability to export agricultural and pastoral products which would be at risk from fallout. Thus nuclear testing, particularly in the atmosphere, was opposed throughout the 1950s and beyond, irrespective of the country conducting it. Furthermore, New Zealand supported the Nuclear Non-Proliferation Treaty of 1968 and has been committed to achieving a Comprehensive Test Ban Treaty or the pursuit of alternatives when the prospect of such a treaty has seemed remote (Campbell).

The current Labour government, reelected in August 1987, has followed the traditional Labour policy; indeed it has gone further than any previous Labour government and entrenched its opposition to what is called "nuclear defense" by passing (in June 1987) the New Zealand Nuclear Free Zone, Disarmament, and Arms Control Act. In this legislation the Labour government not only codified its non-nuclear policy, but also implemented within the national jurisdiction (inter alia) the South Pacific Nuclear Free Zone Treaty of 1985. Accordingly New Zealand law

*Specifically, only two New Zealand publications are relevant here, *New Zealand International Review* and *The Listener*. A third could be allowed as partially relevant—*Pacific Defence Reporter*.

now requires that aircraft and ships which would otherwise be permitted to visit the country must conform to two criteria: ships must not be "wholly or partly dependent on nuclear power" for their propulsion, and neither aircraft nor ships are to be "carrying any nuclear explosive device." In addition, members of the New Zealand armed forces (and other servants or agents of the Crown) are prohibited from aiding or abetting any person to manufacture, acquire, possess, or have control over any nuclear explosive device anywhere in the world. By inference, the New Zealand armed forces are precluded from joining with allied forces for exercises which even remotely have a nuclear character; should the act be interpreted strictly, even exercising with a nuclear (powered or armed) ship could presumably be contravention of its provisions.

As with New Zealand's original impetus toward the ANZUS treaty, the current policy is strongly redolent of an anxiety about the state of the world; it is, moreover, a condition which found official expression over two decades ago. As long ago as 1963, a New Zealand government took the formal decision never to permit the storage, testing, or manufacture of nuclear weapons on New Zealand soil. Since there is no evidence that any of these were serious prospects, this decision serves merely to date official New Zealand opposition to nuclear defense, however that may be defined. Subsequently, the Labour Party after 1966 and the Labour government of 1972–75 came to oppose visits by nuclear-powered craft, however armed, as well as visits by any craft which might be carrying nuclear weapons. A measure of the changed conditions in which the ANZUS alliance operates is apparent from the fact that the Labour government's request of its allies to refrain from bringing nuclear-powered and nuclear-armed craft to New Zealand was honored—as was the succeeding (National Party) government's wish to host such vessels.

CURRENT POLICY ON ANZUS

For the first two years of the Lange Labour government, official statements declared New Zealand's continuing commitment to ANZUS. Two facets of this stance deserve special consideration. First, ANZUS is what the New Zealand government asserts it to be; second, New Zealand's commitment was to ANZUS as a *conventional* alliance. Thus the Prime Minister denied that ANZUS obliged New Zealand to accept nuclear weapons and stated that his country had no wish to be defended by nuclear weapons (*New Zealand Foreign Affairs Review* 1985: 5). He defined its value as follows:

> New Zealand is a member of ANZUS because we see its usefulness as a conventional alliance to us and to our region. It is a useful means of interaction among the conventional forces of three countries of broadly similar outlook and interests in the region (cited in *New Zealand Foreign Affairs Review* 1985: 13).

It was also clear that the Lange government subscribed to the "ultimate guarantee" interpretation of ANZUS. In Canberra in April 1985 Mr. Lange foresaw the "inevitability" of ANZUS operating if one of the three partners were attacked (*The Australian*, 18 April 1985: 2). By so determining the parameters and contingent expectations of ANZUS, the New Zealand policy was in effect a qualified commitment to general alignment.

The above assessment of course begs the question of "alignment to what?" ANZUS clearly was not what it used to be. Indeed the impasse caused by New Zealand had brought into extensive currency the term "inoperative," although this term was taken to apply only to the level and nature of defense cooperation in conditions short of war within the treaty framework. As a result, the core obligations of ANZUS—to consult and act to meet the common danger in accordance with constitutional processes— remained intact; indeed they were reaffirmed by both Australia and the United States, as well as New Zealand. However, a situation in which the lowest common denominator prevailed was far from ideal because it both emphasized the changed character of the tripartite relationship and underlined the potential for further deterioration of the alliance as it had been known.

By 1986 the situation was evidently intolerable. At the thirty-fifth ANZUS meeting, held at San Francisco on 10 and 11 August—and at which New Zealand was not represented—a joint Australia–U.S. communique was issued which "suspended" the U.S. security obligations to New Zealand under the treaty (McMillan 1987: 153–65). Since virtually all trilateral activities had been suspended for most of the previous two years, the San Francisco communique was but the formal conclusion of an already attenuated relationship.

ANZUS IN PUBLIC OPINION AND ELECTORAL POLITICS

Faced with the de facto status of being anathema to ANZUS, the Labour government was still required to consider whether and what type of security relationship it might redevelop with the United States (Mc-Millan 1987: 153–65). Domestic support for ANZUS, consistently at a high level, Australian concern, and regional (Southwest Pacific) anxieties demanded nothing less. Since 1986, however, little progress has been made toward assuaging these various sources of disquiet. Rather, both New Zealand and the United States (*vis-à-vis* its neither-confirm-nor-deny policy) maintained hardened positions which were mutually exclusive and widened the area of disputation—the former by questioning the value and reality of the security guarantee in the first place, and the latter by taking punitive measures in respect of New Zealand's access to U.S. defense equipment and technology (McMillan 1987: 94–113, 153–65, 170–72).

Against this background the best that Prime Minister Lange was able to say of a security relationship with the United States was that *conventional* defense cooperation was and would be "valued" (Lange 1987: 18). He thereby failed to address positively the conclusions of the Defence Committee of Inquiry, which found that although 73 percent of New Zealanders surveyed desired that their country's defense be arranged in a nuclear-free manner, 72 percent also desired an alliance with larger countries, and some 52 percent favored a return to the status quo ante 1984 if the non-nuclear policy deprived New Zealand of operational membership in the alliance (*Defence and Security* 1986: 44). Lange's silence was no doubt partly influenced by the fact that 44 percent were in favor of maintaining the non-nuclear policy even if it meant exclusion from ANZUS. A response was unlikely to satisfy much more than half of the country, which, almost to overstate the obvious, was found to be "deeply divided" (*Defence and Security* 1986: 73).

Counter-intuitively, the ANZUS/non-nuclear policy controversy has so far been devoid of identifiable electoral significance. In the July 1984 election campaign, in which Lange led Labour to its first victory in four attempts, it was topical without being significant. Nor was this unexpected: the 1984 campaign was centered on the National Party's record of government over the previous nine years in general and the abrasive, idiosyncratic, and polarizing style of its leader, Sir Robert Muldoon. Even in 1987, with over two-and-one-half years of controversy and crisis both in ANZUS and in the bilateral relations with Australia and the United States, the ANZUS/non-nuclear issue was never more than a secondary consideration at best. Despite the fact that punitive measures taken by the United States had resulted in the withdrawal of virtually all the valued benefits alluded to at the outset of this chapter, culminating in the termination of the MOU on 21 June 1987, the issue proved incapable of competing with the more traditional domestic fare offered to the New Zealand electorate. Here coincident developments must be seen in perspective.

ANZUS slid into inoperability from early 1985 as "Rogernomics," the radical economic restructuring program of Finance Minister Roger Douglas, dominated political debate and preoccupied the electorate. Essentially the August 1987 poll was foreseen, and then realized, in terms of the mandate it would provide for Rogernomics. Inevitably intervening factors played a role in the handsome victory won by Labour, not the least of which was the inept record of the National Party in opposition and its procession of three leaders in less than as many years. Yet it was indicative of the perceived importance of the economic dimension that the National Party could neither mobilize the domestic support for ANZUS in its favor nor change the terms of the debate away from the economic agenda on which it was so vulnerable.

Lost in this process are the intellectual inadequacies (as opposed to the political utility) of Labour's policy in respect of its assumptions, presumptions, and internal logic or consistency, all of which need to be addressed, albeit briefly, if the New Zealand perspective on ANZUS is to be understood and the future of the alliance contemplated.

POLICY ASSUMPTIONS

It is immediately noticeable that a mode of thinking prevails which assumes that ANZUS is primarily, even solely, a legal document. (Possibly this reflected the fact that the principal parties to the policy in the 1984–87 period—the Prime Minister, the Deputy Prime Minister, Geoffrey Palmer, and the Defense Minister, Frank O'Flynn—were all lawyers in private life.) But it is not just a recourse to legalisms that is noticeable. It is conjoined with an attempt to atomize the elements of the alliance. Using both, Mr. Lange thus presented his view of ANZUS from his first day as Prime Minister-elect. When interviewed by Australian television about the possible inconsistency in Labour's policy (remaining in ANZUS but banning nuclear craft), Mr. Lange's reply was along the lines of "Show me where in the ANZUS treaty it says New Zealand has to accept nuclear vessels in its ports." Later this position was represented as a redress of an absent-minded foreign and defense policy process: "New Zealand never made a conscious decision to join a nuclear infrastructure" (cited in *National Times* [Sydney], 1–7 February 1985: 4).

Mr. Lange does his legal training a disservice here because in two principles of general contract law and one rule of international law there clearly are cautions against the approach he has taken. As regards the former, estoppel and active performance might be considered relevant.* Under estoppel the general principle is that no person can be allowed to dispute his own solemn deed. Thus New Zealand's decision to enter into a security treaty with Australia and the United States in 1951 cannot be affected by any subsequent decision of the United States to acquire nuclear weapons. In any case, the United States by 1951 had proved its willingness to use atomic weapons (some six years earlier), decided upon the development of the H-bomb (nearly two years earlier), developed its first war plan—which included an atomic attack on the Soviet Union in the event of an attack on Western Europe (two-and-one-half years earlier), and deployed atomic weapons on a worldwide basis (over one year earlier). U.S. policy and intentions were therefore quite clear—as is Lange's attempt to refashion history for his own purposes.

It is, furthermore, patently untrue to assert, as Lange does, that "the ANZUS alliance has in the past been regarded by the treaty partners as a *conventional alliance,* not a nuclear alliance" (*New Zealand Foreign Affairs Review* 1985: 5; emphasis added). Nowhere in the official records of ANZUS Council communiques or other statements is there any reference to Australia and the United States defining the treaty as relating only to conventional defense. Even the record of New Zealand in ANZUS after 1951 affirms this. Not until 1984 did a New Zealand government challenge the contractual basis for ANZUS. In positive terms, against a background of steady growth in U.S. strategic and tactical nuclear forces, successive New Zealand governments actively and without demur performed an alliance role which could be taken only as acquiescence to the military direction in which ANZUS headed. It cannot be denied that the Labour Party after 1966 and the Labour governments of 1972–75 and 1984–89 came to oppose nuclear weapons and nuclear-powered vessels, but this stand cannot be justified on legal-historical grounds.

Insofar as international law is concerned—in particular public international law—the ANZUS treaty (like any other treaty among states) is a binding contract which can be amended or terminated only by agreement among the parties to it or voided by a total change of the circumstances

---

*The claim here is not that contract law is or should be applicable in a strict sense, but that the principles of contract law should provide a caution against making claims that are out of keeping with the alliance agreement as recorded.

under the rule of *rebus sic stantibus* implicit in all treaties.* Moreover, it is clear that Lange is sensitive to ANZUS as a binding international contract, although he has unilaterally reinterpreted it in response to influences to which he owes his leadership of a political party. Lange, therefore, would appear to have caused New Zealand to repudiate fundamental principles of security to which the ANZUS treaty gives expression in the form of a political declaration of the reciprocal obligations of the parties to that treaty. Notwithstanding these shortcomings in the legal argument, the government has attempted to seek refuge for its actions in what was not specified; moreover, it has attempted unilaterally to determine what comprises the content of nonspecificity. Clearly the intent is to rob the treaty of any associated understandings, certainly to render them invalid.

A similar habit of mind emerges in the discussion of the joint Australia–New Zealand signals facility in Singapore. This is operated under the authority of the New Zealand force commander in Singapore and is claimed by Deputy Prime Minister Palmer to have "nothing to do with ANZUS." Strictly speaking, he is correct; it relates more to the 1947 UKUSA (secret signals intelligence) agreement among the United Kingdom, the United States, Australia, Canada, and New Zealand. But to regard the cooperation between Australia and New Zealand in isolation is surely stretching credibility because (despite Mr. Lange's assertions) none of the parties to ANZUS have hitherto viewed it in purely legal terms. Indeed it has become a truism in the three countries to speak of it as only the legal expression of a very much wider relationship. The reason is quite simple: the "relationship" and the understanding attendant on it facilitated closer diplomatic liaisons than would otherwise have been the case.

Of greater concern is the question of whether New Zealand's policy is seen by the government as a prescription for other nations or merely a peculiarly national initiative. If the former, two scenarios must be considered. The first is that in all Western alliances which include the United States considerable disruption will result: increasing numbers of states like New Zealand will be "frozen out," and the active alliance members will be reduced to a rump. In all probability this rump will consist of right-wing states whose views differ little from those of the United States. Alternatively, all states allied to the United States will withdraw nuclear visiting rights, with the effect that *all* alliances with the United States will be rendered inoperative. In both cases any restraint which allies such as

*I am indebted to Mr. F. Chalmers-Wright of Wellington for bringing the principle of rebus sic stantibus to my attention via personal correspondence.

New Zealand might have on the United States will diminish, even disappear. In the second scenario, dependent ally unilateralism could very well be met by dominant ally unilateralism. Since U.S. strategic and economic interests are worldwide, it is not credible to suggest that it will abjure them merely because its former close allies have departed the fold. On the contrary, it should be expected that the United States will act according to its own superpower interests and without the restraint that might otherwise have been urged upon it.

In fairness, it must be conceded that the New Zealand government has specifically stated that it was not providing a model for export to Western Europe or Japan. Yet fairness also demands that such declaratory statements be seen in the context of some rather confused thinking and counterindicators. In the course of his debate with the Rev. Jerry Falwell at Oxford University in March 1985, Mr. Lange attacked the proposition that it is the intention of an act which determines its moral character. Accordingly, he argued that nuclear weapons subvert the best of intentions; they pervert the motive of security. (Although not absolutely clear from his address, Mr. Lange appears to have been advancing only a particular case—nuclear weapons—not a general case.) To demonstrate his point he cited the anxiety and insecurity felt by many in the United States and Europe as a result of the nuclear arms race (*New Zealand Foreign Affairs Review* 1985: 8). When discussing the possible disruptive effects on the Western alliance system if his country's example were to be followed, however, Mr. Lange inverted this system of logic. The moral or other consequences of New Zealand's actions are not an issue because there should not be any: as New Zealand *intends* only to pursue a nonnuclear policy itself, no untoward consequences can be held to be caused by it. In other words, not even the possibility—let alone the inevitability—of New Zealand's intentions being subverted is allowed on the basis of nothing more than prime ministerial fiat.* More important, Mr. Lange has thereby succeeded only in drawing attention to the fact

---

*The closest Mr. Lange comes to reasoning his not-for-export claim is his acknowledgment that Western Europe lives in different political and strategic circumstances from New Zealand and that its nuclear deterrent is maintained in good conscience. But this fails to advance his argument: if circumstances determine morality, then Mr. Lange's ultimate objective of eliminating nuclear arsenals is invalid. If, on the other hand, circumstances do not determine morality, then there is no moral distinction to be made between Western Europe and New Zealand. To become "moral" in Mr. Lange's eyes, Western Europe would need to reject nuclear defense—and thus follow his country's example. But by his assertion it is not to.

that his policies are less than soundly based and far too easily identified by a selective, almost Jesuitical form of reasoning.

By this assessment even casuistry has fallen on hard times because it is conjoined with disingenuousness. Helen Clark, a Labour M.P. and chairwoman of both the New Zealand Parliamentary Committee on Foreign Affairs and the Parliamentary Select Committee on Disarmament, clearly believes that New Zealand was slow to join the nuclear protest nations and that its example will give an impetus to other nations to adopt similar policies and condemn the nuclear weapons race (Clark 1985: 10–11). According to this measure, Mr. Lange has obviously failed to convince one of the leading spokeswomen in his party of the party's intentions. But perhaps this gives too much attention to "intentionalism." At best it is a silly defense. As Dr. Johnson said of Rousseau's perceived corruption of young minds, proving bad intentions is impossible; it is sufficient to note that the judge would still hang you for murder if you shot a man through the head although you intended all along to miss him.

Notwithstanding these objections, if New Zealand's policy is not prescriptive but a solution to the country's particular needs, a less profound but more unflattering conclusion may be drawn—i.e., the Labour government has opted out of ANZUS obligations because (implying in the last resort a nuclear guarantee) they are too dangerous for New Zealand. In conjunction with an espoused reliance on ANZUS in time of need, this is tantamount to freeloading: New Zealand is to enjoy the benefits of alliance while allowing other countries to carry the risks and burdens. Even if one does not believe that morality exists in the relations among states, this would still be regarded as questionable behavior by most New Zealanders and a practice quite alien to the country's traditions (argument adapted from Bell 1984: 4–10). If nothing else, it would offend their self-image.

POLICY PRESUMPTIONS

The deficiencies in legal reasoning considered above foreshadow the manner by which certain conclusions have been drawn from propositions concerning the U.S. Navy and New Zealand's ability to determine the character of certain task-force size elements in time of threat or war. This is very largely an extension of the atomistic mode of thinking on ANZUS and refers to the presumption that since the U.S. Navy has combat vessels which are neither nuclear-armed nor nuclear-powered, the U.S. government can and will deploy these and only these vessels in the event that New Zealand needs U.S. military assistance. This policy is summed up in the expression that "New Zealand does not seek nuclear defense." Its proscriptions apply to the forces of allied nations such as France and Great Britain and would apply to Australia should it acquire a nuclear capability.

For the time being, it is the application of these presumptions to the U.S. Navy that requires close inspection.*

The U.S. General Accounting Office claimed in 1976 that 287 warships were certified to carry nuclear weapons of various kinds and some 35,000 navy personnel were involved in work with nuclear weapons. Probably half of the 600 ships in the navy are certified to carry nuclear weapons now. In addition, Cochran, Arkin, and Hoenig note the following:

> A *large percentage* of the navy aircraft carriers, cruisers, destroyers, frigates and attack submarines are equipped with nuclear-capable weapons systems and supplied with nuclear weapons during operations (1984: 93–94; emphasis added).

There is therefore a marked difficulty in determining with a high degree of certainty whether U.S. vessels in general have nuclear weapons on board.

In contrast, nuclear propulsion of U.S. warships is no secret whatever. Indeed the letter "N" is included in the public classification of all nuclear-propelled warships. Thus CVN–68 is a nuclear-powered aircraft carrier, while CV–41 is conventionally powered. The United States has four nuclear-powered carriers in service (*Enterprise, Nimitz, Eisenhower*, and *Carl Vinson*) and two under construction. There are nine cruisers with nuclear propulsion, with the notation CGN (USS *Long Beach, Bainbridge, Truxton, California, South Carolina, Virginia, Texas, Mississippi*, and *Arkansas*). No other surface warships are being built with nuclear propulsion, for budgetary reasons.

For many years all new U.S. submarines have been nuclear-powered because the navy regards diesel-powered submarines as inefficient, short-ranged, and too vulnerable to Soviet attack. Thirty-four ballistic missile-carrying submarines (SSBN series) and ninety-four attack submarines (SSN series) are nuclear-powered. Only five diesel-powered submarines remain in the active U.S. fleet (*SS Grayback, Darter, Barbel, Blueback*, and *Bonefish*). It may be presumed that any U.S. submarine is likely to be nuclear-powered.

For the time being, it seems highly unlikely that any SSBN could become involved in a New Zealand defense situation, so these can be

*Much of the material in this section on the U.S. Navy's nuclear character is from Samuel (1985: 6).

omitted from the following consideration. Nuclear attack submarines cannot be so absolved. All of the SSNs carry weapons armed with conventional explosives; moreover, *most carry the nuclear standoff anti-submarine weapon SUBROC as well.** Furthermore, Tomahawk long-range cruise missiles, which are now being deployed on U.S. battleships, cruisers, some destroyers, and attack submarines, will have conventional and nuclear warheads. The latter will be the W80, which weighs about 120 kg. and is for use against land targets. (The other two variants, anti-submarine and anti-ship, are of shorter range and configured with conventional warheads.)

Surface-to-ship weapons raise another difficulty for New Zealand governments—i.e., the spread of nuclear weapons throughout a fleet in which most of the systems are dual-purpose (that is, the same rocket or aircraft can be armed with nuclear or conventional high-explosive devices). One authority on the U.S. Navy, Norman Polmar, has claimed that there are 850 W44 nuclear warheads deployed on 170 U.S. warships (cited in Cochran et al. 1984: 267–68). Other sources claim that some 1,000 Tomahawk sea-launched cruise missiles will be deployed in the U.S. Navy. In addition, the navy has always had a number of nuclear warheads for fitting on surface-to-air missiles, presumably for last-ditch defense of its big carriers and cruisers against aircraft or cruise missile attack. Almost all varieties of U.S. naval aircraft can carry three different sizes of nuclear bombs (designated B43, B57, and B61).

According to these indicators, there is a wide dispersion of nuclear warheads in both undersea and surface vessels of the U.S. Navy. Moreover, these figures could be conservative. According to the testimony of Deputy Assistant Secretary of Defense for East Asian Affairs Paul Kelly before a U.S. House of Representatives subcommittee, the U.S. Navy is 100 percent nuclear capable. By this account, all navy vessels handle nuclear weaponry from time to time, including even amphibious ships (cited in *The Australian*, 20 March 1985: 1).[†]

---

*SUBROC is no longer being fitted to SSNs, so for the present newly constructed vessels in this class will not have a nuclear standoff anti-submarine capability. However, a replacement weapon for SUBROC is scheduled for the late 1980s.

†Kelly's claim has received support from an unusual quarter (albeit one that might not be universally accepted)—Tam Dalyell, a Scottish MP in the House of Commons whose trenchant criticism of the Thatcher government's handling of the Falklands campaign has become something of a *cause célèbre*. Citing a variety of information and evidence, Dalyell points to the distinct possibility that Royal

In the light of the foregoing discussion, New Zealand presumptions concerning the U.S. Navy take on the hue of fantasy. While this is not the place to enter into an analysis of the tactics and structure of (say) a carrier battle group, it must be apparent that any force likely to be sent to the aid of New Zealand in time of threat is likely to contain nuclear elements as an integral part of its defenses. It follows that the U.S. government could agree to a New Zealand request only by being willing to degrade seriously not only the protection normally afforded to such a force, but also its worldwide deterrent posture.

POLICY LOGIC

At this point, it may be useful to examine the proposition that New Zealand will be a safer place under the government's non-nuclear vessel policy. Allowing nuclear vessels could be dangerous for three reasons—a serious malfunction of a nuclear reactor, the accidental detonation of a nuclear device, and the targeting of a New Zealand port or ports while nuclear-capable vessels are berthed. The first is an ever-present hazard, but to date there has been no evidence of a serious incident. (It is not to say it cannot happen—only that the record is impressive.) The second carries an even more impressive record because there has been no accidental detonation in any nuclear navy.

The third is also an ever-present risk, but it requires irrational strategic decisions, in whole or part, by the Soviet Union, United States, and New Zealand (see, for example, Bunn and Tsipis 1983: 32–41).* For a U.S. Navy ship or task force in New Zealand to be hit by a Soviet nuclear strike implies that the U.S. government, in a time of high tension, would keep important elements of its fleet in port. This is not only contrary to good naval strategy, but it also contravenes U.S. naval practice in such periods. Moreover, it imputes to the New Zealand government a certain dumbness in the face of clear danger—i.e., that it would not order the vessels out of national waters. Even in the face of New Zealand inactivity and the U.S. Navy's contravention of its own principles by remaining in (say) the port of Wellington, what could a task

---

Fleet Auxiliary vessels (merchantmen associated with the Royal Navy for supply purposes) regularly carry nuclear weapons in the normal course of their duties (Dalyell 1983: 32–33). The substance of Dalyell's claim is confirmed in Cochran et al. (1984: 5, 92, 244–45).

*I assume that the buildup to a superpower conflict would be gradual.

force contribute when so far removed from the likely theater of operations? If a Soviet preemptive attack is envisaged, then the Soviets have to be seen as irrational. If this is the case, we observers of international relations are engaged in a futile endeavor. If imputing irrationality to our adversaries becomes our habit, our mode of analysis is no longer rational examination and reflection but something akin to observing the entrails of goats.

If the New Zealand government wishes to make judgments on a nuclear threat to the country, it might consider the priority which the Soviet Union might accord certain of its purely national assets. Among these would be New Zealand's primary production system, its deep water ports, and—above all—the Government Communications Security Bureau facility at Tangimoana (north of Wellington)—assuming that this establishment is rightly classified as purely national—and the New Zealand–based component of an international telecommunications network.

Should such an evaluation be attempted, it is probable that the threat posed to the first two would prove difficult to determine. It is also probable that the facility at Tangimoana, whose direction-finding functions are geared against the Soviet navy in the main, would signify a more substantial, if not primary, risk. Moreover, should it be found that Tangimoana has extensive linkages with the Naval Operational Intelligence Center (formerly the Naval Ocean Surveillance Information System—NOSIS) in Suitland, Maryland, or the anti-ship cruise missile programs code-named Outlaw Shark and Bullseye, then the irony of denying visiting rights to nuclear vessels would be massive. Tangimoana, a New Zealand Defence Department unit ostensibly under New Zealand control, would be facilitating vessels and weapons systems which are denied pier space in New Zealand harbors but which nonetheless increase the likelihood, however marginally, of the country being targeted. The bulk of available evidence and considered opinion at this time point to the conclusion that Tangimoana has linkages with U.S. and other allied signals intelligence networks.*

Even greater irony attends the Wellington terminal, where an 8,152-mile Commonwealth Pacific (COMPAC) cable comes ashore en route from Sydney to Hawaii and Port Albertini, Canada. Because it

---

*In his controversial book Woodward (1987) locates Admiral Bobby Inman in New Zealand during the early days of the Carter-Reagan transition. His purpose, according to Woodward, was a visit to "one of the [National Security Agency's] listening posts" (p. 48).

frequently is the practice of the U.S. government to lease telephone lines from the private (Common Carrier) sector for its military communications system, the COMPAC submarine cable is now the alternative (to satellite-based) means of communication for the Joint Defence Space Communications Station at Nurrungar in South Australia; this facility, previously defended on account of its arms-control and early-warning functions, is now acknowledged to have a nuclear war-fighting role. It is therefore inescapably a primary nuclear target, and by extension the vulnerable shore terminals must share this jeopardy—probably to a lesser, but nevertheless certain extent (see Ford 1985: 66–68, and Ball 1987: 47–49).

In sum, the presumptions of the non-nuclear vessel policy as they relate to aid which might be proffered in time of need appear to be an inadequate basis for the conclusions which the government has reached about guarantees of New Zealand security. This policy, moreover, would appear not substantially to increase the safety of New Zealanders, particularly since two of the country's own defense assets are a prejudicial influence against that very objective.

As an aside, New Zealand might reconsider the proposition that its remoteness provides its security. In July 1985 a small unit of French divers sank the Greenpeace protest vessel *Rainbow Warrior* without any difficulty whatsoever. *Rainbow Warrior* was not strategically significant for New Zealand—it was not even registered there—but the operation which led to its demise carried implications for the country's defense. First, New Zealand is permeable—an obvious consequence of having a coastline longer than that of the mainland United States. Second, in the last quarter of the twentieth century there is no such thing as remoteness; Paris might be half a world removed from Auckland, but such distance cannot prevent tragic results. Third, it is not necessary to mount a full-scale invasion of New Zealand in order to damage it. Fourth, had France been intent on war with New Zealand (instead of administering a murderous lesson to Greenpeace), the costs would have been immense. Overall the implication is *not* that the old New Zealand policies would have prevented such a disaster, but that the relative remoteness of New Zealand, which substantially underpins the new policies, is an unreliable indicator of security.

If, as we have argued, New Zealand's non-nuclear policy has not significantly advanced New Zealand's security by any objective criteria, it is also the case that ANZUS has not been significantly damaged. In the imbroglio which emerged after Labour came to office, this point was often lost because insufficient attention was paid to the details of New Zealand's contribution to ANZUS. At best it was slight.

GEOSTRATEGIC POSITION AND ANZUS MEMBERSHIP

In geostrategic terms, to be in New Zealand is to be lonely. So many negative indicators can be adduced in support of this fact that it is perhaps more useful to concentrate on the few positive indicators which make the same point. Surrounded by vast oceans, New Zealand is remote from anywhere except Polynesia, Australia, and the southern polar ice— so much so that one is tempted to apply Henry Kissinger's famous deprecation of Latin America to New Zealand: "a dagger pointing at the heart of Antarctica." Whereas some Australians fear that their country's endowment of natural resources could provoke some form of attack or incursion, New Zealand's main bounty is agriculture, and the notion that someone might want to invade for this is universally held to be fantastic. Again, whereas Australia is preoccupied with the near north of its strategic environment, in 1969 New Zealand Prime Minister Keith Holyoake met with considerable derision when he attempted to explain his country's minimal commitment to the Vietnam War in terms of the "logic" of geography. As was quickly pointed out by McIntyre, New Zealand's front line could be placed in Southeast Asia only with the aid of a spurious "logic":

> It is helpful to remember that London is closer to Hanoi than Christchurch is. Even Disraeli, who said the "key of India" was Constantinople, never claimed that the outer defences of the Straits of Dover stretched to the Gulf of Tonkin (1967: 342; see also McIntyre 1969: 19–32).

Against this background, New Zealand is very much cast into shadow—a small group of islands behind an island continent. This is not to say that New Zealand is a "pissant little country south of nowhereville" (as one U.S. commentator chose insensitively to describe it; quoted in "Stronger Alliance" 1985: 1), but neither does it possess the geostrategic importance that Gibraltar enjoyed in previous times, or that Australia in relative terms has had thrust upon it now. This means that it is possible for New Zealand's policymakers to posit a no-threat environment with greater confidence than would be the case in Australia. It also means that if New Zealand did not exist, it would not have to be invented. The readiness of the Reagan administration to cut off intelligence to and take punitive measures against Wellington in the current impasse suggests that the U.S. government is well apprised of the distinction between convenience and necessity with regard not only to the value of its facilities in New Zealand, but also the country's strategic assets.

NEW ZEALAND CONTRIBUTIONS TO ANZUS

DEFENSE FORCES

In 1983–84 the cost of New Zealand's defense totaled U.S.$470 million.* This represented 2.3 percent of GDP and 4.2 percent of government expenditure. By way of comparison, Australia spent over U.S.$5 billion, accounting for 9 percent of the total budget. By 1985–86 the disparity was even more striking. In June 1985 New Zealand allocated U.S.$469 million to defense—an 18 percent boost over 1984–85 and 5.1 percent of government expenditure.† Australia increased its 1985–86 defense outlay by 10 percent over the 1984–85 levels. Total expenditure forecast thus rose to U.S.$4.67 billion. To place these figures in perspective, the *total* New Zealand defense budget was just U.S.$2 million more than the *increase* allocated to defense in Australia for 1985–86. As of 1986–87 the defense outlay had climbed to U.S.$561 millions (just over 2.1 percent of GDP).**

Approximately half of the annual total is accounted for by expenditure on personnel, 17 percent on capital equipment, and 6 percent on forces overseas, mainly a presence in Singapore (which includes one of the country's two infantry battalions). Although defense expenditure has increased in real terms since the late 1970s, New Zealand's military capabilities are, to say the least, modest even for a country of 3 million people.

In practical (yet not hypercritical) terms most of the defense forces establishment represents a working museum, a memorial to the bygone

*Data on the defense forces are from *The Military Balance* (1984–85, 1985–86, 1986–87, and 1987–88).

†The wildly fluctuating NZ dollars (against the U.S. dollars) make allocations look like a decrease in June 1985. Effectively New Zealand devoted more dollars, but they bought fewer American dollars than previously.

**One other comparison is revealing: among the Western industrialized nations, only Austria, Finland, and Luxembourg spend a smaller proportion of GDP on defense.

era of forward defense strategy. The strike elements without exception are artifacts belonging to modes of thinking which did not survive intact beyond the 1960s; moreover, their obsolescence is so consummate as to render a comparison with any regional power invidious (further discussion in Beaglehole 1984: 15–19; Miles 1984: 36–38; and West 1984: 2–6). The New Zealand air force, for example, must be one of the few in the world which possesses fighter-type aircraft slower than its transport aircraft. In capability, sophistication, and size, the gap between Australia and New Zealand is currently profound and must be expected to increase substantially.* In a strictly military sense, ANZUS's resources were not improved by New Zealand's active membership, nor should they be disadvantaged by its removal.

ECONOMIC INFLUENCES ON NEW ZEALAND DEFENSE CAPABILITIES

The prospects for strengthened capabilities are not bright because New Zealand has suffered from certain structural disadvantages which are likely to persist. These are outlined by Beaglehole:

> New Zealand has had to face the difficult task of creating and maintaining a viable defence force in a society whose wealth is still largely agricultural, with a small population and reliant entirely for its armed forces on a volunteer system in a relatively prosperous society. The task has been further complicated by the fact that the defence environment is principally maritime, and therefore requires a defence profile which includes a viable sea and air capability. These areas of defence, however, are at the same time the most capital intensive and technologically sophisticated. However, the changes that have taken place in New Zealand's defence situation over the last decade have been accompanied by spiralling equipment and training costs, in an economic climate which has brought increasing financial constraints (1984: 20).

The magnitude of such constraints can be gauged by reference to just a few economic indicators. For most of the 1980s New Zealand has been beset by double-digit inflation: 15.8 percent in 1982, 12.6 percent in 1983, and 16.9 percent in late 1987. Growth in GDP has been

*While we have not entered into either a regional nor an ANZAC comparison here because of the constraints of space, sources such as *The Military Balance* and the various *Jane's* publications have observed arms procurement programs under way in Southeast Asia. The inference is clear that New Zealand has fallen well behind according to the objective indicators of military power in the region.

unspectacular—3.2 percent in 1982, 0 percent in 1983, and -.8 percent in 1986–87. At the same time, burdens on the economy have been increased by an exchange rate rigidly fixed 25 percent too high. Moreover, there was a budget deficit in 1983–84 equal to 9 percent of the GDP and a foreign debt in 1982 of U.S.$10.2 billion (against a 1982 GDP of only U.S.$22.8 billion). As a result, New Zealand incurred a higher foreign debt per dollar of GDP than even Brazil, and it lost the top credit rating it had previously enjoyed among the banks of New York.

Some hope is held for the long-term future of the economy because the strategy of the Lange Labour government is currently in the control of what can only be described as "free marketeers." This would seem out of character for any Labour government anywhere, but nevertheless the evidence abounds that New Zealand is in the grip of a radical economic experiment. Not only have all exchange controls been terminated and the exchange rate floated (effectively devaluing the New Zealand dollar considerably), but also under the direction of Finance Minister Douglas the government has abolished all the price controls, wage controls, interest-rate controls, most industrial subsidies, agricultural subsidies, export subsidies, and state corporation subsidies introduced or increased by the previous *conservative* government. It has introduced a goods and services tax on everything (including food) and hopes to use the tax revenue so gained to make deep, across-the-board reductions in income tax. Just as surprising, it is also dismantling much of its welfare state—which, ironically, was once held to place New Zealand in the forefront of "progressive" nations. Little wonder that *The Economist* chose to describe this process as an "abattoir session for Labour's sacred cows" ("NZ Labour Is Getting It Right" 1985: 18).

If this experiment works, New Zealand might return to genuine economic prosperity, but this will not necessarily presage improvements in the country's defense capabilities. Despite Mr. Lange's embrace of the free market, he is still ideologically in the Labour mold as regards social if not socialist causes. He is especially keen to expand education, both by competition and government stimulus ("NZ Labour Is Getting It Right" 1985). In particular, he is concerned with improving the lot of New Zealand's indigenous Maori youth. It must be assumed that both education and the Maori will take precedence over defense needs in terms of a sustained commitment to necessarily high levels of expenditure.

In large part, the economic experiment will depend on how the rest of the world treats New Zealand. There are grounds for pessimism here because New Zealand's foreign-exchange–earning agricultural export industry faces serious competition from grossly subsidized production, such as that within the EEC. Efficiency, therefore, will not of itself ensure a prosperous New Zealand, nor even one capable of providing for its own defense. Thus inside or outside of ANZUS, New Zealand can be seen as the Turkey of the Southwest Pacific—the "sick man" of the alliance.

WIDER CONTRIBUTIONS TO ANZUS

For New Zealand as well as for Australia various assets have been provided by the United States to further the aims of the security relationship, but it should be clearly understood that the U.S. contributions in New Zealand are very much less significant than some of the American installations in Australia (Ball 1983: 71–75, 86; see also Wills 1985: 27–30). In a war-fighting sense, the most important New Zealand installation is the Defence Communications Unit at Tangimoana, a signals intelligence operation under the national control of the Government Communications Security Bureau. Its particular function is to provide High Frequency Direction Finding data to a global network directed by the Naval Operational Intelligence Center at Suitland, Maryland (Wills 1985: 29). The end product of this intelligence is the location of all naval vessels, especially those of the Soviet Union (including submarines), on a worldwide basis.

On its own Tangimoana is of extremely limited strategic value; it is a clear case of the whole (i.e., the surveillance system) being very much greater than the sum of its parts. If Tangimoana were to be lost to the system, a replacement could be located elsewhere in the South Pacific without undue inconvenience and without the alliance suffering any serious intelligence degradation.

In sum, the infringements of New Zealand sovereignty and other costs associated with alliance-relevant defense installations are not comparable with those in Australia. Under certain conditions the installations in Australia would invite a priority nuclear strike; those in New Zealand would appear not to (Ball 1983: 88–93). On the whole, New Zealand's military and strategic contribution to ANZUS had more to do with its presence than with any other attribute.

CONCLUSIONS

The New Zealand perspective on ANZUS as outlined in this chapter obviously reflects a view of the world profoundly different from that in Australia or the United States. Regardless of how New Zealand's policies might be judged according to political or other criteria, in the very least they ought to be rational and internally consistent. However, the New Zealand government has created a set of policies that resemble a collection of ad hoc measures which cannot logically serve the nation's security.

If the objections outlined above to the ANZUS and non-nuclear policies are valid, their creation and pursuit is an indulgence. In times of relative peace this is a relatively harmless consolation. In other circumstances it will become a costly delusion. A danger exists that a sudden break with the past will be cherished for its own sake—just as the habits of the past came to be—and what is cherished then transcends intelligence or even common sense. Yet it is clear that something other and better is required of New Zealand's policy on both ANZUS and non-nuclear policy.

REFERENCES

"ANZUS Expert Sets Record Straight." 1985. *Evening Post* (Wellington), 14 February.

Ball, Desmond. 1983. "The ANZUS Connection: The Security Relationship between Australia, New Zealand and the United States of America." In *Arms, Disarmament and New Zealand: The Papers and Proceedings of the Eighteenth Foreign Policy School 1983*, ed. T. J. Hearn. Dunedin: University of Otago, Department of University Extension.

―――. 1987. *A Base for Debate: The US Satellite Station at Nurrungar*. Sydney: Allen and Unwin.

Beaglehole, J. H. 1984. "New Zealand: Highly Professional but Upgrading a Slow Process." *Pacific Defence Reporter*, July.

Bell, Coral. 1984. "The Case Against Neutrality." *Current Affairs Bulletin*, September.

Brunt, Tony. 1983. "In Search of Values." In *Right Out: Labour Victory '72*, ed. Brian Edwards. Wellington: A. H. and A. W. Reed.

Bunn, Mathew, and Tsipis, Kosta. 1983. "The Uncertainties of a Pre-Emptive Nuclear Attack." *Scientific American*, November.

Campbell, David. "New Zealand and the Nuclear Issue: A Comparative History." Unpublished seminar paper prepared for a program of study in the Honours School, Department of Political Science, University of Melbourne.

Clark, Helen. 1985. "No Nukes Meeting in Athens." *New Outlook*, March/April.

Cochran, Thomas B.; Arkin, William M.; and Hoenig, Milton M. 1984. *The Nuclear Weapons Data Book*, vol. 1: *U.S. Nuclear Forces and Capabilities*. Cambridge, Mass.: Ballinger.

Dalyell, Tam. 1983. *Thatcher's Torpedo: The Sinking of the Belgrano*. London: Cecil Woolf.

Defence and Security: What New Zealanders Want. Report of the Defence Committee of Inquiry. 1986. Wellington. July.

Defence Review. 1978. Wellington: New Zealand Department of Defence.

Ford, Daniel. 1985. *The Button: The Nuclear Trigger—Does It Work*. London: George Allen and Unwin.

Holsti, Ole R.; Hopmann, P. Terrence; and Sullivan, John D. 1985. *Unity and Disintegration in International Alliances: Comparative Studies*. Lanham: University Press of America.

Jackson, Keith. 1980. "New Zealand and the Vietnam War: A Retrospective Analysis." In *Beyond New Zealand: The Foreign Policy of a Small State*, ed. John Henderson, Keith Jackson, and Richard Kennaway. Auckland: Methuen.

Kennaway, Richard. 1984. "Changing Views of ANZUS." *New Zealand International Review* 9 (November/December).

Lange, David. 1987. "Facing a New Reality." *New Zealand International Review*, November/December.

McIntyre, W. David. 1967. "The Future of the New Zealand System of Alliances." *Landfall* 84 (December).

————. 1969. *Britain, New Zealand and the Security of South East Asia in the 1970s*. Wellington: New Zealand Institute of International Affairs.

McMillan, Stuart. 1987. *Neither Confirm Nor Deny: The Nuclear Ships Dispute between New Zealand and the United States*. Wellington and Sydney: Allen and Unwin/Port Nicholson Press.

Miles, Robert. 1984. "Will God Defend New Zealand?" *New Outlook*, November/December.

The Military Balance. Various years. London: International Institute for Strategic Studies.

New Zealand Foreign Affairs Review 35. 1985. Three addresses by Prime Minister David Lange (pp. 3–17) and one address by the High Commissioner to Australia, Graham Ansell (pp. 47–51). January/March.

"NZ Labour Is Getting It Right." 1985. *Economist* article reprinted in *Weekend Australian,* 8–9 June.

Samuel, Peter. 1985. "Samuel's Manual for Nuclear Protesters." *Weekend Australian,* 26–27 January.

"Stronger Alliance Rises from ANZUS Ashes." 1985. *The Australian,* 8 April.

Thakur, Ramesh. 1986. *In Defense of New Zealand: Foreign Policy Choices in the Nuclear Age.* Boulder, Colo.: Westview.

West, Dalton. 1984. "The 1983 Defence Review: Prospects and Implications." *New Zealand International Review* 9 (May/June).

Wills, Peter. 1985. "Spy vs. Spy." *New Outlook,* March/April.

Woodward, Bob. 1987. *Veil: The Secret Wars of the CIA 1981–1987.* London: Simon and Schuster.

Chapter 3

FRANCE IN THE SOUTH PACIFIC

Robert Aldrich

France's interests in the South Pacific center in, but are not limited to, its Oceanic territories of French Polynesia, New Caledonia, and Wallis and Futuna. These three archipelagos cover a land area of 23,227 square kilometers and are home to a population of 310,672 French citizens. Thanks to the Law of the Sea Agreement of 1982, France enjoys control over an exclusive economic zone of seven million square kilometers of maritime area in the South Pacific. Through its participation in multinational accords, such as the Lomé Conventions for aid to developing countries, and by bilateral agreements, France maintains significant contacts with several Oceanic micro-states and has important relations with the larger regional powers—Australia, New Zealand, and Papua New Guinea. Yet no European country's activities in the South Pacific have been so contested as those of France, especially in regard to nuclear tests in French Polynesia, changes in the statute of New Caledonia, and the sinking by French agents of the Greenpeace vessel *Rainbow Warrior* in Auckland, New Zealand, in 1985. Despite two centuries of activities in the region, France has been treated by many as the pariah of the South Pacific (Paringaux 1986: 2).

French explorers voyaged in the South Seas in the late 1700s, and a British fleet beat the French by only a week to establish sovereignty over Australia and set up a colony at Botany Bay in 1788. In 1840 the English similarly arrived a few days earlier than the French in New Zealand and precluded French takeover of those islands. France was successful, however, in establishing a protectorate over Tahiti and the Marquesas Islands in 1842; France gradually extended its control over the five island clusters which now make up French Polynesia and annexed the Etablissements Français d'Océanie (EFO), as it was then called, in 1880. In 1853 France had taken over New Caledonia and the Loyalty Islands in the western Pacific. A protectorate was established over the small islands of Wallis and Futuna, which lie between New Caledonia and French Polynesia, in 1887, and they were officially annexed in 1912. France also had interests in the New Hebrides but was unable to acquire sovereignty over that archipelago; in 1906 France and Great Britain worked out an arrangement for joint administration of the New Hebrides—the Condominium, which lasted until Vanuatu became independent in 1980. Finally, France claimed the small uninhabited island of Clipperton off the coast of Mexico; Mexico disputed ownership, but international arbitration awarded France possession in 1931. (On the EFO, Newbury 1980; on New Caledonia, Connell 1987; on the New Hebrides, McClancy 1980. There are no major works on Wallis and Futuna in English but the standard French text is Poncet 1976.)

France initially became interested in the South Pacific because of rivalry with Britain. Missionary interests also played an influential role, as French Catholic orders sent priests to many of the islands of Oceania. France maintained economic interests as well. It was the largest European importer of copra in the nineteenth century, and the Pacific was a major supplier of the dried coconut meat used in the manufacture of soap and margarine. France became the second largest purchaser of Australian wool, a commodity essential to France's expanding textile industry. The discovery of vast nickel reserves in New Caledonia in the 1860s provided stimulation for economic exploitation of the islands' resources; by the end of the century, New Caledonia was the world's largest exporter of nickel, essential as an alloy in steel and in increasing demand for armaments. Phosphate was later mined in French Polynesia. The islands were a source of various tropical products, including coffee, vanilla, pearls, and (for a time) cotton. In addition, France used New Caledonia as a penitentiary and transported some 10,000 convicts and political prisoners to Oceania between 1863 and 1897.

The economic development of the French possessions, however, was slow because of a lack of labor, capital, markets, and—in the case of Tahiti—direct shipping connections with France. Settlers were slow in migrating to the French Pacific. Colonists then imported Asian workers for their plantations and mines. New Caledonian settlers first recruited in other islands, then in a more systematic way in Japan, Java, and Indochina. In the EFO, colonists imported Chinese to work on plantations; most soon left their agricultural employment and became shopkeepers. The native Melanesian and Polynesian islanders were largely marginalized. The indigenous population diminished considerably after the European arrival, not to begin a recovery until the 1920s. In the EFO and Wallis and Futuna, Polynesians retained much of their land, but in New Caledonia, Melanesians were confined to reservations (which totaled one tenth of the land area on the main island, plus all of the outer islands). By the end of the nineteenth century, therefore, a capitalist economy had been implanted in the islands, the indigenous population had been Christianized and partially Westernized, and a multiracial demographic structure was in place. These structures were consolidated in the first half of the twentieth century with programs for economic development and continued Asian immigration. Even though World War II temporarily cut off the colonies from France and saw thousands of American troops stationed in the French Pacific, at the end of the war France reasserted its authority and maintained direct rule over the possessions (see Aldrich forthcoming). The history of the Pacific territories in the last thirty years reveals a mixture of local alliances and strategies, the effects of international developments, and particularly the changing policies of the metropole.

NEW CALEDONIA

In New Caledonia the major post–World War II development was a nickel boom in the late 1960s. New Caledonia remained a major world producer of nickel, which accounted for over 90 percent of the territory's exports. The boom drew many Melanesians into the Western economy and was accompanied by an influx of European settlers and migrant workers from Wallis and Futuna and Tahiti. The Europeans, Polynesians, and Asians came to outnumber the native Melanesians, confirming the latter's marginal position and sparking Melanesian nationalism. At the same time, the European and Asian settlers increasingly identified with the land where many had lived for generations.

Politically movements for greater autonomy in local affairs emerged in the late 1940s. At first based in a multi-ethnic and moderate political party, the consensus evaporated as Melanesians became more radical. The influence of the anticolonial New Left and frustration with French attempts to maintain direct rule over the territory and favor the interests of the white New Caledonians, the Caldoches, led Melanesian activists to demand independence by the late 1960s. Militants pointed out that Melanesians still owned little property, the economy was totally controlled by European interests, and Melanesians were absent from the economic, political, and cultural elite—the first Melanesian to be awarded a high school diploma graduated in the 1960s. Paris formulated plan after plan for economic development and political reform, and a prime minister of the 1970s, Pierre Messmer, encouraged French immigration to New Caledonia in an effort to drown the budding Melanesian nationalism by demographic means. The reform plans failed to obtain support from either the Melanesians or the Caldoches, and positions polarized.

The election of a socialist government in France in 1981 brought new hopes and fears to New Caledonia. The plan for "independence-association," advanced by French High Commissioner Edgard Pisani in 1984, provoked even greater criticism than previous reform efforts. Melanesian pro-independence activists formed a coalition, the Front de Libération Nationale Kanak et Socialiste (FLNKS), under Jean-Marie Tjibaou, which demanded a "Kanak and socialist" independence. The whites rallied to the conservative Rassemblement pour la Calédonie dans la République (RPCR), which, under the leadership of Jacques Lafleur, opposed independence. Some whites supported the FLNKS, and the RPCR prided itself on having Melanesian members, but the battle lines divided on ethnic as well as political grounds. (The Asians, Tahitians, and Wallisians, fearful of their status in a future "Kanaky," supported the Caldoches.)

Violence erupted in 1984, and two years of turmoil followed with two dozen Melanesians and Caldoches killed. With the rejection of the Pisani plan, an intermediate arrangement, the Fabius plan, divided New Caledonia into four regions; elections brought pro-independence Melanesians to power in three of these, leaving the fourth—the capital, Nouméa—in the hands of the RPCR. Both the socialists and their opponents in metropolitan France promised a referendum on the status of the territory, but the conservative government elected in March 1986 did everything possible to strengthen the RPCR. New Caledonians finally voted in September 1987; only those with a minimum of three years' residence in the territory were allowed to vote, and the pro-independence parties boycotted the ballot. The 59 percent of the eligible voters which cast a ballot voted almost unanimously in favor of continued association with France. The French minister of overseas departments and territories, Bernard Pons, who called the referendum, heralded the vote as a victory; supporters of independence condemned it. A number of metropolitan political figures, including President François Mitterrand, expressed reservations about the utility of the exercise. The government of Prime Minister Jacques Chirac nevertheless promised another plan for economic and political development, including a redrawing of the regions to equalize RPCR and FLNKS control. (On the events of the last two decades, see Connell 1987; Dornoy 1984; Spencer, Ward, and Connell, eds. 1988; and Kohler 1987: 6–7.)

In April 1988, at the time of the French presidential elections, a group of Kanaks attacked a police station on Ouvéa island and killed four gendarmes. More than two dozen policemen were taken hostage; some were soon released, but the others were hidden in a cave on the island. The Chirac government ordered soldiers to storm the cave to free the hostages; in the operation, two French soldiers and nineteen of the Kanaks were killed. Newspaper reports in France claimed that some of the Kanaks had been killed in summary executions and that the government had even considered dropping napalm on the island. Chirac and Pons proclaimed the success of the operation, while regretting the loss of life. The action did not apparently aid Chirac, whose presidential aspirations were dashed by the victory of Mitterrand. However, the subsequent legislative elections failed to give a clear majority to the president's supporters. The election results, combined with the unprecedented casualties in New Caledonia, created a climate for a new approach to the territory's problems.

France's new socialist prime minister, Michel Rocard, sent a fact-finding mission composed of clergymen and public servants to New Caledonia and arranged meetings with both Lafleur and Tjibaou in Paris. In negotiations which would have seemed impossible only weeks before, Rocard worked out an agreement between the FLNKS and the RPCR and persuaded Lafleur and Tjibaou to shake hands in front of cameras. The Matignon Accord, as the agreement was labeled, was approved by both major parties in New Caledonia and, with varying degrees of enthusiasm, by metropolitan parties. According to the accord, New Caledonia will be ruled directly by the high commissioner, the representative of the French government, for one year dating from July 1988. The territory will then be divided into three provinces—a largely European south, the Melanesian Loyalty Islands, and a mixed north—each with an assembly and executive and substantial autonomy. This structure, coordinated by the high commissioner, will stay in place until 1998, when another referendum on the future of New Caledonia will be held. Only those voters living in New Caledonia in 1988 and their descendants will be eligible for this ballot, which will decide whether New Caledonia will become independent or remain part of France. In the meantime, France promises to pour large amounts of money into the territory to support economic development, train Kanak public servants, and address various Kanak grievances. So that the Matignon Accord could not be substantially altered by future governments, Rocard submitted it to the French electorate (including voters in the metropole) in November 1988; despite an unprecedented rate of abstention in the referendum, voters overwhelmingly approved the proposal.

The arrangements worked out by Rocard for New Caledonia were intended to provide a cooling-off period when economic and social development in the territory could be promoted. Both the pro- and anti-independence factions hoped that the ten years before the supposedly definitive vote on independence would provide them time to win greater numbers of supporters for their respective causes. Critics charged that the French government was only buying time and that anti-independence parties were hoping for some partition of the territory, with Nouméa and the south remaining French even if the rest of New Caledonia became independent. In general, the Matignon Accord has been applauded by French political circles and by international observers who had previously been critical of French policy in New Caledonia (*Pacific Islands Monthly* [*PIM*], June, July, August 1988).

FRENCH POLYNESIA

Like New Caledonia, French Polynesia has undergone significant changes since the 1960s, prompted initially by the opening of an international airport in the capital, Papeete, and the beginnings of large-scale tourism. But the central issue in the recent history of French Polynesia has been the creation of the Centre d'Expérimentation du Pacifique (CEP) and its tests on the atoll of Mururoa. French nuclear testing had been carried out in the Algerian desert before the independence of that country in 1962; the following year President Charles de Gaulle announced his intention to transfer testing to the South Pacific. The first atmospheric tests were conducted in Polynesia in 1966, and they continued until 1974; since that time France has done underground testing on Mururoa. The CEP has had immense effects on French Polynesia, providing a great number of jobs and transforming the economy of the territory from one of subsistence production and export of agricultural products (and phosphate) to an economy which lives largely off transfer payments and subsidies from the metropole. Large numbers of Polynesians abandoned farming, migrating from the rural districts of Tahiti or from peripheral islands to Papeete. The city swelled to count half the territory's population, and the tertiary sector became the major employer.

French Polynesia has also witnessed increasing demands for autonomy since the 1950s, led by the *demis*, the mixed Polynesian and European group which controls most economic power in the territory. France for many years rejected such demands, even jailing the main pro-independence activist, Pouvanaa a Oopa. As part of its decentralization program, the Mitterrand government gave a new statute to French Polynesia in 1984. This gave the territorial government—composed of a president, cabinet, and legislature—substantial control over economic and social issues. French Polynesia also gained a distinctive flag and an anthem. The French government, represented by a high commissioner, maintains control over security, defense, and external relations. Several political parties, which garner about one fifth of the total vote, continue to demand independence (Shineberg 1986).

WALLIS AND FUTUNA

Wallis and Futuna are totally dependent on France. Exports of copra and handicrafts are minimal, and most income comes from metropolitan transfers and migrant remittances. Approximately ten thousand of the islanders live in New Caledonia, and the money they send home from their jobs as miners and laborers is a major source of revenue. The traditional social structure remains in place in the islands. Wallis is governed by a king, Futuna by two kings. The French administrator manages the bureaucracy. The Catholic Church retains great influence in the totally Christianized archipelago. Wallis and Futuna could have strategic importance, and various suggestions for development have been put forward. But change is slow, and neither the Wallisians nor the French officials want to rush it (Rensche 1983).

CONTEMPORARY PROBLEMS

In both New Caledonia and French Polynesia substantial political difficulties remain. The Matignon Accord provides a good basis for bringing about the recovery of New Caledonia, but the failure of numerous plans in the past and the ultimate incompatibility of extremist pro- and anti-independence demands casts a shadow over the current mood of optimism. Disputes exist inside the FLNKS and the RPCR, and the personal leadership of both Tjibaou and Lafleur has been contested. Hardliners in the pro-independence movement are unhappy with the ten years of French rule mandated by the Matignon Accord, and far right-wing Caldoches feel they have been sold out. In French Polynesia, extreme fragmentation of political parties has marked politics. In spite of this, local politics were long dominated by Gaston Flosse, a local businessman, head of French Polynesia's main conservative party, chief of the territorial government, and Chirac's secretary of state for the South Pacific. Flosse came under great criticism in 1987 for his political empire-building and shady business dealings and was forced to relinquish his presidency of the French Polynesian government. With the elections of 1988 he lost his ministerial portfolio and his seat in the National Assembly. Former supporters had turned against him, and the new territorial government, led by Alexandre Léontieff, is a coalition of anti-Flosse conservative parties, centrists, and even a pro-independence party. It is uncertain how long the coalition government can survive or whether Flosse is capable of a political comeback (Bohin 1987; Rollat 1987: 32–33).

In both territories major economic challenges exist: the unequal development of the territories—overdevelopment and a congested population in the capital cities and underdevelopment in the interior regions and the Loyalty Islands of New Caledonia and the outer islands of French Polynesia; a maldistribution of income; underrepresentation of Melanesians and pure Polynesians in the upper ranks of the economy and in the political class; the effects of urbanization, salaried employment, education, and Christianity on the indigenous islanders; and overreliance on metropolitan money. The volatile price of nickel has adversely affected New Caledonia, while political upheaval came near to destroying the growing tourist industry. Paris is thus obliged to subsidize the territory's budget. French Polynesia has only a few exports of tropical products and pearls—only 5 percent of the budget is covered by exports—and tourism is not able to take up the slack. The territory lives on metropolitan transfers; much of the money and employment is linked directly or indirectly with the CEP.

For critics this state of affairs is indicative of continued French colonialism, characterized by the exploitation of islanders and island resources for the profits of an entrenched European elite and the needs of the French capitalist economy and military machine. For others, however, the problem is more complex and demands that such issues as the resource endowment of the islands, political clientelism, and the socialization of the indigenous population be taken into account. Proposed solutions to the political problems range from total integration with France (*départementalisation*) to various sorts of autonomy or "free association" to total independence. Economically a variety of possibilities for development has been mooted—tourism, free ports, high-technology industry, etc.—but for the foreseeable future metropolitan transfers and possibly renewed nickel development in New Caledonia and tourism in Polynesia will be the motors for growth.

OPPOSITION TO FRENCH ACTIVITIES

Opposition to French activities has ranged from outright condemnation of the French presence and demands that France immediately cease nuclear testing and grant independence to French Polynesia and New Caledonia to much milder reservations about current French policy. France's European partners and the United States have refrained from criticism, although it is unclear whether their silence implies wholehearted support for French activities or a desire to preserve cordial relations with Paris. Some Third World countries have castigated the French, but France's political and commercial clients have been discreet in their disagreement with French policy. The centers of opposition have been the South Pacific Forum (SPF—an association of independent states in the region), the United Nations, and the Nonaligned Movement. Especially loud in their protests have been the independent island states of the South Pacific, as well as Australia and New Zealand.

Two major areas of opposition against France exist. The principal criticisms concern the French policy on nuclear testing. As late as 1972 Australian authorities said that French nuclear tests posed no hazard to Australia, but the Australian position reversed with the election of a Labor government in that year. In 1973 Australia joined New Zealand in taking France to the World Court of Justice to try to stop atmospheric tests. The court ruled in favor of Australia and New Zealand, but France said it would take no heed of the decision. Soon afterward, however, it abandoned atmospheric tests for subterranean ones. Protests continued, particularly in Australia, where dockers refused to unload French vessels in 1974, protesters occupied the French consulate in Melbourne in 1978, and various groups called for a boycott of French goods. The Labor government of Bob Hawke, which came to power in 1983, temporarily suspended shipments of uranium to France, arguing that it could be used for military purposes, yet when Australia's balance of payments worsened two years later, Hawke again began the shipments. The French invited scientists from Australia, New Zealand, and Papua New Guinea to visit Mururoa in the early 1980s; the tests that the scientists performed did not provide evidence of danger, but the results did not quieten criticism (Danielsson 1986).

Condemnation of the CEP has been based on questions about the safety of the exercises, both seismic dangers from the explosions and radioactive pollution. But such scientific questions often spill over into a denunciation of French nuclear policy in general and charges of weapons testing in the Pacific. For their part, the French point out first of all that Mururoa is only a giant laboratory. Vice-Admiral Pierre Thireaut, chief of military forces in French Polynesia and commander of the CEP, categorically notes the following:

> We are not testing weapons. Mururoa is only a physics laboratory. We do laboratory tests for testing the elements [of nuclear devices]. . . . There are no French nuclear weapons in the Pacific (1986: 24–25).

Asked about ecological risks, Thireaut replies:

> There is no radioactive risk. There is no risk of radioactive substances going into the ocean. Everything is totally capped in the basalt, not the coral. There are some seismic vibrations down in the atoll. Part of the atoll is slowly going down without any risk for anybody (*ibid.*; see also Lewin 1984).

Similarly a French publication, *French Nuclear Tests in Mururoa: The Reasons Why*, states the following:

> [The basalt base of Mururoa with its] particularly stable geological substrata makes it possible to carry out in-depth underground tests in all safety. . . . Beyond a few hundred meters the shock waves generated by underground nuclear explosions turn into a seismic wave whose energy equals about one per cent of the energy released by the explosion. A few dozen kilometers away, the ground movement is less than a tenth of a millimeter (quoted in *Islands Business*, January 1987, p. 19).

As evidence of the safety of the tests, the French cite scientific experiments carried out on Mururoa, in the vicinity of the atoll, and elsewhere in Polynesia which show no abnormally high levels of radiation; in fact the inhabitants of Tahiti exhibit a lower level of exposure to radioactivity (both natural and artificial) than most residents of the northern hemisphere. The French also point to the reports of a French scientific delegation, led by the respected geologist Haroun Tazieff, in 1982 and a mission composed of foreign scientists the following year. To charges that France is polluting the "backyard" of Pacific nations, Paris argues that the Mururoa site is 1,200 kilometers from Tahiti and 6,000 kilometers from the coasts of Australia, Chile, and Mexico. Paris is closer to the Soviet testing station in Kazakhstan than is Sydney to Mururoa. Furthermore, the French point out that only 200 residents live in a range of 500 kilometers around the French site, whereas 1.2 million live in the same radius from the Soviet site and 15 million live 500 kilometers or less from the American test site in Nevada. The French do not dispute that there are seismic effects from the tests but argue that these are not dangerous in the isolated region of Mururoa. Moreover, these effects explain why the tests cannot be conducted in metropolitan France; an area of approximately 30 kilometers around the site devoid of rail lines, buildings, bridges, or underground conduits is necessary to safeguard against any damage from the explosions (Thireaut 1986: 24–25).

Critics of French testing counter that the foreign scientists making a quick visit to Mururoa were not able (or allowed) to carry out exhaustive tests to determine lingering radioactivity or seismic effects. They argue further that the incidence of such diseases as leukemia and thyroid cancer has increased dramatically in French Polynesia since the start of the testing and that radioactivity has poisoned large numbers of fish in the territory. They also say that the continued drilling of the atoll has turned it into a Swiss cheese and that this, and the possible sinking of part of the coral reef, could risk greater pollution (Danielsson 1987). They add that both Britain and the United States have ceased testing on Pacific islands and argue that France should either stop or transfer testing. However, the same critics have expressed great fear that France might eventually move its testing site to uninhabited Kerguelen Island in the southern Indian Ocean, as has been rumored (but denied by Paris); Kerguelen is closer to Australia than is Mururoa.

Australia and New Zealand have led opposition to French testing, and most of the South Pacific micro-states have followed suit. Criticism against French testing is a regular battlehorse at the annual meetings of the SPF.* SPF opposition to French testing crystallized at the 1985 meeting with the adoption of the South Pacific Nuclear-Free Zone (Rarotonga)

*French territories are excluded from the forum, and the SPF has even denied them observer status at meetings.

Treaty, which forbids nuclear testing, the storing or use of nuclear weapons, and the disposal of wastes in the area. Three of the world's nuclear powers—France, the United States, and the United Kingdom—have declined to sign the agreement. Nor did Vanuatu sign, arguing that the treaty was too limited. The Soviet Union, which did sign, noted that if the international context changed, so could Soviet policy. The treaty is thus a toothless tiger. (See *PIM*, September 1985, pp. 10–13; see also X. Pons 1987; for the Australian viewpoint, Hayden 1987; for the other side, B. Pons 1987b.)

The second aspect of French policy in the South Pacific which is generally contested by neighboring nations is the status of New Caledonia. The micro-states of Oceania, which acceded to independence in the 1960s and 1970s, assume that New Caledonia (as well as French Polynesia) should become independent under the control of the local population; Australia, New Zealand, and the SPF are careful to say that they want a multiracial and peaceful independence, but the Melanesian spearhead nations—a front line of support led by Vanuatu and including Papua New Guinea and the Solomon Islands—stress Melanesian rights to organize a newly independent state. Politicians have criticized both the structural inequalities in New Caledonia and French administration of the territory. The Pisani plan of 1984 was popular with several Pacific governments, and the Fabius plan was greeted as an acceptable short-term compromise which at least allowed Melanesians control of several regions and permitted a certain economic and political apprenticeship for the indigenes. However, the pro-RPCR Chirac government and the September 1987 referendum inflamed passions among France's opponents to an unparalleled degree. The Matignon Accord has again quietened criticisms.

Even before the 1986 change in government in Paris, SPF members took the issue of New Caledonia to the United Nations. The United Nations maintains a roster of dependent territories which should be decolonized. Its Committee of Twenty-Four monitors the listed territories and, if the administering power allows, sends its own investigators. France itself had listed New Caledonia on the roster in the late 1940s but, with a vote by the New Caledonian electorate in 1958 that the colony become an "overseas territory" of France, had it removed from the list. The SPF members of the United Nations, including Australia and New Zealand, moved in 1986 for New Caledonia to be once again placed on the roster. France canvassed hard for a no vote on the proposal but failed to convince a majority of members of the General Assembly. Paris then announced it would take no notice of the decision and would not cooperate with the UN committee. A second vote by the General Assembly, after the September 1987 referendum in New Caledonia, resulted in a much smaller "anti-French" majority: more nations voted against a motion critical of France or abstained on the ballot than voted to support "decolonization." Paris labeled the vote a triumph, proof of the efficacy of the referendum in convincing world opinion about French intentions.* More recently the Committee of Twenty-Four has expressed satisfaction with the Rocard government's initiatives.

As noted above, the Nonaligned Movement has also criticized France. At its meeting in Harare in 1986 the movement received a delegation from the FLNKS and adopted a resolution based on the previous UN and SPF pronouncements.† The Harare resolution favored self-determination and the rapid accession of New Caledonia to independence, conforming to the rights and aspirations of the territory's original inhabitants but with guarantees of rights for all residents. The FLNKS welcomed the resolution, while the French viewed it as a predictable *prise de position* by the Nonaligned Movement (*Bwenando*, 26 September 1986).

Individual nations have also raised questions about French policy in New Caledonia. Most surprising to the French was the politely worded criticism advanced by Japan just before the September 1987 referendum; the French greeted the criticism with quiet anger (*Le Monde*, 6 August 1987). Paris has responded more strongly to criticism from Libya, with which France is embroiled in Chad. Colonel Muamar Ghaddafi has condemned the French presence in New Caledonia on expected grounds. In late 1987 he invited several FLNKS activists to Tripoli for an international meeting of "liberation" groups. Rumors circulated that Libya had provided training in terrorism to the FLNKS members. Those opposed to independence used the Libyan connection as a major plank in their platform, while New Caledonia's neighbors became concerned about a Libyan entry into the South Pacific, even though French intelligence sources were unable to find evidence of Libyan arms entering New Caledonia. Moderates in the FLNKS disapproved of contacts with Tripoli, and the head of the pro-Libyan faction lost his post as foreign relations spokesman for the coalition.**

*The meetings of the SPF and the United Nations are regularly reported in *PIM*.

†An FNLKS submission to the United Nations is reprinted in *Bwenando* 78–79, April 1987.

**Around this time Australia closed the Libyan People's Bureau in Canberra.

Continuing opposition to French policy in New Caledonia and Polynesia found a rallying point in the sinking of the *Rainbow Warrior* in 1985. The vessel, operated by the ecology organization Greenpeace, was on its way to protest nuclear testing in Mururoa. French agents, launching their mission from New Caledonia, sank the ship in the harbor of Auckland. The prime minister of New Zealand, David Lange, one of the bitterest of France's critics, charged Paris with terrorism, and Australian and South Pacific leaders joined the chorus. For many it seemed as if France was willing to resort to violence against protesters to defend its interests and that it had little respect for the sovereignty of independent nations. In the scandal which ensued several top French officials resigned, and Paris agreed to pay indemnities to New Zealand, Greenpeace, and the family of a photographer killed in the sinking. French authorities downplayed the incident; the French minister of defense and the two French agents arrested and convicted in New Zealand were hailed as heroes by some sectors of public opinion. France showed its muscle by threatening to engineer EC retaliations on New Zealand exports if the two agents were not released. The countries came to an arrangement for the pair to be detained on the island of Hao in French Polynesia for the balance of their sentence.* The affair has left a black mark against France and is a theme regularly invoked by Paris's critics in the Pacific (see Shears and Gidley 1985).

FRENCH VIEWS OF THE SOUTH PACIFIC

Mururoa, New Caledonia, and Greenpeace have brought the South Pacific to the attention of the French—and disabused them of images of Oceania modeled on the novels of Pierre Loti and the paintings of Gauguin. The new interest has prompted efforts to coordinate French policy in the region. In February 1986 President Mitterrand set up a South Pacific Council, consisting of the French ambassadors in the region and various other officials, presided over by presidential counselor Régis Debray. The council has become inactive since the conservative electoral victory of March 1986. As noted, Prime Minister Chirac appointed a secretary of state for the South Pacific (Flosse), but the position was not renewed in the Rocard government of 1988. Such policy initiatives have responded to recent events as well as to the French perception of its global

*Both agents have now returned to France, repatriated on medical grounds over the opposition of New Zealand.

role and to a new analysis of the place of the Pacific in world politics. Understanding the interpretations by French geostrategists and political scientists is vital to comprehending French behavior in the South Pacific.

In the face of challenges to French authority and great problems for the development of its islands, the obvious question is why France has hung on to the Oceanic territories while decolonizing most of the rest of its empire in the 1950s and 1960s. The most apparent reason is the simple desire of the majority of residents in the Pacific territories to remain French: the pro-independence Melanesians in New Caledonia are outnumbered; the electorate in French Polynesia shows little support for local pro-independence groups; in Wallis and Futuna there is no independence movement. Certainly the demographic balance has been altered by the immigration of metropolitan French and the importation of outside laborers, particularly in New Caledonia; probably too a number of residents have been convinced to vote pro-French through various direct or indirect incentives. Nevertheless, in a constitutional state such as France, ignoring majority wishes and unilaterally granting independence would be not only unprecedented, but also illegal.

For supporters of French policy, New Caledonia, French Polynesia and Wallis and Futuna are not colonies. Under the provisions of the constitution of the Fifth Republic, promulgated in 1958, the three archipelagos voted on their future and decided to become *territoires d'outre-mer* (TOM). As such, they are represented in the French Senate and National Assembly and in other national bodies. All inhabitants of the territories (except foreigners) are French citizens and vote in all local and national elections. They enjoy an unrestricted right of residence and work in metropolitan France—there is no French equivalent, for example, of a British overseas passport. Laws passed by the French parliament must be officially labeled as applicable to the TOM if they are to be in force in these territories, but the laws and institutions of metropolitan France and the TOM are similar. Although the TOM are not so integrated into the metropole as the *départements d'outre-mer* (DOM), they are fully a part of France. They have the constitutional right to become independent if a majority of the electorate so decides. As the French point out, however, this has not been the case for the Pacific TOM.

France reaps various benefits from the Pacific TOM. They provide a number of useful commodities, an outlet for business and administrative work, and a cultural stake in the Pacific. Yet France has been able to maintain these advantages in almost all of its former colonies: more Frenchmen live in black Africa now than before the independence of the African colonies, French companies are major entrepreneurs in Africa, French troops are stationed in six independent African states, and French culture thrives in sovereign states on several continents. So these advantages cannot explain the continued sovereignty over the Pacific TOM. More important in material terms, the vast exclusive maritime zones surrounding the French archipelagos may prove a useful source of minerals if it becomes profitable to exploit the seabed, continental shelves, and polymetalic nodes under the water. The exact wealth of such resources is unknown, but the possibility (or hope) that they may provide great returns is enough to make France think twice about abandoning its Pacific territories. Furthermore, the waters contain vast stores of exportable seafood, and overseas territories can provide useful registries for ships sailing under flags of convenience (as in the case of Kerguelen).* Together with France's other territories, the Pacific islands give France the third largest exclusive maritime zone in the world—a maritime area in the Caribbean, North Atlantic, Indian Ocean, and the Pacific. Current excitement about undersea resources underlines the potential value to France of the exclusive maritime zone surrounding its overseas territories. Without its overseas possessions, France would lose 97 percent of its exclusive economic zone in the world's oceans, thereby falling from third to forty-fifth in world rank (see Gallois 1986).

Another benefit is space exploration and tracking. The French space station at Kourou in South America is the base for the Ariane program, which has launched satellites on behalf of the French, the EC, and various other groups. With the crisis of the American space program, Kourou has assumed even greater importance. Meanwhile, President Ronald Reagan's Strategic Defense Initiative proposal implies that earth stations for monitoring outer space activities could become vital, not just for telecommunications and science, but also for military purposes. With territories scattered in the Pacific and elsewhere, France has a prime position for undertaking or keeping track of a variety of maneuvers in space. Economic, political, and strategic benefits may accrue from such a position, and reasons of security make it preferable that activities be carried out in areas over which a nation exercises complete sovereignty. As General Jeannou Lacaze, chief of staff of the French armies, explains:

> The nuclear testing center of the Pacific at Mururoa and the space center at Kourou in Guyana are absolutely essential to the maintenance

*France agreed to register ships in Kerguelen Island so that they could employ a smaller proportion of French sailors than is usually required on French flagships.

of our technological level and to the coherency of our defense capacity (cited in Gallois 1986).

GEOPOLITICS AND FRENCH STRATEGY

It is thus strategic interests which overshadow other uses of the Pacific TOM. The French concept of France's political and military identity, first formulated by de Gaulle and continued by his successors, is that France ought to maintain a global presence. That presence must be backed by an independent military and defense capacity. As the world's fourth largest economy, a leader in European affairs, and a permanent member of the UN Security Council, France has a responsibility to be present in an active way all over the world. It must look after its own interests and maintain a certain distance from the superpowers and international organizations. To do so, it needs a strong and modern military, which in the atomic age means a nuclear force. An independent nuclear deterrence force, therefore, has been the centerpiece of Gaullist and post-Gaullist international strategy. To ensure that such a force is of maximum modernity and strength, continual tests are necessary. Mururoa provides the ideal location for the safety and security of such tests, and other islands can serve as extra testing sites (Fangataufa), backup airports and stations (Hao), and administrative and military headquarters (Papeete). In this perspective Mururoa becomes the heart of French defense policy.

New Caledonia did not enter into this original articulation of French defense policy; indeed the government has hesitated in developing the strategic potential of the territory. But in recent years strategists have referred to its importance as a backup base for conventional forces or as the "aircraft carrier" of the South Pacific. In 1985 the French minister of defense announced the creation of a major naval base in New Caledonia, but that plan soon was put on hold. The Chirac government was surprisingly noncommittal about strengthening military capacity in Nouméa, although it deployed some 8,000 military and paramilitary personnel in the territory to maintain order. Nevertheless, New Caledonia is not without interest as a base for French ships, a troop garrison, and a telecommunications center.

The French global military perspective and the importance of France's nuclear force have provided one rationale for a continued presence in the Pacific. Other theories take different (if often complementary) approaches to defend French Pacific activities. One has been a reevaluation of the Pacific basin.

THE PACIFIC: CENTER OF THE WORLD

The French have periodically rediscovered the Pacific (Aldrich 1988). In the 1880s plans for the Panama Canal prompted a wave of interest in the South Seas. In the 1980s new interest has emerged with the growing economic and political importance of Pacific states, particularly Japan. Most interesting and most comprehensive of the many new groups which discuss France and the Pacific has been the Institut du Pacifique, founded in Paris in 1983. Members include academics, journalists, businessmen, and political figures; since many are prominent in their fields and have good connections with the administration (although the institute is an independent organization), the Institut du Pacifique enjoys considerable influence in official circles.

The Institute's collectively authored work, *Le Pacifique, "nouveau centre du monde,"* first published in 1984, is a manifesto for its work and an analysis of the region. The first part of the volume, an exposition of the economy and politics of the Pacific, argues that the Pacific basin now contains some of the major trading links in the world and is also one of the most coveted areas for political influence. The remainder of the book presents three "scenarios" for the future of the Pacific basin. The first, which the authors see as the present trend, is a "triumphant capitalism" based on an economic dyarchy of Japan and the United States drawing in their wake the newly industrialized nations of South Korea, Singapore, Hong Kong, and Taiwan. The second scenario, which could either follow from this Japanese-American hegemony or replace it, is a general destabilization of the Pacific region with extended influence by the Soviet Union and China and the advent of Castro-style regimes in Oceania. Both of these prospects seem undesirable, particularly because of the lack of possibilities for French participation. The third scenario, the optimum choice, is what the authors term "multipolarity plus non-infeudation equaling coresponsibility"—in other words, an effort by Pacific nations to steer clear of the overlordship of either the Americans or the Soviets and the creation of more substantial ties among the nations of the Pacific basin and other countries with an interest in the area. In this setting France has a major role to play because of its TOM and because of Paris's independent position between the United States and the Soviet Union. In this scenario France's task must be to create amicable relations which encourage coresponsibility in the South Pacific. The authors therefore favor technical and economic aid, political friendship, and greater cultural activity to increase French influence. They also suggest that the solution to the New Caledonian problem lies in a quasi-independence, in which New Caledonia would gain autonomy but would agree on a "compact of free association" with France through which Paris would retain control of the archipelago's foreign affairs and defense (Institut du Pacifique 1987).

In a second edition of its book, the Institut du Pacifique maintains these theses. In addition, the president of the Institute, Georges Ordonnaud (1985), has formulated the concept of the "southwest Pacific," which includes Australia, the Melanesian islands, and the states of the Association of South East Asian Nations (ASEAN) but not the eastern or northern Pacific. The southwest Pacific is particularly important, Ordonnaud says, because the Straits of Malacca control access from the Pacific to the Indian Ocean and because of the political turmoil which has racked Southeast Asia in recent decades (including the regime change in the Philippines). Peace and security in this area depend on the maintenance of ASEAN, good relations between Australia and its Asian neighbors, an Australian defense policy which goes beyond "fortress Australia," and a French presence acceptable to both Australia and the other states of the region. Ordonnaud also emphasizes the importance of the American bases of Subic Bay and Clark in the Philippines and the possibility of their being transferred to Palau if the Philippines becomes anarchic or anti-American.

With the increasing importance of the Pacific, observers consider it necessary that France maintain an active presence; such a presence can be best assured by continued control over the foreign policy and defense of its islands, nuclear testing and strong conventional defense forces, and harmonious relations with the states of Australasia, Oceania, and Southeast Asia. The interest of other powers in the South Pacific—symbolized particularly by the Soviet Union's short-lived fishing treaty with Kiribati and General Secretary Mikhail Gorbachev's 1986 speech in Vladivostok on Soviet-Pacific relations (emphasizing the Soviet Union's interest in the Pacific but promising not to intervene in domestic questions in Pacific states)—makes a French presence even more vital.* The new Soviet interest in the region, in fact, is a prime element in arguments for French activities. Some of the more fanciful geopolitical amateurs have dreamed of conspiratorial plans by which France's (or the West's) enemies aim to penetrate the Pacific or use France's Oceanic territories as stepping-stones from Asia to South America or Australia (Zeldine 1985).

---

*See *Politique étrangère* 52 (Spring 1987), especially the articles by François Godement and Georges Ordonnaud. This special issue on "La France et le Pacifique Sud" is essential reading.

THE DOM-TOM

Another French approach to its presence in the Pacific is not to link the TOM to the southwest Pacific or the entire Pacific basin but rather to France's other DOM and TOM.* These ten bases around the world give France a stake in global affairs, and maintaining complete sovereignty allows France the possibility of intervention with complete liberty, in conjunction with (or even in spite of) various regional alliances. Moreover, the DOM and TOM complement each other: the nuclear testing in French Polynesia and the space station in French Guyana benefit from backup provided by the Pacific and Caribbean territories respectively, and Réunion and Mayotte provide a base in the Indian Ocean for French fleets and shore bases. Even unoccupied islands, such as Kerguelen or Clipperton, could provide airstrips and bases for French activity should they be needed. (See Guillebaud 1976.)

The DOM-TOM in this perspective provide more than just strategic interest, for they give France an exclusive maritime zone in the world, markets, venues for Francophone cultural activities, and "windows" on the regions in which they lie. The DOM-TOM are thus a great advantage for France (Gomane 1985: 419–35; Vallin 1987). In addition, Bernard Pons (1987a) has argued that the DOM-TOM should be seen in a European focus, particularly in light of the greater unification of Europe planned for 1992. The DOM-TOM, Pons suggests, are not just the "luck" of France, but also of Europe, the way in which the EC can maintain a presence in the Atlantic, Pacific, and Indian Oceans. Were it not for the French territories and the overseas possessions of other EC states, there would be no bases of European presence around the globe.

In this perspective independence for one of the DOM-TOM, such as New Caledonia, could have a "domino" effect on the others, particularly those with nascent pro-independence movements (such as French Polynesia or Guadeloupe). The cohesiveness of French policy demands that such an evolution be nipped in the bud. In the worst scenario pro-independence agitation in the overseas possessions could even infect metropolitan France, particularly such regions as Corsica and Britanny.

Of course there are dissidents to the viewpoint that the Pacific and the DOM-TOM are important to France. Some inside the French military

*In addition to the Pacific territories, the DOM-TOM are Martinique, Guadeloupe, and Saint-Pierre et Miquelon in North America and the Caribbean; French Guyana in South America; and Réunion, Mayotte, and the Terres Australes et Antarctiques Françaises in the Indian Ocean (see Connell and Aldrich forthcoming).

establishment disagree with arguments about the strategic use of New Caledonia as an "aircraft carrier" in the South Pacific. Admiral Alexandre Sanguinetti, the most outspoken dissident, argues as follows:

> What gives interest to an aircraft carrier, which some laymen tend to confuse with an ordinary air base, is its mobility, which permits it, in the case of uncertainty of the adversary about its exact position, in carrying out an attack on him then immediately to withdraw out of reach of a possible counter-attack. New Caledonia, geographically fixed, is in a position only to attack Australia and New Zealand, who are friends—furthermore, no French attack aircraft has the necessary radius of action necessary to do so. New Caledonia thus has no aeronaval interest for us Frenchmen (1986).

In general, Sanguinetti suggests that the contemporary navy prefers ships rather than land bases, as they are more effective defense stations. He adds that historically New Caledonia has never been a major defense base for France.

Prominent commentators, such as Jean Chesneaux, have criticized the French position in New Caledonia and Tahiti (and in the other DOM-TOM). A pro-FLNKS Paris-based organization, the Association d'Information et de Soutien au Peuple Karak, holds meetings and publishes *Kanaky*, a journal regularly criticizing French policy and demanding independence for New Caledonia. Marches in support of the Melanesians regularly draw several thousand in Paris. There is a French antinuclear organization (as well as a branch of Greenpeace). The Communist Party, the United Socialist Party, and a variety of far left groups have argued against French policy and the suppositions on which it is based. These individuals and groups, however, are a minority (Chesneaux 1985, 1987, 1986: 18–20, 41).

THE FUTURE OF FRANCE IN THE SOUTH PACIFIC

The point of departure of France and its opponents regarding the South Pacific is different. For France the right to a Pacific presence is irrefutable, given the nation's sovereignty over the TOM in Oceania and France's global status. For opponents, however, France is an interloper, maintaining colonial rule and carrying out dangerous (or even fatal) activities in the South Pacific. The two positions seem irreconcilable, and efforts at compromise have been unsuccessful. The SPF effectively declares Paris persona non grata in Oceania. France, for its part, has been apt to dismiss the concerns of local governments in an arrogant and unconciliatory manner. Both sides have engaged in name-calling, no better exemplified than in the insults exchanged by Australia and France over their respective treatment of aborigines and Melanesians. The expulsion of the Australian consul general from Nouméa and the French ambassador from Vanuatu in 1987 typifies the impulsiveness of both sides.

Neither side is so righteous as it may claim. The small Pacific countries which denounce French colonialism are dependent on handouts from international institutions or other aid donors just to survive. France in 1980 gave Aus$286,000 to Papua New Guinea, Aus$96,000 to Tonga, Aus$20 million to Vanuatu, Aus$92,000 to Western Samoa, and Aus$572,000 to regional institutions. It also contributed money channeled (under arrangements with the EC) to Pacific states which are members of the Africa Caribbean Pacific group (Knapman 1986). The SPF members criticize a lack of democracy in the French territories, but few are themselves shining examples of democracy: Tonga is ruled by an authoritarian king, only a small group of Western Samoa's citizens vote for that country's legislature, the prime minister of Vanuatu has barred his principal opponent from parliament, a cabinet minister in Papua New Guinea accepted an Aus$200,000 gift from an Indonesian general, and two coups d'état in Fiji in 1987 blatantly show that the island championed as the exemplar of the "Pacific way" is not immune to undemocratic and racist political movements. *Islands Business*, a Pacific monthly magazine not noted for its friendliness to France, could not help remarking on the double face of the 1987 SPF meeting, which resulted in calumny cast on the French position in New Caledonia and a blind eye cast on the Fiji coups (July 1987, p. 3).

Australia and New Zealand defend a non-nuclear and independent Pacific, but it is clear that both countries are thereby trying to ingratiate themselves with Pacific micro-states. Australia wishes to consolidate its position at the frontier of Southeast Asia and Melanesia, and New Zealand wishes to establish a strong presence in Polynesia. Both nations control dependent offshore territories; Australia, which controls two thirds of investment in Papua New Guinea, maintains close relations with its former colony. Moreover, Labor prime ministers Hawke (Australia) and Lange (New Zealand) are responsive to pressure from domestic lobbies, particularly trade unions, which support them and which have been in the forefront of anti-French actions. Neither Australia nor New Zealand has been willing to attack France commercially (except for the short-lived ban on uranium exports from Australia). Probably neither would dare do so: France is a major purchaser of Australian wool and minerals and through its influence in the EC could affect both Australian and New Zealand sales (see Aldrich 1984).*

Nor can France be too self-righteous. The platitudes mouthed by conservative politicians in New Caledonia do not go very far in calming tensions or in reassuring the other Pacific governments about French intentions. The unswerving support of the Chirac government for Lafleur and Flosse seemed only to underpin the position of local white chieftains. Bernard Pons's policy in New Caledonia—including the dismantling of the land office, which tried to increase Melanesian holdings, and of the Melanesian Cultural Institute—looked blatantly provocative. Incessant talk of FLNKS "terrorists" and continued mentions of Libyan, Cuban, or Soviet influence have similarly stirred up emotions among the opposition rather than making friends of local governments. The Greenpeace affair, which even Frenchmen now characterize as a mistake, seriously damaged France's reputation. When Chirac stopped to visit the French agents convicted of the *Rainbow Warrior* sinking—on his way to exult in the 1987 referendum victory in New Caledonia—many in the South Pacific regarded his action as insulting. It has taken a change of government in Paris to reverse these trends and improve France's reputation in the South Pacific.

France's position in the South Pacific remains relatively strong, and none of the criticisms of its policies need lead to serious challenges to that position. The most recent institutional criticisms—the Rarotonga Treaty, the UN Committee of Twenty-Four relisting of New Caledonia as a colonized territory, and the Harare·resolution of the Nonaligned Movement—from a French perspective are sterile gestures. The Rarotonga Treaty is a totally voluntary arrangement with no provision for enforcement. France can safely take no notice of the Committee of Twenty-Four action. That group is notoriously inconsistent in its listing of territories; a territory can be rostered only through the action of neighboring states, and the list of territories so listed is an exercise in irrationality.[†] France's clientelistic relations with former colonies assure it of votes in the United Nations, and its own veto on the Security Council is a final guarantee of

---

*In 1984–85 Australian exports to France totaled Aus$680 million, making France the twelfth largest purchaser of Australian goods; Australia bought Aus$637 million of French exports, making France the eleventh largest supplier of Australia (*Australian Year Book*, 1986).

†Thus, for example, New Caledonia is listed, but not the other DOM-TOM; the American Virgin Islands is, but Puerto Rico is not.

freedom of action. Neither the United States nor the United Kingdom—both of which have a nuclear force and dependent overseas territories—is liable to criticize French policy in strong terms. Britain's refusal to sign the Rarotonga Treaty indicates that London's primary concern is with its EC partners, not with the former British colonies in the South Pacific, and the inaction of the Commonwealth on the Fiji coups—particularly at the 1987 meeting of the Commonwealth Heads of Government in Vancouver—is further proof of British disengagement from the South Pacific. France has always had a privileged position in relations with the Soviet Union and China. Both Moscow and Peking are likely to increase their presence in the Pacific—as is normal for two states on the Pacific littoral—but rumors of a Communist menace in Oceania are greatly exaggerated.* The French presence in the South Pacific neither safeguards against nor encourages Soviet activities any more than in Africa or elsewhere. France is not likely to be swayed by the micro-states of the South Pacific, with a few thousand inhabitants and no economic resources; moreover, France holds the leverage of giving or withdrawing aid to the Oceanic nations.

In any case, international law recognizes French sovereignty over New Caledonia and French Polynesia, which gives France a free hand to carry out the policies it sees fit. Domestic contention in those territories could lead to continued problems, but outright independence against the wishes of Paris seems unlikely. In New Caledonia the French have the military means to prevent such a step, and the main opponents there to French policy in the future could as easily be the Caldoches—in the scenario of greater Melanesian control—as the Kanaks. Independence for French Polynesia seems just as unlikely. Even if that territory became independent, French nuclear testing need not stop: as one writer points out—and it is very important—French Polynesia has ceded the islands of Mururoa and Fangataufa to Paris, which administers them directly, so that even if French Polynesia became independent, France would retain these bases (Ordonnaud 1987).

Few countries, however, are willing to carry out their foreign and domestic policy simply by ignoring critical regional opinion. France thus faces the task of currying favor in the South Pacific. It can take advantage of dissensions and of opportunities to recruit support from the Pacific micro-states. Ordonnaud (1987: 41) notes rather straightforwardly that France can thus drive a wedge between its opponents. Certainly attempting to win friends was Flosse's brief as secretary of state for the South Pacific. He traveled widely through Oceania, talking with government

*The USSR maintains embassies only in Canberra and Wellington.

and business leaders. He arranged for Tonga's King Tupou and a West
Samoan leader to visit Mururoa. Both said they saw very little to consider
dangerous. The French courted Sir Thomas Davis, the conservative prime
minister of the Cook Islands; he was subsequently defeated at the polls,
but one of the first actions of his successor, Pupake Robati, was to visit
Paris and accept several million francs in aid. Some of the French efforts
have backfired. In the Solomon Islands, Paris offered money to Prime
Minister Peter Kenilorea for reconstruction after cyclone damage; a scandal broke when it was discovered that the money was to be funneled to
Kenilorea's own island, and it led to his resignation. In Vanuatu the
French were accused by Prime Minister Walter Lini of giving money to the
leader of the opposition, the moderate Vincent Boulekone; the French
denied the payments, but Lini expelled the French ambassador. The coups
in Fiji have provided a chance for the French to capitalize on regime
change, despite their condemnation of the actions of the coups' leader,
Brigadier Sitiveni Rabuka. French aid has been offered to and accepted by
the new government in Suva. (See the reports in *PIM* for 1987.)

France needs a more coherent and long-term strategy in the South
Pacific. Clément Meunier (1987), a French diplomat, has sketched one
program. Institutionally he recommends that France take an "evolution-
ary perspective" on its Pacific TOM, gradually putting into place statutes
which recognize the specificities and autonomy of each territory;
however, Paris should not budge in the exercise of its sovereign rights
regarding nuclear testing. In terms of cultural and financial cooperation
France should develop the new French University of the Pacific and other
research organizations and increase bilateral and multilateral aid. Politically it should open dialogues with the micro-states, Australia, and New
Zealand, as well as draw the United States and Japan into South Pacific activities. In the domain of information and communications, France should
develop possibilities for regional information-sharing, audiovisual and
telecommunications projects, and scientific research. Time will tell
whether the Rocard government formed in June 1988 will be able to ar-
ticulate and implement a comprehensive and constructive policy and
whether it will be similar to or different from the one Meunier proposes.

When all is said and done, Pacific politics will be best served by a
modus vivendi between France and its opponents. A French statement of
the *possibility* of discontinuing nuclear testing if conditions make it
feasible and a more concerted effort at promoting Melanesian interests in
New Caledonia (through appointments, job training, funds to the regions
controlled by Melanesians, and land reform) might well defuse tensions.

At the same time, an invitation to France's TOM to participate in the SPF might make France feel less of a pariah in the Pacific. Such a concerted effort would go far to aiding alliance problems: to keep outside powers at a distance from the South Pacific and make possible the economic and political cooperation that is vital for the economies of the micro-states to develop and for democracy to work in Oceania.

CONCLUSION

From an historical perspective the recent confrontation between France and its neighbors in the South Pacific is not the first episode of tension. On several occasions in the nineteenth century English and French interests clashed, notably at the time of French takeover of Tahiti and New Caledonia. Similarly hostilities emerged in the 1880s. Australian expansionists and Protestant missionaries organized public meetings in Sydney and Melbourne to protest against French activity in the New Hebrides and to demand Australian annexation of that archipelago. If the two countries did not rattle sabers, lobbyists on each side worked hard to arouse sentiment for their causes throughout the 1880s, and anti-French feeling helped develop Australian nationalism: the first intercolonial conference among the Australian colonies occurred in response to the French "menace" in the western Pacific. Several Australian businessmen were particularly outspoken on the French in the South Pacific, and military commanders warned of the danger of French colonies on Australia's doorstep. Journalists wrote about the chances of French prisoners escaping from the penitentiary in New Caledonia or exiles from the Paris Commune of 1871, confined in New Caledonia, spreading revolutionary philosophy if they escaped to Australia (Aldrich 1987).

The French-Australian hostilities of the 1880s put the opposition to the French position in the contemporary South Pacific in perspective. However, outside pressures have never led to French decolonization. In fact, it has been only the agitation of local populations sufficiently determined to gain independence which has led to French decolonization. Yet even the granting of independence has not meant, in most cases, the end of French economic, political, and even military presence in its former colonies. Moreover, the precedent for a division of territory exists. When the Comoro Islands gained independence in 1975, France retained sovereignty over Mayotte, one of the archipelago's islands which had voted against independence. Even in the unlikely event of New

Caledonia or French Polynesia becoming independent in the near future, Wallis and Futuna would probably not follow, and there is no assurance that the New Caledonian and Polynesian archipelagos would not be divided. Such an event would be unacceptable to most parties, but it indicates the range of alternatives open to France in the South Pacific.

France has been singled out as the scapegoat for criticism in the South Pacific. Critics call it a colonial power, yet the United States, the United Kingdom, Australia, New Zealand, and Indonesia all control islands in Melanesia, Micronesia, and Polynesia. France is charged with militarization of the region, yet the United States maintains military installations in Australia, and rumored Soviet missiles in Vietnam would have the South Pacific in their range. The economies of the French territories are accused of being artificial, yet most of the Oceanic micro-states rely on aid from overseas. Tuvalu is so devoid of resources that it successfully pled with donors to set up a permanent trust fund on its behalf. Critics demand independence for France's TOM, but some observers point to the higher standard of living in these territories than in neighboring islands, and others are reassessing the benefits of political independence (Antheaume and Lawrence 1985; Fairbairn 1987: 49–51; Bilney 1987: 17). Just as France has at various times been considered the bad boy of NATO or the *enfant terrible* of the EC, so it is seen as a menacing intruder in the Pacific. Current changes in the wider Pacific region—*glasnost* in the Soviet Union, the uncertain future of the Philippines, the coups in Fiji—may lead to a reassessment of France's presence.

France will not soon quit Oceania, and any change in its position in the South Pacific depends more on decisions made in Paris than actions in Nouméa or Papeete and least of all on pronouncements in Canberra, Wellington, or the capitals of the island states. Less important in the long run than the particular status of the territories under French control is a genuine and perceived willingness that Paris is ready to undertake programs of local development (in particular to recognize and act upon the legitimate grievances of the indigenous populations) and is able to cooperate with states in the region. France's presence in the South Pacific results from the era of colonialism and European expansion. Inequalities and anomalies of the colonial past certainly persist. If the French government can overcome those problems, it may be seen as having a useful and progressive role in the region.*

*Articles of interest in understanding the historical development of the French view of the Pacific are Gilles (1975 and 1977: 27–28, 30), Chaussan (1978), Dalton (1981), Gomane (1983), Baumel (1984), Servoise (1985), and Leymarie (1985: 1, 13).

REFERENCES

Aldrich, Robert. 1984. "Commercial Relations between France and Australia: An Historical Overview." In *The French-Australian Cultural Connection*, ed. Anne-Marie Nisbet and Maurice Blackman. Sydney: University of New South Wales.

―――. 1987. "L'Australie et la France dans le Pacifique: Contentieux actuels et arrière-plan historique." *Journal de la société des océanistes* 87: 93–98.

―――. 1988. "The French View of the Pacific: A Critique of Geopolitical Analysis." Sydney: University of Sydney, Research Institute for Asia and the Pacific. Occasional Paper no. 3.

―――. Forthcoming. *The French Presence in the South Pacific, 1842–1940*. London: Macmillan.

Antheaume, Benoît, and Lawrence, Roger. 1985. "A l'aide ou trop d'aide: Evolutions des économies vivrières dans le Pacifique insulaire." *Etudes rurales* 99–100: 367–87.

Baumel, Jacques. 1984. "La France et les enjeux du Pacifique." *Revue des deux mondes* 25: 48–54.

Bilney, Gordon. 1987. Speech reported in *PIM*. September. Mr. Bilney is an Australian member of parliament.

Bohin, Frédéric. 1987. "Les Déçus du 'Lafleurisme' s'organisent." *Le Monde*, 29 September.

Chaussan, Pierre. 1978. "La France dans le Pacifique." *Défense nationale*.

Chesneaux, Jean. 1985. "'Les Dernières colonies françaises': Objectifs communs et grande diversité des mouvements indépendantistes." *Le Monde diplomatique* 377.

―――. 1986. "France in the Pacific." *Peace Studies* 2.

―――. 1987. *Transpacifiques*. Paris: La Découverte.

Connell, John. 1987. *New Caledonia or Independent Kanaky?* Canberra: Australian National University.

Connell, John, and Aldrich, Robert. Forthcoming. "Remnants of Empire: France's Overseas Departments and Territories." In *France in World Politics*, ed. R. Aldrich and J. Connell. London: Routledge.

Dalton, John. 1981. "France in the South Pacific." *Dyason House Papers* 8: 2–9.

Danielsson, Bengt. 1986. *Poisoned Reign*. Harmondsworth: Penguin.

―――. 1987. "Les Essais nucléaires français dans le sud-est Pacifique." *Bwenando* 67–68 (14 January). (*Bwenando* is the journal of the FNLKS.)

Dornoy, Myriam. 1984. *Politics in New Caledonia*. Sydney: University of Sydney Press.

Fairbairn, Te'o I. J. 1987. "Pacific States and Development Options." *Islands Business*. April.

Gallois, Pierre-Marie. 1986. "Du Bon usage des confettis de l'Empire." In *Pour une nouvelle politique étrangère*, ed. François Joyaux and Patrick Wajsman, pp. 115–31. Paris: Hachette.

Gilles, René. 1975. "Pacifique-Sud 1974: Evolution interne et rôle des puissances extérieures." *Défense nationale* 31: 59–73.

———. 1977. "France in the Pacific." *Pacific Defense Reporter* 4.

Gomane, Jean-Pierre. 1983. "Les Perspectives de la France dans le Pacifique." *L'Afrique et l'Asie moderne* 138: 26–44.

———. 1985. "Perspectives de la France outre-mer." *Politique étrangère* 50: 419–35.

Guillebaud, Jean-Claude. 1976. *Les Confettis de l'empire*. Paris: Seuil.

Hayden, Bill. 1987. Speech reprinted in *PIM*, June, pp. 16–17.

Institut du Pacifique. 1987. *Le Pacifique, "nouveau centre du monde."* Paris: Berger-Levrault, 2d ed.

Knapman, Bruce. 1986. "Aid and Dependent Development of Pacific Island States." *Journal of Pacific History* 22: 139–51.

Kohler, Jean-Marie. 1987. "Les Contradictions coloniales de la démocratie néo-calédonienne." *Le Monde diplomatique*, July.

Lewin, Guy. 1984. "Le Centre d'expérimentation du Pacifique." In *Pacifique Sud et Océanie*, pp. 192–203. Paris: Institut du Pacifique. (This volume, papers from a 1984 colloquium, includes articles on a number of questions of interest, such as geostrategy, maritime links, the law of the sea, economic resources, and French policy.)

Leymarie, Philippe. 1985. "Les Enjeux stratégiques de la crise néo-calédonienne." *Le Monde diplomatique*, March.

McClancy, Jeremy. 1980. *To Kill a Bird with Two Stones*. Port-Vila: Vanuatu Cultural Centre.

Meunier, Clément. 1987. "Une Politique française pour le Pacifique.". *Politique étrangère* 52: 71–86.

Newbury, Colin. 1980. *Tahiti Nui*. Honolulu: University of Hawaii Press.

Ordonnaud, Georges. 1985. "Pacifique Sud-Ouest: Un nouveau théâtre." *Le Monde*, 22 August.

———. 1987. "La France et le Pacifique Sud. Enjeux stratégiques, diplomatiques et économiques." *Politique étrangère* 52: 35–46.

Paringaux, Roland-Pierre. 1986. "La France—mal aimée du Pacifique." *Le Monde*, 3 April.

PIM. Pacific Islands Monthly.

Poncet, Alexandre. 1976. *Histoire de l'Ile Wallis*. Paris: Société des Océanistes.

Pons, Bernard. 1987a. Remarks at a conference in Paris on "La Vocation océanique de l'Outre-mer français," 16 June.

————. 1987b. "The French Viewpoint." *PIM*, September, pp. 21–22.

Pons, Xavier. 1987. "L'Australie, le nucléaire et la présence française en Nouvelle-Calédonie." *Politique étrangère* 52: 47–60.

Rensche, Karl. 1983. "Wallis and Futuna: Total Dependency." In *Politics in Polynesia*, ed. Ahmed Ali and Ron Crocombe, pp. 4–17. Suva: University of the South Pacific.

Rollat, Alain. 1987. "Problems Come to Paradise." *PIM*, October.

Sanguinetti, Alexandre. 1986. "Nouvelle-Calédonie: Summum jus summa in-juria." Reprinted in *Bwenando* 46 (3 July 1986) and 47 (10 July 1986).

Servoise, René. 1985. "Le Pacifique, nouveau 'nouveau monde.'" *Politique étrangère*, January, pp. 101–17.

Shears, Richard, and Gidley, Isobelle. 1985. *The Rainbow Warrior Affair*. Sydney: Allen and Unwin.

Shineberg, Barry. 1986. "The Image of France: Recent Developments in French Polynesia." *Journal of Pacific History* 21: 153–68.

Spencer, Michael; Ward, Alan; and Connell, John, eds. 1988. *New Caledonia: Essays in Nationalism and Dependency*. St. Lucia: University of Queensland Press.

Thireaut, Pierre. 1986. Interview in *Islands Business*, November.

Vallin, Paul. 1987. *Les "Frances" d'outre-mer*. Paris: La Pensée Universelle.

Zeldine, Georges. 1985. *L'Hémisphère Sud*. Nouméa, n.p.

Chapter 4

SOVIET INTERESTS IN THE PACIFIC: IMPLICATIONS FOR THE ANZUS PARTNERS

Graeme Gill

At the beginning of the 1980s, the USSR was not popularly seen in the West as a major challenger in the Pacific region. Despite the American defeat in Vietnam, the growth of Soviet military force in the Soviet Far East, and the presence of Soviet allies in North Korea and Vietnam, the weight of the American alliance structure in the region (embracing Australia, New Zealand, the Philippines, South Korea, and Japan) and the strength of pro-Western sentiment in the micro-states of the South Pacific seemed to constitute a significant barrier to Soviet penetration. The effect of this pro-Westernism was buttressed by the coolness of the relationship between the USSR and the People's Republic of China and by the apparent containment of Soviet forces by the Japanese archipelago. But this appearance of the Pacific as a "Western lake" seemed significantly shakier by the late 1980s, when the USSR was being seen as a real challenger to the maintenance of Western hegemony in the region. This was in part due to the erosion of the Pax Americana—a development evident for some time in many parts of the world, but coming much later to the Pacific region. Its local manifestations included the disruption to the ANZUS Pact caused by New Zealand's policy of barring nuclear weapons and nuclear-powered ships from its ports, increased Filipino questioning of the value of an extension of U.S. base rights in the Philippines, and the growth of more radical and anti-Western sentiments in some of the micro-states of the region. It is clear that in some instances the USSR has taken direct advantage of these sorts of developments to expand its role and influence in the region, but also important in explaining the Soviet challenge has been the new thinking in foreign affairs that has accompanied the rise of Mikhail Gorbachev to leadership in the Soviet Union.

During the long period of rule of Leonid Brezhnev, the Soviet approach to foreign affairs was dominated by an overwhelming concentration upon East-West relations, and particularly upon the relationship with the United States. In large part, Soviet relations with other states were pushed into the background behind this primary focus, and were seen in significant measure as dependent upon the Soviet-American axis. Soviet foreign relations were stolid and inflexible, conducted more with an eye to their effects on the larger relationship with Washington than to their implications for bilateral relations between the USSR and the particular state or region directly concerned. The main arenas of superpower rivalry were those of immediate significance to the USSR (principally Europe) or those areas where American hegemony did not extend (mainly Africa and Asia). Areas like the South Pacific which appeared to be firmly in the American pocket, and which, because of geography, would have imposed major strains on Soviet resources were Moscow to attempt to establish a profile in them, did not become major scenes of East-West tension.

During this period the dominant thrust of Soviet foreign policy was military in nature. In response to setbacks the USSR had experienced in the early 1960s—in particular, the Cuban Missile Crisis—Soviet policymakers embarked on a major expansion of Soviet military capacity. But this approach tended to blinker the policymakers, encouraging them to see international relations primarily in military terms. The principal emphasis of Soviet policy during the 1970s was to achieve arms limitation agreements with the United States, primarily to prevent the Americans from attaining an unbridgeable military superiority over the USSR. In its relations with the rest of the world too, the USSR saw the military aspect as paramount. The spread of Soviet influence was seen to be furthered through support for "progressive movements" in their struggle against pro-Western forces, particularly in Africa, and even Soviet trade with and aid to the Third World was strongly oriented around military hardware. This combination of a focus on the relationship with the United States and the primacy of the military element made Soviet foreign policy particularly inflexible. Soviet decision-makers were not sensitive to the demands and perspectives of other states, and by viewing them through the prism of the American relationship, they were unable to respond appropriately to changed conditions in those countries.

The inflexibility of Soviet foreign policy was recognized by Gorbachev and his supporters, and upon coming to power they acted to rectify the problem. Organizationally this was reflected in the replacement of Andrei Gromyko as foreign minister by Eduard Shevardnadze, the purge and reorganization of the Foreign Ministry in Moscow, the transfer of significant responsibility for foreign affairs formulation from the Foreign Ministry to the International Department of the Central Committee Secretariat, and the replacement of veteran Comintern official Boris Ponomarev as head of this department by Anatolii Dobrynin, former ambassador to the United States. These changes brought into significant policy-formulating roles many people who had not been on the top rung of the foreign policy establishment under Brezhnev—people who were able to question the orthodoxies of the past, draw on the range of debates occurring within the foreign policy community, and implement policies which diverged from those carried out under Brezhnev (see Hough 1986; Breslauer 1987: 429–48).

But the response has not been only organizational: the principal emphases of Soviet foreign policy have also been changed.* There has been a greater willingness to break Western alliance structures down into their component parts and to attempt to deal with those components on a more realistic bilateral basis. Individual states have been approached on their own terms rather than as components of a larger Western bloc, with greater attention to bilateral interests and concerns rather than global strategic perspectives. This shifting of priorities has been very important for Soviet bilateral relationships.

An equally important change has been the downgrading of military power as a diplomatic weapon and its supersession by economic and cultural diplomacy. Parallel with the attempt by the Gorbachev leadership to reduce military expenditures, reflected most graphically in its search for an arms reduction agreement with the United States, Moscow has sought to reduce the military element in its bilateral relations with other countries. Without rejecting the assumption that the United States in particular and the West in general remain hostile to the USSR, the Gorbachev leadership has accepted the proposition that war is not inevitable and that security has important nonmilitary aspects. This is seen principally in terms of economic interdependence: if economic ties are strengthened, peace and security can be consolidated between states with widely different social and economic systems. Economic cooperation and interdependence with the capitalist world are seen as the path to lasting

---

*This is most evident in Soviet practice, but it is also reflected in many of Gorbachev's speeches. In particular, see his address to the XXVIIth Congress of the Communist Party in February 1986 and his speech at Vladivostok in July 1986 (*Pravda*, 26 February 1986; 29 July 1986).

peace and security, while any security based purely on military factors will be transitory. Such an emphasis constitutes the basis for a flexible foreign policy which is likely to be much more effective than that followed throughout most of the 1970s.

The new approach to foreign policy has also been reflected in the increased attention devoted in recent years to the Pacific region. How this has been manifested will be discussed below, but first we must consider what interests the Soviet Union has to pursue in the region.

SOVIET INTERESTS IN THE PACIFIC

Soviet aims in the Pacific are part of the overall thrust of Soviet policy, both domestic and international. Since Gorbachev came to power, the link between domestic and foreign policy has become more direct than in the past. The new General Secretary's chief priority has been economic reform. One way of increasing the resources that can be devoted to such reform is by reducing defense expenditures, but this can only be achieved if the USSR sees itself in a strategic environment which is stable and not threatening. The attempt to move toward such an environment is behind recent arms reduction initiatives and efforts to improve relations with the United States. In regional terms, a reduction in tensions with China and Japan and stabilization of the Pacific security environment would facilitate cuts in the Soviet defense forces in the Far East, thereby freeing up funds which could be directed into regional economic development.

But even if tensions in the Pacific and Far East were to be substantially reduced, Soviet relations with the United States would remain tinged with an element of distrust. Under these circumstances, attempts to build up friendships and closer relations with the states of the region must be seen as an attempt to expand Soviet influence and weaken U.S. hegemony in the Pacific.* Ideally, in the Soviet view, this would mean rupturing the relationships the United States currently has with the states

---

*A clear example of this can be seen in the South Pacific Nuclear Free Zone Treaty. The USSR wanted this treaty to deny even the right of passage of nuclear-powered warships because this would disrupt the passage of U.S. vessels while having no effect on their own ships. (No Soviet surface warships are deployed in this region.) However this position, held at the time of the treaty signing, was changed prior to ratification. There was little regional support for it (except for Vanuatu), reflecting the continued strength of pro-American sentiment (Dibb 1985: 71).

of the region, weaning the Japanese away from their close alliance with the Americans, and the substitution of pro-Soviet sentiment for the existing Western orientation in the micro-states of the South Pacific. Moscow is not so sanguine as to believe that U.S. influence could be expelled from the Pacific altogether, but if it could be balanced by Soviet influence—perhaps reflected in an expansion of Soviet diplomatic, commercial, and cultural ties with the states of the region—then in the continuing superpower rivalry this region would not be quite so hostile to the USSR. In concrete terms, the Soviet objective is to ensure that in a global conflict this region would not be an unchallenged springboard for attacks on the USSR.

Defense considerations are also important in a more direct sense. Regardless of the content of international agreements, the Soviet Union, like the United States, will continue to plan for a worst-case scenario. Soviet decision-makers must plan what they would do in the event of a conflict with the United States. In such a situation, the Pacific would be a major arena of conflict, and the Soviets must therefore take steps to ensure that they are not unfamiliar with it. If the Soviet Union could gain access to docking or port facilities in the micro-states of the South Pacific, its flexibility in the event of tensions would be greatly increased. The systematic mapping of the Pacific floor that can proceed as a result of the transit of Soviet vessels through the area could have significant military implications, particularly in facilitating the operations of missile-carrying submarines. The western Pacific has direct military significance because it is through this area that the only all-weather sea route from European Russia to the Far East passes. Given the vulnerability of the trans-Siberian rail link, even with the duplication provided by the Baikal-Amur main line, it is imperative that the sea route be made as secure as possible for the transit of Soviet ships. It is also through this area that the supply of Soviet forces based in Vietnam must proceed.

The Pacific region is also important to the USSR in a direct economic sense. Not only economic reform but short-medium term improved economic performance depends in part upon international factors. The Soviet authorities are seeking foreign investment in their economy, and while the major potential sources of this are Europe and North America, the Pacific region—chiefly Japan—is of some potential import. Trade is also important for Soviet economic welfare, and the Pacific is a region in which the USSR generally has a trade deficit. It would like to expand its exports to the region and thereby reverse the drain on the economy such a negative trade balance has. Indeed the

Soviet leadership would like to hook the Soviet economy into the vigorous and dynamic economies of the region and benefit from the domestic stimulus that would provide.

Despite the trade imbalance, the Pacific region makes an important contribution to the Soviet economy. Significant in this regard is the hard currency which is earned as a result of the activities of Soviet cruise ships in the Pacific and, more importantly, through the operations of the Far East Shipping Company (FESCO). FESCO is a cargo carrier throughout the Pacific, serving both Australia and New Zealand, which has achieved the position of being the single largest carrier between Japan and the west coast of the United States (Dibb 1985: 73). The Pacific is also a major source of supply for the Soviet domestic fish market, which has more than doubled in the last two decades (*ibid.*); some two-thirds of Soviet domestic needs comes from the South Pacific region.

In sum, the attempt to expand Soviet influence and raise its profile throughout the Pacific region is aimed at improving the Soviet strategic environment and at gaining the economic benefits Moscow believes will flow from greater involvement in the economic activities of the Pacific. These general aims are sought in both the northwest Pacific and in the South Pacific, although it has been in the latter that most scope has existed for a higher Soviet profile. But the attempt to expand Soviet influence is a recent development. Why has the pursuit of Soviet advantage been so retarded?

OBSTACLES TO AN EXPANSION OF SOVIET INFLUENCE

The Soviet government has never been unaware of the potential importance of the Pacific region, but for most of the life of the Soviet regime its interest has been manifested in specific foreign policy concerns—most particularly support for its Communist allies in China, North Korea, and Vietnam. The broader Pacific region seemed out of reach. There were five main reasons for this perception.

The first reason is the Eurocentric view characteristic of the Soviet leadership. The top priority in foreign policy has always been Europe. Geographically and culturally closer to Moscow, it was also the region from which the most direct threats to the Soviet Union were perceived to stem. Even after World War II, when the United States was seen as the principal opponent, the main thrust of its challenge was believed to come through Europe. Such a perception left little room for a major focus on Pacific affairs.

Second, for most of this century the Pacific has appeared to be a Western and, especially since World War II, an American lake. The islands were either colonial dependencies of the Western powers or closely allied to them, while the overlay of culture that was superimposed upon the indigenous cultures was strongly Christian and Western in orientation. Consequently there seemed to be little room for Soviet influence.

A third reason has been the weakness of the Soviet position on the Pacific littoral. The development of the Soviet Far East had always been sluggish. The population was never large, and the industrial base was limited, fuelled principally by the military imperatives of having Vladivostok as the main focus of Soviet forces in the region. Separated from the main centers of the Soviet Union by vast distances, difficult terrain, and, for much of the time, indifferent transport and communications systems, the area remained something of a backwater. Despite the stimulus to the local economy provided by the buildup of military forces in the region in recent times, the Far East remained a weak basis from which to project Soviet power into the Pacific.

Fourth, any attempt to project Soviet power into the Pacific had to overcome the blocking effect of two hostile gatekeepers. Throughout most of this century, including most of the postwar period, China and Japan have performed symbolic gatekeeper roles. Their political opposition combined with their geographical positions have seemed to cut the USSR off from the Pacific at large, both physically and symbolically; they have loomed as barriers keeping the Soviet bear in his northwest Pacific den. In particular, Japan has been a physical obstruction in that Soviet vessels must work their way through narrow straits under the gaze of potential opposition to reach the open ocean. As symbolic barriers locking the Soviet Union away in its Pacific backwater, they have prevented the development of a sense of Soviet strategic overhang in the Pacific. In concrete terms this has meant that the USSR has not been widely perceived by the states of the region as a legitimate political actor in Pacific affairs.

The fifth factor which prevented the projection of Soviet power into the Pacific region was the USSR's naval weakness. The navy had always been a junior partner in the Soviet military establishment, and it was not until the Soviet backdown in the Cuban Missile Crisis that naval development was given a high priority. As a result, the vast military growth which characterized the Brezhnev period included a significant expansion of naval forces. This has been reflected in a heightened naval presence in the Far East, where the Soviet Pacific fleet, the largest in the Soviet navy, is based. By the middle of the 1980s, Soviet military deployments in the Far East were estimated to include 53 divisions of troops, 785 aircraft, 250 helicopters, 160 mobile SS-20 IRBMs, and a Pacific fleet numbering 88 submarines and some 300 surface ships (IISS 1985: 16, 29). A major submarine base is located at Petropavlovsk on the Kamchatka peninsula, and a number of backfire bombers have been deployed in the region. In addition, existing deployments have been reinforced on the Northern Territories, which are claimed by Japan. The size and power of the Soviet military in the Pacific region is significant, and even though the operation of the navy may be hindered by the need to pass through the potential choke points around the Japanese archipelago, and doubts exist about military efficiency following the KAL 007 affair (see Johnson 1986), the Soviet military now constitutes a powerful means of projecting Soviet power throughout the Pacific.

But if the naval expansion provided the Soviet Union with a means it did not earlier possess to project its power into the Pacific, and the erosion of the Pax Americana seemed to provide the opportunity for increased influence, neither of these overcame those aspects of geopolitics which seemed to limit the USSR to being a marginal actor in Pacific affairs: its weak domestic base and the hostile gatekeepers. That the Soviet leadership recognizes this is evident from Gorbachev's seminal speech in Vladivostok on 28 July 1986 (*Pravda*, 29 July 1986).*

THE VLADIVOSTOK INITIATIVE

In his address Gorbachev argued that the Soviet Far East should become a "highly developed economic complex." Believing that a strong economic infrastructure already existed in the region, he called for the intensive development of the regional economy so that it could become a self-sufficient component of the Soviet economy. He criticized the recent failures in economic development of the region, blaming them principally on deficiencies in central decision-making and in local implementation, and called for a comprehensive program of long-term Far Eastern development. This was to include the expansion of the fishing industry, self-sufficiency in manufacturing and energy, and the growth of export trade. There was to be a massive expansion of the Soviet presence on the Pacific littoral, and the Soviet Far East was to become a dynamic economic center for the north Pacific region (*Pravda*, 26 August

*See also Gorbachev's comments in his book *Perestroika i novoe myshlenie dlia nashei strany i dlia vsego mira* (Moscow, 1987): 187–91 and his September 1988 speech in Krasnoyarsk (*Pravda*, 18 September 1988).

1987). It would expand from being basically a military complex into a regional economic leader, thereby changing not only the magnitude of the Soviet presence in the region, but its nature as well. The development of the Far East would involve an expansion of linkages with neighboring states and their direct involvement in that process of development. The law on joint enterprises adopted in January 1987 (*Pravda*, 27 January 1987), which provided the mechanism for major foreign investment in enterprises in the USSR, potentially was a means of tying the Far East into the broader regional economy.

Gorbachev then turned his attention to the two gatekeepers. He noted the improved nature of the USSR's relationship with China and expressed a willingness to engage in discussions with the Chinese on "additional measures for creating an atmosphere of good-neighborliness." Acknowledging their common desire to accelerate social and economic development, he called for cooperation in the implementation of their development plans, as well as in space, education, and cultural fields. Although he did not mention China's "three obstacles" to improved relations directly, Gorbachev did address them in the speech. He implied a refusal to bring pressure to bear on the Vietnamese to force them to withdraw from Kampuchea by referring to the undesirability of trying to impose a solution, thereby suggesting no change in the Soviet position on that issue. However, his comments on the other two "obstacles"—Soviet troops in Afghanistan and on the Chinese border— did reflect a degree of Soviet flexibility which had not been evident before. The announced withdrawal of six regiments from Afghanistan and the mention of a timetable for the complete withdrawal of all troops did not meet the Chinese demand for an end to Soviet involvement, but it reflected a desire to disengage and was clearly meant to be seen as a concession to the Chinese position. His call for discussions with China aimed at proportionate reductions of land forces was clearly directed at Chinese concerns about Soviet troop concentration on the Chinese border, but more important was the declaration that a "substantial part" of the Soviet troops in Mongolia would be withdrawn. The border situation was further stabilized by the declaration that the USSR was willing to accept the main ship channel in the Amur as the boundary with China rather than the Chinese bank, as Soviet spokesmen had hitherto claimed.* Islands over which the two countries had fought in the recent past would now be recognized as Chinese territory—a clear concession to the Chinese.

*This also applied to the Ussuri River, as Vice-Foreign Minister Kapitsa acknowledged (Klintworth 1987).

Turning to Japan, Gorbachev spoke critically of what he called the "militarized triangle" of Washington-Tokyo-Seoul, and of the ways in which Japan's "non-nuclear principles" and the peace provisions of its constitution were increasingly being openly circumvented. However, despite this, Soviet relations with Japan had been improving, and what was needed was increased cooperation "on a sound realistic basis, in a calm atmosphere free from problems of the past." Gorbachev particularly emphasized economic cooperation, referring to existing commercial links between the Soviet Far East and Japanese firms and calling for the establishment of joint enterprises and cooperation in the investigation of marine resources and the study of outer space.

Gorbachev's speech was an attempt to improve relations with China and Japan and thereby overcome the effect of these hostile gatekeepers in restricting the Soviet Union to the role of marginal actor in Pacific affairs. But his speech was also an attempt to project the USSR as a legitimate regional actor. Openly declaring that the USSR was an Asian and Pacific power, he suggested a broad program for the achievement of peace and stability in the region which was clearly designed to project the USSR as a responsible participant in the affairs of the Pacific. He acknowledged that the United States was a power with legitimate economic and political interests in the Pacific and that problems of security in the region could not be resolved without U.S. cooperation. With regard to the other states of the region, Gorbachev declared that relations with the socialist states would be strengthened and invigorated, while the Soviet Union was "prepared to expand ties" with Indonesia, Australia, New Zealand, the Philippines, Thailand, Malaysia, Singapore, Burma, Sri Lanka, Nepal, Brunei, the Republic of the Maldives, and the micro-states of the Pacific.*

Gorbachev's Vladivostok speech was an important statement of the Soviet perspective on Pacific affairs. It represented formal Soviet acknowledgment of the importance of this region and reflected its higher profile in the Soviet Union's overall foreign policy outlook.† Rather than being simply an aspect of the broader East-West balance, as it had been before, the region was now seen as having an integrity of its own and therefore as needing a much more complex and sophisticated foreign

---

*India was discussed elsewhere in the speech, and Papua New Guinea was included among the micro-states. Pakistan, Taiwan, and South Korea were ignored.

†When the Soviet Foreign Ministry was reorganized, a Department of Pacific Ocean Countries was established for the first time.

policy approach than in the past. But the speech was more than a formal acknowledgment of this fact: it was part of that new foreign policy. It alerted the states of the region to the Soviet intention of playing a much more active role in the Pacific, and it made suggestions and concessions designed both to structure the agenda of international debate and discussion in the region and to advance Soviet objectives within that debate. As such it was a major component of the drive for an enhanced Soviet profile in the Pacific.

A HIGHER SOVIET PROFILE?

Only limited success has been achieved in the strengthening of the economic base of the Soviet Far East since the Vladivostok speech. Soviet economic growth rates have not improved to the extent desired, and levels of foreign investment in the Far East have been disappointing. There is no indication thus far that the economy of the Far East is going to become the dynamic economic center of this part of the world hoped for by Gorbachev. The problems of weak infrastructure, poor investment, inefficiency, and low worker morale which afflict many sectors of the Soviet economy continue to plague the economy of the Far East, but here their effects are exacerbated by the problem of distance from the major centers of the Soviet economy.

There has been some improvement in relations with China. Since 1980 there has been a gradual increase in bilateral contacts, mostly at the nonpolitical level; cultural, sporting, educational, and commercial relations have grown in a process which appears to have been seen by both sides as creating an infrastructure upon which solid political advances could be made. Since October 1982, normalization talks have been held twice a year, and in February 1987 border talks were resumed. Visits to Beijing have been made by First Deputy Premier Arkhipov in December 1984 and Politburo candidate member Talyzin in September 1986, and during the course of these contacts, agreements have been reached on a wide range of issues, including Soviet help with industrial development, increasing trade, expanding consular facilities, and improving border contacts. There has also been talk of a summit between Gorbachev and Chinese leader Deng Xiaoping.

The improvement in relations between the two countries is clear from the increased contacts, network of agreements, and drop in the levels of mutual abuse, but the Chinese would argue that "normalization" has not taken place and cannot take place until the USSR has acted to overcome the "three obstacles." However, it is clear that substantial improvement in relations has taken place without any Soviet movement on these issues. Indeed, except for relations at the party level which still remain awkward, it is difficult to see how relations could be made any more normal. In terms of the usual relations between states, those between the USSR and China fit the norm. This means that the three obstacles are not real obstacles, but diplomatic mechanisms used by the Chinese leadership to keep some distance between themselves and Moscow. When they want to accentuate Chinese independence from the USSR, the obstacles will be highlighted; when they want to emphasize friendship, the obstacles will be downgraded. If the Soviet leaders were to overcome the three current obstacles, the political line being followed by the Chinese would ensure that other obstacles appeared in order to maintain that sense of distance which Beijing seems to desire.

Thus, while the relationship between the USSR and China has greatly improved during the 1980s, it does not approach the closeness of the 1950s. That is not surprising because the relationship of the 1950s was at odds with the traditions of Chinese history, the sensibilities of Chinese nationalism, and the demands of Chinese *realpolitik.*

Despite concerns in Moscow about increased Japanese military spending and support for President Reagan's Strategic Defense Initiative, Soviet relations with Japan have also improved. The visit of Soviet Foreign Minister Shevardnadze to Tokyo in January 1986, and the return visit by Japanese Foreign Minister Abe five months later, signalled increased Soviet attention to its neighbor after a prolonged period in which Japanese relations were given a low priority in Soviet foreign policy. Increased efforts have been made to attract Japanese investment in Siberian development, with limited success; a Japanese company was one of the first foreign firms to enter the Soviet Union under the provisions of the joint enterprises legislation introduced in 1987.* At times, Soviet spokesmen have implied the possibility of some movement in the Soviet position on the disputed Northern Territories—the four islands of the Kurile chain taken over by the USSR at the end of World War II. However, so far Soviet determination to keep the islands remains firm. Without Soviet concessions on this issue, and while Soviet force levels remain high in the region, there is not likely to be significant impetus for an improvement in relations coming from the Japanese side.

*This is the Tairiku Trading Co. Ltd., which has reached agreement with the Irkutsk timber industry on the production of timber for export to Japan (see Gurevich 1987).

Although the Chinese and Japanese gatekeepers have not been neutralized, there is a channel for Soviet influence in the Pacific through Vietnam. Despite Soviet denials that they have a base at Camranh Bay (see, e.g., Samoteikin 1987: 12), Soviet forces clearly enjoy extensive use of the naval facilities at both Camranh Bay and Da Nang. These facilities enable at least part of the Soviet navy to escape the constrictions imposed by frozen seas and Japanese choke points. They also provide the USSR with a basis from which to project Soviet power into the South Pacific and Indian Ocean regions, and to mount intelligence-gathering operations. A treaty with a mutual defense clause remains in force between the USSR and Vietnam, and significant quantities of Soviet aid (both military and civil) are channelled into Vietnam. It was doubled in the current Vietnamese five-year plan to some US$2 billion annually (USIS 1988: 3; Rosenberger 1983: 210–13). The effect of this has been to solidify the links between the USSR and Vietnam.

Perhaps the most significant evidence of the higher Soviet profile in the region, at least as publicly perceived in the ANZUS states, has been the negotiation of Soviet fishing agreements with Kiribati and Vanuatu. From at least the early 1970s, the USSR had sought to establish a presence in the South Pacific, chiefly through offers of aid and assistance to the island states. Some attempts had also been made to establish fisheries agreements with some of the island states, but to no avail. However, in the light of the breakdown of the agreement between Kiribati and the American Tuna Boat Association at the end of 1984 and charges of illegal American fishing in the exclusive economic zones (EEZs) of some of the micro-states, the Kiribati government reached an agreement with the USSR. This gave Soviet tuna fleets fishing rights in Kiribati's EEZ for twelve months on payment of a license fee, but no access was given to its territorial seas (within 12 miles of the coast) or its ports (Doulman 1986). When the agreement expired, it was not renewed, and the Kiribati government refused to accede to the Soviet demand for a reduction of $300,000 in license fees, made on the grounds that fishing yields were below expectations. However, in January 1987, an agreement was reached between the USSR and Vanuatu providing for access by Soviet ships to Vanuatu's EEZ and its ports, although they would have no right to fish in its territorial seas. This agreement also ended after one year, with the Soviet side again complaining that the terms were not economically viable (*The Australian*, 21–22 May 1988). Approaches have also been made by the USSR to Fiji, Tonga, and Papua New Guinea (IISS 1987b: 179). Although Soviet fishing fleets had been operating in the Pacific before the Kiribati and Vanuatu agreements, these agreements seemed to represent a consolidation of the Soviet presence in a way that it had not been before.

At the formal diplomatic level, Soviet relations exist with all of the states on the Pacific west rim with the exception of South Korea and Taiwan. There is no permanent Soviet diplomatic presence in the micro-states of the South Pacific (at least partly because of resistance by some of the micro-states), but there are nonresidential relations with Fiji, Tonga, Vanuatu, Kiribati, Nauru, Tuvalu, Western Samoa, and Papua New Guinea. The Soviet embassies in Canberra and Wellington combine to service the South Pacific area. On top of this established network of relationships, the USSR has sought to play a larger, much more active diplomatic role in the Pacific region during the 1980s, and particularly after the Vladivostok speech.

A heightened Soviet profile has been evident in recent diplomatic activities. The USSR signed and later ratified the Treaty of Rarotonga, which established the South Pacific nuclear-free zone,* in December 1986, it gained observer status at the Pacific Economic Cooperation Conference at Vancouver, and has since requested "dialogue partner" status with ASEAN. Soviet diplomats in many of the countries of the region seem to have been more outgoing and publicly approachable than in the past.[†] Anatoly Zaitsev, chief of the Southeast Asia section of the Foreign Ministry, visited the region in September 1986, while Foreign Minister Shevardnadze visited Australia, Indonesia, Thailand, Laos, Kampuchea, and Vietnam in early 1987. These visits were very important in highlighting the new Soviet emphasis on the region; Shevardnadze was the first Soviet foreign minister to visit Australia and Thailand and the most senior Soviet official in Indonesia since 1964.

It is clear that by the late 1980s the Soviet profile in the Pacific region had been considerably raised above its level at the beginning of the decade. Gorbachev's Vladivostok speech suggests that if he has his

---

*This was trumpeted as evidence of the Soviet desire to transform the Asia-Pacific region into a zone of peace and friendship, and was contrasted with the U.S. reaction to the New Zealand policy of barring nuclear ships from its ports: while the USSR sought to bolster peace and friendship by signing the treaty, the United States not only refused to sign the treaty, but also sought to punish an ally which refused entry to nuclear weapons and nuclear-powered ships.

†This is reflected most clearly in the greater willingness to talk openly to the press of their host states. See, for example, the extensive interview with Soviet Ambassador to Australia Samoteikin in *The Age* (Melbourne), 28 January 1987.

way, the Soviet presence will become even stronger in the future. What implications does this have for the ANZUS partners?

The type of response that will be forthcoming to an increased Soviet presence will depend upon the way in which the ANZUS partners interpret Soviet actions and motives. "New thinking" is required on the part of Western policymakers to match that so evident in Gorbachev's USSR. In times past, the West's relationship with the USSR has been seen in zero-sum terms: what benefitted one side was disadvantageous to the other. This was accompanied by a significant measure of hypocrisy. It was wrong for the USSR to send arms to the Nicaraguan government, to support one side of the civil war in Angola, to invade Afghanistan, and to send ships into the Pacific Ocean, but it was legitimate for the United States to arm an anti-Soviet Pakistan and Afghan mujahadeen fighting Soviet troops, to support the opposite side in the Angolan civil war, to invade Grenada, and to station ships in the Indian Ocean. This sort of attitude springs from the strongly moralistic tone in which American foreign policy has usually been couched—a tone which has consistently portrayed the United States as defending the "free world" from the ravenous clutches of an expansionist Communism centered in the Soviet Union. Such a perspective, which for most of the postwar period has had its mirror-image counterpart in the Soviet Union, has been a major factor in fuelling the arms race and, more importantly, in hindering a clear perception about Soviet foreign policy goals and reacting realistically to them. As long as international relations are seen as a zero-sum game, with results measured in terms of gains or losses of influence and advantage, the likelihood of long-term stability is small. What is needed is an approach which is not characterized by the stereotypes of the past, but which acknowledges Soviet interests and aims and reacts to developments on the basis of a realistic evaluation of Soviet actions.

The starting point of such an approach must be recognition of legitimate Soviet interests in the Pacific region. Geographical factors alone establish them in the northwest Pacific. Soviet domestic development aims envisage a significant growth of the Soviet Far East, and this means that what happens in the waters that lap the Soviet coast is of immediate concern. The South Pacific is not geographically contiguous to the USSR, but it remains an area of legitimate concern because, as noted, the only all-weather sea route between the eastern and western parts of the Soviet Union runs through it. Commercial considerations, in the form of cartage, fishing, and cruise ships, are also important, and while military competition exists between East and West, the Soviet Union will continue to seek to offset any advantage which the West is perceived to enjoy in the region.

Some could seek to deny the legitimacy of the Soviet presence in the South Pacific by referring to the existence of American and Soviet spheres of influence, recognized by both superpowers, into which the rival superpower should not enter. Such a conception has its roots in the postwar settlement in Europe, and has been widely accepted at both the official and popular levels. However, any superpower consensus on this question seemed to be evaporating by the beginning of the 1980s. The Soviet invasion of Afghanistan and the American reaction to it clearly reflected differing conceptions of where the boundaries of such a Soviet sphere lay: in Moscow's view, Afghanistan was within its sphere, but this attitude was not shared by Washington. More importantly, much of the early rhetoric of the Reagan administration implied a lack of recognition of a Soviet sphere in Eastern Europe, which not only cast doubt on the terms of the postwar settlement but also undercut the notion of discrete spheres of influence.* Soviet assistance to the government in Nicaragua also seems to undercut such a concept. With both superpowers at least questioning the notion of discrete spheres of influence, arguments against Soviet involvement in the Pacific based upon the view that it is an American sphere are considerably weakened.

Of course accepting the legitimacy of Soviet interests in the Pacific region is not the same as accepting all forms of Soviet action or all ways in which those interests are pursued. The main thrust of the response of the ANZUS partners should be based upon a recognition of legitimate Soviet interests and of the need to channel them into forms which are both applicable to and valuable for the region as a whole. What this demands is flexibility in ANZUS policy and the pitching of responses to the different aspects of the changing situation.

Fundamental for developments in the Pacific are Gorbachev's plans for the Soviet Far East. In his Vladivostok speech he outlined plans for the intensive development of this region in the industrial, raw materials, and agricultural spheres. However, given the priorities he has placed on his plans for overall economic development (in particular, his emphases

---

*This was particularly clear in many official statements at the time of the Polish unrest in the early 1980s. For a more recent argument which undercuts recognition of Eastern Europe as a Soviet sphere, see Pipes (1984: 259–73).

upon renewal of existing stock rather than the construction of new plant, upon the machine-building sector in the European part of the Soviet Union, and upon the energy complex in eastern Siberia), it is unlikely that there will be significant extra resources coming from within the Soviet economy to foster Far Eastern development. Consequently, if the plans for development are to succeed the Far East must hook into the dynamic economy of the region as a whole. The most obvious way to achieve this is through Japanese involvement in Siberian development.

In his address at Vladivostok, Gorbachev specifically recommended joint ventures with Japan. The USSR has been attempting to attract Japanese capital into Siberian energy development for some time, but the likelihood of a major increase in Japanese involvement is small—on commercial grounds. Investment in Siberia has become less attractive to Japanese investors over time because of the decline in oil prices and the restructuring of the Japanese economy away from imported natural resource-based industries (Berton 1986: 1282). Furthermore, the conditions under which joint ventures can be established have been sufficiently restrictive to deter many potential investors.* Under these conditions, a substantial inflow of Japanese capital into Siberia is unlikely, even if the issue of the Northern Territories is resolved in the near future.

China is unlikely to be a major source of capital because of the level of its economic development and its own programs of economic reform; South Korea is also unlikely because of the mutual hostility between it and the USSR. In principle, the ANZUS partners could be a source of such investment, although in practice the shortage of investment capital in Australia and New Zealand would impose a significant limitation. Moreover, the same type of commercial considerations which are likely to discourage the Japanese will discourage potential investors from these states. However, if it is true that the interweaving of economic relations provides a useful basis for building peace and stability, it is in the interest of the ANZUS partners to encourage the proliferation of such links with the Soviet Far East. But given the limited capacities they have to control the overseas activities of their own companies, and the objections

*These include a maximum non-Soviet equity share of 49 percent, with profits shared in proportion to each partner's contributions, a two-year tax holiday, a tax of 30 percent on profits, and an additional tax of 20 percent on repatriated profits. Also, the chairman and director must both be Soviet citizens, and financial arrangements must be conducted through Soviet institutions or according to Soviet procedures.

to any policy which looks like subsidizing the USSR, their role in fostering such links will probably have to be restricted to the negative one of not placing barriers in the way of businessmen who seek to develop them, and the positive one of encouraging commercial interests to investigate the possibilities.

Expansion of the Soviet presence in the Pacific generally will depend not only on the development of the Soviet Far East, but also on overcoming the effects of the hostile gatekeepers blocking Soviet access to the region. The military aspect of this blockade is important not only because of U.S. involvement, but also because any outbreak of conflict in this heavily militarized region would be likely to have direct implications for the Pacific as a whole. The arms race that has occurred there in the last decade, both in terms of the USSR versus the United States/Japan and North versus South Korea, is dangerous because there is nothing in the region similar to the network of understandings, regulations, treaties, and agreements which structures the armed relationship in Europe. Superpower arms control has not yet come to the Pacific region, and it is clear that the different sides recognize the dangers in such a situation. What is needed is a regionally based effort to both reduce armament levels and introduce confidence-building measures, but this can only occur if the various parties recognize the legitimacy of the others' presence in the region. "New thinking" on all sides is required.

Turning again to the gatekeeper relationship with Japan, in the absence of Soviet movement on the Northern Territories issue and the improbability of substantial Japanese investment in the USSR, it is unlikely that the Japanese attitude will shift in favor of closer relations with the Soviet Union. Japan will therefore remain, at least symbolically, an immovable barrier to the extension of Soviet influence directly into the Pacific. This will be particularly true while Japan remains close to the United States, but even if there were to be some estrangement between these two states, Japanese wariness of the USSR would make a significant warming of their relationship unlikely.

Nor is the other major gatekeeper—China—likely to leave the way clear for an expansion of Soviet influence in the Pacific. Despite the signs of increased friendship, a return to the relationship of the 1950s will not occur, so that the prospect of a united Communist monolith in the Pacific region is fanciful. Both states will pursue their own interests, and in doing so they will agree on some issues and differ on others. It is in the interests of all the regional countries that the relationship between these two states should become soundly based enough to weather the bad times without either side having to resort to arms or the relationship descend into hostility. The ANZUS partners should thus welcome the *rapprochement* and should not attempt to play one off against the other as was done in the 1970s. Such a tactic not only would be likely to fail, but also could embitter relations among all the parties involved.

In practical terms, the blockading effect of the gatekeepers is in part undermined by the strategic reach enjoyed by the USSR through its relationship with Vietnam. As long as the Vietnamese economy remains heavily dependent upon Soviet aid, Hanoi will continue to be closely aligned with Moscow. Such dependence is unlikely to end in the short term: the invasion of Kampuchea is a continuing drain on the Vietnamese economy, and recently introduced economic reforms are unlikely to bring about significant improvement quickly. One way the ANZUS partners could try to lessen Hanoi's dependence is through increased aid and trade with Vietnam. The United States is clearly in the best position to do this, but it would require a reversal of American policy of the past ten years. However, this is made especially difficult by the continuing emotional impact on the American psyche of the Vietnam War, reflected most graphically in the continuing issue of the MIAs (American soldiers missing-in-action). Such a policy would also require greater Vietnamese flexibility on the Kampuchean issue; expanded Western aid to Vietnam while its forces remained in Kampuchea would not be greeted very favorably by the ASEAN states. Perhaps the best the ANZUS partners can do is continue to press for a Vietnamese withdrawal from Kampuchea using the promise of increased aid and trade as a carrot.

Also important in this situation is the Soviet military presence in Vietnam. Much has been made in the West about the expanded reach and increased flexibility provided to the Soviets by their access to Vietnamese ports (see, e.g., *The Australian*, 10 & 27 February 1987). Clearly these facilities do provide increased flexibility for Soviet forces: the constraints imposed by the northern climate and the choke points around Japan are evaded, the distances that have to be covered for effective force projection into the South Pacific and the Indian Ocean are greatly reduced, and the capacity for signals interception is greatly increased. However, too much should not be made of this. Supply and reinforcement lines between Vietnam and the Soviet Far East are extended and vulnerable to interdiction, particularly while American forces remain in the Philippines. Furthermore, because the Vietnamese bases themselves are vulnerable in the event of conflict, they would be unlikely to play a major part after the initial clashes. For the ANZUS partners, therefore, the

Soviet presence in Vietnam is less a military issue than a political one, as the Australian Defence Minister has argued.* More important than the military factor is the basic Soviet-Vietnamese relationship.

Concerns raised regarding the expanding Soviet presence in the South Pacific arise partly because of the sheer novelty of the Soviet action, but they also reflect anxiety about the effects a Soviet presence in a hitherto Western lake might have on the interests of the ANZUS partners. The principal focus has been on the potential military consequences of this presence, including possible Soviet interdiction of trans-Pacific ANZUS traffic (both vehicular and electronic), the movement of missile-carrying Soviet submarines into the deeper parts of the ocean in the event of heightened military tension or conflict, the conduct of research which could have military utility, the opportunities for surveillance of American missile-testing facilities in Kwajalein, and the turning of the states of the region against their traditional, pro-Western affiliations (see Herr 1986).

Concerns about the Soviet presence also rest upon the increased instability that has been evident in the region in recent years. The coups in Fiji, the struggle for independence in New Caledonia, the civil disturbances in Tahiti and Vanuatu, and the apparent breakdown in parliamentary procedures in Papua New Guinea—all combine to create a picture of instability which seems to present opportunities for expanded Soviet influence. Indeed, it is the Soviet ability to take advantage of such situations which some statesmen have cited to argue that the USSR should be prevented from gaining a land footing in the region.[†] Such worries have some validity. When there are conflicts in a society, the opportunities for external interference increase, if only because of the temptation to seek external support against the opposition. If such conflicts arise, there is little the ANZUS partners can do to prevent one side from looking to the Soviet Union for support. The most appropriate response would be to seek to nudge the authorities toward a resolution that is satisfactory to all, possibly using increased economic aid and assistance to expedite the

*In March 1987 he said: "We see it [the Soviet presence at Camranh Bay] as a serious political problem, as a serious political threat. . . . The Soviet buildup there, not as great as many make out, poses serious political problems. . . . The Americans only want to talk about the military problem in Cam Ranh Bay, even though it is quite clear that the Americans would destroy it in 20 minutes in a nuclear war and within 12 to 48 hours in a conventional one" (*Sydney Morning Herald*, 5 March 1987). For the U.S. Department of Defense view that these forces could be neutralized with "relative ease" in a global war, see USIS (1988: 6).

†For example, see Australian Foreign Minister Hayden's comments at press conferences in Kiribati (15 May 1986) and Auckland (13 December 1986).

process. Even though thus far none of the parties to intra-island disputes has been disposed to seek Soviet assistance, the only way of ensuring that this does not occur is to resolve the issues at the heart of the disputes. This must primarily be a domestic matter.*

While a state of subdued hostility and competition continues to exist between the USSR and the United States and its allies, concerns about the military potentialities of the Soviet presence in the Pacific will have some validity. However, the extent of Soviet military power in the region should not be exaggerated. Despite the significant growth and qualitative improvement of the Soviet Pacific fleet over the past decade, it still does not match the forces of the major ANZUS power—the United States. The potential impact of the Soviet forces would be reduced by the enormous distances over which any reinforcements would have to be carried—an element of crucial importance in any sustained conflict.† Furthermore, the U.S. fleet is significantly superior to that of the USSR in all of the major combat capacities, including early warning, air defense, anti-ship and anti-submarine warfare, and amphibious capabilities.** While precise Soviet planning for action in the event of a crisis in the region is unknown, the U.S. Department of Defense view in 1986 was that the task of the Soviet fleet would be primarily defensive, aimed at blunting the American policy of taking any conflict to points of Soviet vulnerability, which would include the Far East (Acharya 1987: 158). In any case, regardless of intention, the Soviet capacity to project military power into the Pacific in times of tension is significantly less than that of the United States.

There is nothing that the ANZUS partners can do to stop Soviet vessels from sailing through the region or from conducting oceanographic

---

*Despite many claims about Soviet influence in the region exercised through trade unions, church organizations, and youth groups, there is little direct evidence. For example, one author spends considerable time discussing various organizations in the South Pacific which he believes are acting to further Soviet aims, but then admits that "The exact Soviet role in all this is unclear because the principal actors are non-Soviets, and some participants are communists who do not support the Soviet Union, although pro-Soviet union leaders from downunder do play an important role" (Tanham 1988: 93). It is important to distinguish between criticism of Western or American policy and support for the USSR.

†Crude numbers alone tell us little. The latest estimates of Soviet and American force levels in the Pacific region will be found in IISS (1987: 29–30, 45–46).

**According to U.S. Department of Defense estimates, the United States maintains an overall margin of naval superiority, but this is being reduced, and the balance is not favorable in all aspects of naval operations (USIS 1988: 8).

research on and below the surface of the high seas. This is as much the legal right of the USSR as any other states, and in terms of those unwritten rules which structure superpower relations, it is the prerogative of either superpower if it believes it to be in its best interests. Indeed, given the use of the area by Soviet commercial vessels, Soviet research can be justified on commercial grounds. While right of free passage exists, ship-based surveillance of activities in the region will continue to be a useful supplement to the information that can be gained from satellite activity.

But if the ANZUS states can do little about the presence of Soviet vessels in this region, they can have some effect on the ability of the USSR to establish a permanent landed presence. Fishing agreements in themselves pose a challenge only to the commercial interests of Western fishermen, and these presumably must survive according to the operations of the market, about which the ANZUS governments have been quite forceful. If the Soviet fishing fleet offers better terms to island governments, so be it. It may be that the ANZUS partners would see it as in their interests to bolster the commercial competitiveness of their fishermen by underwriting or subsidizing their fleets in an attempt to block the USSR out of the market, but this would be in effect simply a subsidy to one sector of the domestic economy to enable it to succeed in the marketplace. This could be very expensive, and it would not stop Soviet transit or conduct of research, which could continue in the absence of any formal fishing agreement.

The main ANZUS fear has been that a fishing agreement would involve the acquisition of a more permanent landed presence by the USSR, and that this would provide a secure basis from which to interfere in local domestic affairs, to conduct surveillance and subversion, and to project Soviet influence. While a landed presence would facilitate such activity, the fear that this is the aim behind fishing agreements seems to be exaggerated. The breakdown of the Soviet fishing agreements with Kiribati and Vanuatu on the basis of claimed Soviet dissatisfaction with the economic returns suggests that the Soviet authorities believe there is little to be gained from such agreements that cannot be obtained without them. If such agreements were perceived in Moscow to have significant strategic implications, they would not have been allowed to lapse. Alternatively, if they were seen primarily in commercial terms, with few other dimensions, disappointing economic returns would be sufficient reason for their abandonment. In the light of past experience, the ANZUS partners should not overreact to the likelihood of further fishing agreements should the Soviet Union seek them. Indeed, the fact that the USSR already has a fishing agreement (with port access) with New Zealand, and that there has been talk of one with Australia, means that a negative reaction to such an agreement with any of the island states would appear paternalistic and hypocritical.

Fears about expanded Soviet influence should stimulate the ANZUS partners to work on strengthening the pro-Western orientations that still remain in the region. The predominantly peaceful process of decolonization, the transfer of democratic institutions and Christian beliefs, the continuing links through aid and trade, and the defense arrangements between Australia and Papua New Guinea and the United States and Tuvalu and Kiribati have all created a basis upon which the islands' traditional pro-Western orientation has rested. What the ANZUS states should do is work at reinforcing these links, but this will involve some careful policy implementation. They must be careful not to be seen to be attempting a heavy-handed control or attempting to exercise powers which infringe the sensibilities and sovereignty of the island governments. The aim is influence through friendship, not control through subterfuge. The latter would only backfire, and could encourage the micro-states to look to the USSR or even Libya or Cuba, which have shown some interest in the region, as a source of support.

The most important aspect of this policy is economic aid and trade—areas in which the USSR has not played a major role in the region. With the exception of fish and possibly natural resources from the seabed (in particular, manganese nodules, which are believed to be a commercially viable source of manganese, copper, nickel, and cobalt), the islands have little to offer the USSR in a trading relationship. The USSR has not been a major source of economic aid, and generally the type of aid it has offered Third World states has not been particularly appropriate to their needs. As long as Western aid and trade relations remain satisfactory to the island states, there is likely to be only limited room for expanded Soviet access. The danger to the island states' economies and national security which some see to lie in a Soviet presence would thereby be avoided.* But skillful management will be required of the ANZUS

---

*For example, see Australian Foreign Minister Hayden's comments in a press conference at Auckland, 13 December 1986. Australia reflects the common ANZUS position in seeing increased Soviet activity or presence as "an unwelcome development." See the speech by Defence Minister Beazley to the House of Representatives, "The Defence of Australia," March 1987, p. 17, and the Executive Summary of the "Review of Australia's Defence Capabilities" [the so-called Dibb Report], *Current Affairs Bulletin* 63, 2 (July 1986): 8.

partners. They must tread a careful path between responding to every attempt by island leaders to "play the Russian card" in an endeavor to screw greater aid from them, and being too parsimonious in their aid and too hard-nosed in their trade. If the ANZUS states are to tread this path successfully, they will need both a clear idea of their aims and priorities in the region and a high level of understanding of regional sensibilities.

In order to maximize their influence, they must resolve three problems. The first is the U.S. refusal to sign the treaty bringing the South Pacific Nuclear Free Zone into existence. This clearly shows the United States unfavorably compared with the USSR, which has signed the treaty. It places the Americans at odds with a substantial weight of opinion in the region, and it constitutes a source of strain on the U.S. relationship with the islands. So too does the American position on French nuclear testing. As long as the United States fails to condemn the continuation of French testing at Mururoa atoll, and to bring pressure to bear on Paris to shift its testing elsewhere, it will remain out of step with regional opinion. Once again it compares unfavorably with the USSR, which publicly opposes this testing. Continued U.S. support for the French presence in New Caledonia will have the same effect.

The third problem that needs to be resolved concerns commercial matters and trade. The ANZUS partners must ensure that their commercial actors in the region behave themselves. Given the size of the economies of the micro-states, foreign commercial interests can have an overwhelming effect on those economies. The micro-states are not sufficiently powerful themselves to be able to exercise effective control over foreign corporations, and therefore it is up to the metropole states to impose some restraint. The action of members of the American Tuna Boat Association in fishing illegally is probably the most egregious recent case to come to the public notice. If the ANZUS powers are to prevent the poisoning of their relations with the micro-states, they must make certain that this sort of thing does not happen again.

Of course nothing the ANZUS partners do can guarantee that the Soviet Union will be excluded from the region; that aim, even if desirable, is unrealizable. What the ANZUS states must ensure is that the relationship between them and the micro-states of the region is sufficiently well-founded that the Soviet presence is not seen by the latter as an alternative source of succor and support. The ANZUS approach is most likely to succeed in restricting Soviet influence and directing it into acceptable channels if it is positive in offering the islands assistance with their future rather than being overbearing or purely negative in denying the Soviet Union any role. The potential benefits of Soviet involvement should be recognized alongside the potential costs, something which Canberra appears to have been more willing to do than Washington.* If relations in the region are not viewed in a zero-sum way, there is no reason why the micro-states cannot and should not have good relations with the USSR as well as the ANZUS partners. As long as the relationship between the ANZUS partners and the micro-states remains good, the Soviet profile will remain restricted. It may also be positive, in that the USSR may become a worthwhile source of aid and a useful, if minor, trading partner. However, if the relationship with the ANZUS states becomes strained and the micro-states begin to look to the USSR to replace the support which they are currently getting from the West, the scope for Soviet influence to grow and to develop in ways that are less acceptable will increase. If a healthy relationship exists between the ANZUS states and the other states of the region, there is no reason why the USSR should not be accepted as a useful partner in the course of regional and global intercourse.

REFERENCES

Acharya, Amitav. 1987. "The Asia-Pacific Region: Cockpit for Superpower Rivalry." *The World Today* 43, 8–9 (August); citing U.S. Department of Defense 1986.

Berton, Peter. 1986. "Soviet-Japanese Relations: Perceptions, Goals, Interactions." *Asian Survey* 26, 12 (December).

Breslauer, George W. 1987. "Ideology and Learning in Soviet Third World Policy." *World Politics* 39, 3 (April).

Dibb, Paul. 1985. "Soviet Strategy Toward Australia, New Zealand, and the South-west Pacific." *Australian Outlook*, 39, 2 (August).

Doulman, David J. 1986. "Some Aspects and Issues Concerning the Kiribati/Soviet Union Fishing Agreement." Pacific Islands Development Program, East-West Center, May.

*For example, see Foreign Minister Hayden's comments in his interview with Soviet commentator Joe Adamov, 19 November 1986. In the 1987 Singapore Lecture, Australian Prime Minister Hawke declared that, although Soviet actions had to be watched carefully, "I would welcome a constructive involvement by the USSR in political and economic developments in the Asia-Pacific" (*Sydney Morning Herald*, 28 November 1987).

Gurevich, Anton. 1987. "Joint Ventures with the West: Recent Developments." *Radio Liberty Research Bulletin*, RL263/87, 5 July.

Herr, Richard. 1986. "The Soviet Union in the South Pacific." Australian Development Studies Network, Briefing Paper, Canberra, October.

Hough, Jerry F. 1986. *The Struggle for the Third World: Soviet Debates and American Options*. Washington: Brookings Institution.

IISS [International Institute for Strategic Studies]. 1985. *The Military Balance, 1985–1986*. London.

―――. 1987a. *The Military Balance, 1986–1987*. London.

―――. 1987b. *Strategic Survey 1986–1987*. London.

Johnson, R. W. 1986. *Shootdown: The Verdict on KAL 007*. London: Chatto & Windus.

Klintworth, Gary. 1987. "Mr. Gorbachev's China Diplomacy." In Thakur and Thayer 1987.

Pipes, Richard. 1984. *Survival Is Not Enough: Soviet Realities and America's Future*. New York: Simon & Schuster.

Rosenberger, Leif. 1983. "The Soviet-Vietnamese Alliance and Kampuchea." *Survey* 27, 118 (Autumn-Winter).

Samoteikin, Evgeny. 1987. Address by Soviet ambassador to conference on "Gorbachev's Vladivostok Initiative: New Directions in Asia and the Pacific." Australian Defence Force Academy, Canberra, 20 March; reprinted in Thakur and Thayer 1987.

Tanham, George K. 1988. "Subverting the South Pacific." *The National Interest*, Spring.

Thakur, Ramesh, and Thayer, Carl, eds. 1987. *The Soviet Union as an Asian-Pacific Power*. Boulder: Westview Press.

U.S. Department of Defense. 1986. *Soviet Military Power 1986*. Washington.

―――. 1988. *Soviet Military Power 1988*. Washington.

USIS [United States Information Service]. 1988. "Allies, Bases Remain Vital to Pacific Security." *Backgrounder*, 10 May; citing U.S. Department of Defense 1988.

Chapter 5

THE ASCENDANCY OF THE ECONOMIC DIMENSION IN AUSTRALIAN-AMERICAN RELATIONS

Richard Higgott

Nurtured during World War II, the relationship between Australia and the United States has evolved from strength to strength as Australia has stood beside its senior partner in Korea, Vietnam, and on a wide range of other politico-strategic issues. As a member of the Western alliance in general and ANZUS in particular, host to strategically significant "joint facilities," and the provider of unfettered port access to U.S. Navy vessels, Australia is correctly seen as one of the United States's strongest international supporters. Indeed numerous works have attested to the strength, depth, and amicability of the relationship.[*]

At first glance, then, the history of the relationship is abundantly, if somewhat uncritically documented.[†] Yet if we look closely at the literature—and by implication analysis—of the relationship, we see that it is very narrow in focus. To date analyses have concentrated overwhelmingly on the politico-strategic dimension of the relationship at the expense of the economic dimension. (For exceptions see Esthus 1964 and R. Bell

---

[*]Books and articles on this most written about of Australia's relationships stretch back to World War II. For example, over this period see *Australian Outlook: The Australian Journal of International Affairs*, in which dozens of articles have appeared on the subject; see especially issue 38, 3 (1984), devoted to the security relationship. For recent analyses of the relationship, see (inter alia) Barclay (1987), Albinski (1981 and 1987), Harper (1987), and C. Bell (1988).

[†]Two notable exceptions are the books by Camilleri (1980 and 1987) and Phillips (1988), which take a more critical approach.

NOTE: *This chapter was originally drafted in June 1987. Updates have been made where essential, but data in the tables remain unchanged, and it has not been possible to rewrite the paper in toto to take account of broader events in the global economic environment such as the progression of the Uruguay Round. The argumentation of the paper remains, however, still relevant to a 1989 publication date.*

1977.) The prevailing tendency—*pace* Coral Bell (1984: 3), for example— has been to focus on economic issues only to the extent that they impinge on politico-strategic concerns in a manner that treats the two spheres as semi-autonomous. There is as yet no major study of the *politics* of Australia's international economic relations in general, nor of the *politics* of Australia's economic relations with its major ally in particular. This is as important an omission from the policy perspective as it is from the scholarly one.

This chapter is divided into four parts. It begins by briefly tracing the evolution of the economic relationship after World War II through the end of the government of Gough Whitlam in 1975, and it provides an insight into the contextual arena of the post–World War II economic order within which to analyze the contemporary bilateral economic relationship. The central feature of this arena is the demise of the United States as hegemon of the post–World War II liberal international economic order and the emergence since the early 1970s of a more anarchical and hostile international economic environment. The second part details the contemporary bilateral economic relationship. The third part attempts to clarify the politics-economics nexus of the bilateral relationship. The fourth part considers the current political management of the relationship, especially with regard to the manner in which politico-strategic and economic considerations interact with each other in a hitherto unprecedented manner.

We shall contend specifically that the search for national economic well-being in the international order for a state such as Australia is as significant as the search for national security (traditionally defined in politico-strategic terms) as we head toward the last decade of the century.* For a variety of reasons, neither analysts nor practitioners of Australia's foreign relations have given the relationship between economic and foreign policy issues the attention it deserves. Australian national economic welfare, influenced and constrained by the international economic order, has always been considered secondary to national security in the international political system. By contrast and for heuristic purposes, we shall assert that Australia is unlikely to be at war outside of an all out global nuclear war. This is not to suggest that Australia does not have broad strategic interests as a member of the Western alliance, nor that it may not face limited regional hostilities; rather, economic issues—for reasons to be

*The contention is in keeping with an increasingly influential (but general) genre of international political economy literature emanating from the United States and Great Britain during the 1980s.

outlined—constitute the most pressing dimension of its contemporary international relations. In short, it is in the international political economy in the 1980s, rather than the international system of states, that Australia faces its most severe challenges.

The recognition of the importance of economic issues has been a long time coming at both the scholarly and policy levels, but the learning curve would appear to be turning. Not only is there now a burgeoning literature traversing the ideological/political spectrum which recognizes the problems that Australia faces as an "open," vulnerable economy in hostile regional and international *economic* environments (see Higgott 1987a: 14–23, 29–38, and 1987b), but there is also an awareness of these problems in policy circles.* Changes in the policy environment were evidenced in the appointment of an economist to head the Department of Foreign Affairs, followed by the amalgamation of this department with the Department of Trade. Furthermore, the policymaker and the scholar come together in their focus on Australia's need to adjust to the rapid changes in the international political economy in the 1980s. Here let us briefly sketch Australia's current problems as an actor in the international economic order for a nonantipodean audience.

Even prior to the global stock market slump of October 1987 and ignoring the hyperbole of analysts who talk of "the death of the Lucky Country," "the Land of Lost Opportunities," or "the Latin Americanization of Australia," Australia's economic downturn in the first half of the 1980s was stark indeed. By 1986 Australia's *gross* debt stood in excess of Aus$70,000 million. The growth of *net* external debt from Aus$30,475 million in 1984–85 to Aus$52,002 million in 1985–86 represented an increase from 16.3 to 25.1 percent of GDP. (See *The Age*, 14 February 1986, p. 3, and Higgott 1987b for an explanation of this growth.) Furthermore, this external debt has increased sixfold in the 1980s; debt-servicing by 1985–86 required 36 percent of export earnings—the highest figure since the depression years of the 1930s. These requirements place Australia in a league with several developing countries such as its neighbor the Philippines rather than its OECD partners. The outpacing of income growth by debt-servicing requirements has been exacerbated by the decline in the value of the Australian dollar, not only against the U.S. dollar throughout the 1980s, but also in relationship with the U.S. dollar against other major currencies such as the yen and the deutsche mark.

*The notion of an "open" economy is taken, albeit liberally interpreted, from Peter Katzenstein's pioneering work on small states in the international political economy (see, inter alia, 1986 and 1983).

More important has been the decline in the import purchasing power of Australia's commodity exports, which give Australia an export profile similar to many LDCs. The World Bank (1985) demonstrated the decline in a basket of thirty-three export commodities from LDCs when measured against the import of manufactures from developed countries. These export commodities included wheat, sugar, beef, copper, tin, nickel, bauxite, aluminum, iron ore, lead, and zinc—many of which are of considerable importance to Australia (see Table 1). With an average for 1977–79 as a base of 100, an index of the purchasing power of Australia's exports shows a decline from 160 in 1974 to 84 in 1984. Similar calculations illustrate a deterioration in Australia's terms of trade (export price index divided by import price index). Over the period 1978/79–1984/85 they declined from 115 to 94 (*Financial Review*, 5 March 1985, p. 12).

This decline has brought Australia back to a position similar to one before 1960, when solving balance-of-payment problems continually took precedence over growth creation. The mineral expansion of the 1960s and 1970s—the so-called "resources boom"—would appear to be well and truly over, and the prospects for a recovery in the commodity markets in which Australia trades are slight. Notwithstanding the current improvement in prices of some rural exports, resisting long-term cuts in export prices for many of Australia's commodities may well prove overwhelming. Consequently the days in which Australia was able to use its agricultural and mineral sectors to subsidize its protected and less competitive manufacturing industries would also appear over. More analytically, these specific problems are part of a broader structural process through which Australia has become marginalized from the new international division of labor that has evolved over the last couple of decades, especially in the Asia-Pacific region. I have discussed this in detail elsewhere (Higgott 1987b: 192–202), but a general outline of the process will be helpful here.

The dynamic process of growth and the centrality of the Asia-Pacific region to the evolution of a new international division of labor can be contrasted with the manner in which Australia has been marginalized from much of this growth throughout the 1960s and 1970s. (Table 2 presents some comparative data.) This is not to argue that Australia has not been part of that growth, but rather that its position has become less significant. For example, an absolute growth of Australia's trade with the Western Pacific needs to be contrasted with a post–World War II decline (threefold from 1960 to the early 1980s) in the degree of penetration of regional markets. In addition, exports as a share of Australia's GDP have

Table 1

Principal Exports From Australia, 1950–1985
(Percent of total exports)

Export	Year (ending in June)							
	1950	1955	1960	1965	1970	1975	1980	1985
Aluminum alloys	- -	- -	- -	- -	- -	- -	0.4%	2.6%
Aluminum oxide and hydroxide	- -	- -	- -	- -	- -	- -	5.1	4.5
Coal	- -	- -	0.5%	2.0%	4.1%	7.9%	8.9	15.0
Crustaceans, molluscs	- -	- -	- -	- -	- -	- -	1.1	1.2
Dairy products	5.8%	4.9%	4.7	3.9	2.4	1.9	1.3	1.3
Drugs, chemicals, and fertilizers	0.5	0.6	0.8	1.2	3.4^d	5.6^d	- -	- -
Fruit	1.7	4.2	3.3	3.2	1.3	0.6	1.0	0.7
Hides and skins	2.5	2.5	3.5	3.1	2.2	1.2	2.5	0.9
Iron and steel	0.3	- -	2.5	2.4	- -	- -	- -	- -
Iron ore and concentrates^a	- -	- -	- -	- -	7.0	8.4	5.7	6.1
Other ores and concentrates	0.9	1.8	2.4	3.1	3.0	2.9	1.7	1.5
Lead, pig	2.1	2.2	1.7^c	2.3^c	- -	- -	- -	- -
Lead and lead alloys	- -	- -	- -	- -	2.7	1.6	2.9	0.8
Other metals and alloys	- -	- -	- -	- -	3.3	2.6	1.3	1.3
Machines, machinery^b	0.6	1.1	0.9	1.6	- -	- -	- -	- -
Machinery and transport equipment	- -	- -	- -	- -	5.2	5.3	4.5	5.0
Meat	5.7	4.5	9.1	10.7	10.8	5.4	8.7	4.2
Petroleum, petroleum products	- -	- -	1.7	0.9	0.7	1.9	2.2	3.8
Sugar (cane)	2.3	4.0	2.8	4.4	2.9	7.7	3.5^e	1.9^e
Wheat	10.2	5.8	6.6	11.5	8.5	12.3	11.5	9.1
Other grain, cereal	6.3	4.0	4.2	3.7	1.3	3.0	2.9	3.8
Wood chip	- -	- -	- -	- -	- -	- -	0.7	0.7
Wool	51.5	45.6	41.2	31.2	19.2	9.0	8.4	7.9
Percent of total exports	90.5	81.2	85.9	85.2	79.1	77.2	69.9	67.3

Sources: Australia, Commonwealth Bureau of Census and Statistics, *Official Year Book* (1953, 1956, 1961, 1966, 1971); Australia, Bureau of Statistics (ABS), *Official Year Book* (1975–76, 1981, 1986).

^{a}Excludes roasted iron pyrites.

^{b}Excludes dynamo, electric.

^{c}Includes bullion.

^{d}Excludes fertilizers.

^{e}Except icing sugar.

Table 2

Australia and the Asia-Pacific Region: Selected Comparative Data, 1960–1982

Country[a]	Total Population (Millions) Mid-1982	Gross Domestic Product (Millions of U.S. dollars)		Gross National Product (Per capita, U.S. dollars) 1982	Gross Domestic Production (Percent average annual growth)		Exports as Share of Gross Domestic Product (Percent)		Gross Domestic Investment as Share of Gross Domestic Product (Percent)		Gross Domestic Investment (Percent average annual growth)	
		1960	1982		1960–70	1970–82	1960	1982	1960	1982	1960–70	1970–82
Australia	15.2	$16,370	$164,210	$11,140	5.6%	3.1%	15%	15%	28%	22%	6.7%	1.1%
Indonesia	156.2	8,670	90,160	580	3.9	7.7	13	22	8	23	4.6	13.7
Malaysia	14.5	2,290	25,870	1,860	6.5	7.7	54	51	14	34	7.5	11.4
Philippines	50.7	6,960	39,850	820	5.1	6.0	11	16	16	29	8.2	9.3
Singapore	2.5	700	14,650	5,910	8.8	8.5	163	196	11	46	20.5	8.7
Thailand	48.5	2,250	36,790	790	8.4	7.1	17	25	16	21	15.8	6.4
China	1,008.0	42,770	260,400	- -	5.2	5.6	- -	28[b]	23	28	9.8	6.4
Hong Kong	5.2	950	24,440	5,340	- -	- -	82	100	18	29	6.9	13.6
Japan	118.4	44,000	1,081,920	10,080	10.4	4.6	11	15	33	30	14.6	3.3
South Korea	39.3	3,810	68,420	1,910	8.6	8.6	3	39	11	26	23.6	11.0
United States	231.5	505,300	3,009,600	13,160	4.3	2.7	5	9	19	16	5.0	1.3
New Zealand	3.2	3,940	23,820	7,920	3.6	1.8	22	29	23	25	3.2	-0.1

Source: World Bank (1984: 218–27).

[a]Some states of the region are not included: the socialist states of East Asia, the small states of the Southwest Pacific, Australia's former colony Papua New Guinea, and Brunei, the newest but smallest member of the Association of South-East Asian Nations (ASEAN). Those included in the table are Australia's major economic partners in the region.

[b]Estimate.

declined from a high of about 40 percent at the time of the Korean War commodity boom of the 1950s to just under 14 percent in 1982. Recently Australia's exports as a share of GDP have been static, contrasting with the more dynamic pattern of other developed countries (see Table 3). This trend is complex and explanations are contested, but two main points stand out.

Table 3

**Exports as a Share of GDP for Selected
Industrial Countries, 1960 and 1982**
(Percent)

Country	1960	1982
Australia	15%	15%
Canada	18	27
France	15	21
Germany	19	31
Sweden	23	33
United States	5	9

Source: World Bank (1984: 227).

First, Australia exports more primary produce and raw materials than do most developed countries (with the exception of its regional neighbor New Zealand). Natural resources have throughout the twentieth century accounted for between two thirds and four fifths of total exports. Even though the mix of these exports has undergone change (note the shifting position of wool and minerals in Table 1), the basic structural pattern has altered little. In addition, Australia imports more manufactures (as a percent of total imports) than is the case for the industrial market economies in aggregate. (See Tables 4 and 5.)

Second, Australian trade has grown more slowly than world trade generally. For example, between 1970 and 1980 the volume of world trade grew at 5.6 percent per annum, while Australian trade increased by only 3.6 percent per annum. Over the period 1939–75 Australian trade dropped from 2.5 percent to 1.25 percent of world trade overall. Australia has failed to hold its share of world trade in an era when growth through trade (especially in manufactures) has been the order of the day for the world's most economically successful developed and developing countries. In short, Australia would appear to be undergoing marginalization through its specialization in export commodities with a low value-added component that are unable to hold their share of overall trade (see Caves and Krause, eds. 1984: 278–81).

Table 4

**Exports of Primary Produce and Raw Materials from Australia and
Industrial Market Economies, 1960–1983**
(Percent of total exports)

Exporter(s)	1960	1965	1981	1983
Australia	92%	86%	75%	77%
Industrial market economies	34	30	27	26

Sources: World Bank (1984: 236–39; 1986: 198–201).

Table 5

**Imports of Manufactures to Australia and Industrial Market Economies,
1960–1983**
(Percent of total imports)

Importer(s)	1960	1965	1981	1983
Australia	68%	78%	77%	79%
Industrial market economies	43	50	54	58

Sources: Same as Table 4.

These problems must be understood in order to understand the
critical nature of Australia's important bilateral relationships—such as
that with the United States. The economic relationship with the United
States must consequently be seen two-dimensionally. Not only is the
relationship crucial to Australia in its specifically bilateral sense. It is also
crucial because much of Australia's wider foreign economic policy is contingent on policy initiated by the United States as a major actor in the
international economy. Therefore, in addition to discussing the bilateral
relationship, we shall also discuss the way in which Australia, as a third
party, is affected by the policies of the world's major economic actors
(especially the United States) in their dealings with each other.

AUSTRALIA, THE UNITED STATES, AND THE INTERNATIONAL ECONOMIC
ORDER SINCE WORLD WAR II

The economic relationship between Australia and the United States
evolved more slowly than the politico-strategic one. Indeed between the
1930s and Britain's entry into the European Community (EC) in the early
1970s the relationship was such that U.S. policymakers could have been
forgiven for thinking that Australia was practicing political expedience—

sheltering under the American military umbrella while preserving its economic relations with the United Kingdom.

As can be seen from Tables 6 and 7, the United Kingdom was still the overwhelmingly dominant economic partner for Australia following World War II. In 1949–50 Britain provided over half of Australia's imports and was the destination for well over a third of Australia's exports. In contrast, the United States, although statistically significant, imported far less of Australia's primary commodities and raw materials. It was not until the late 1950s and early 1960s, as Britain began to look toward EC membership, that major diversification began to take place. By 1969–70 a greater percentage of Australia's exports was going to the United States (13.5 percent) than to the United Kingdom (11.8 percent). Similarly, a greater percentage of Australia's imports flowed from the United States than from the United Kingdom (24.9 and 21.8 percent respectively). Most important, by the 1970s Japan had emerged as a major trading partner for Australia. (For a full discussion of the post–World War II relationship with Japan, see Rix 1986.)

The chief characteristic of the Australia-U.S. economic relationship, established at the outset and current in the 1980s, is the perpetually favorable balance of trade for the United States. As high as 6:1 in the United States's favor at the height of the depression, it has (with the exception of 1949–51) never been much less than 2:1 (see Table 8). Another major characteristic of the relationship is that it has been very harmonious with the exception of two short periods. The first was a conflict over the introduction by Australia of the Trade Diversion Act in 1936 (see Esthus 1964), and the second was between 1972 and 1975, when the United States took exception to what it considered the excessively nationalist posture of the Whitlam government vis-à-vis American capital in Australia. (Current tensions in the relationship will receive full treatment below.)

U.S. investment had grown steadily since World War II to establish itself inside Australian tariff and quota barriers. While it is important, it warrants no treatment here. I am not arguing that international investment does not have major influence over economic development in a country. Rather I am suggesting that apart from the early 1970s, when the issue of foreign domination was a weapon in the armory that brought Whitlam to power (see Cuddy 1980), it has not affected the *bilateral* relationship at a political level as directly as the more tangible relationship of trade. Furthermore, U.S. business interests in Australia, especially in the automobile and resource industries, appear to have contracted in

Table 6

Principal Sources of Australian Imports, 1949/50–1985/86

(*Percent of annual totals*)

Source	1949–50	1954–55	1959–60	1964–65	1969–70	1974–75	1979–80	1984–85	1985–86
Arabian states									
ASEAN[a]	2.5%	3.3%	4.0%	3.6%	3.9%	3.0%	6.2%	5.7%	4.6%
Canada		2.8	3.2	4.0		2.7	2.8		
EC[b]					12.6	14.5	13.3	14.2	16.9
France[c]	2.0			2.3					
Germany, Federal Republic[c]		3.7	5.8	5.6					
India	5.1	3.1	2.0						
Indonesia[d]	2.8	2.7	3.2	2.2					
Iran	2.1								
Japan		2.2	4.5	8.9	12.4	17.6	15.6	22.1	23.8
Netherlands[c]			2.0						
New Zealand						2.3	3.4	3.7	4.2
Saudi Arabia							3.9		
Sri Lanka		2.3							
United Kingdom	51.9	44.9	35.6	26.2	21.8	15.0	10.2	6.7	7.3
United States	9.7	12.1	16.2	23.8	24.9	20.6	22.1	22.7	21.0
Percent of total imports	76.1	77.1	76.5	76.6	75.6	75.7	77.5	75.1	77.8

Sources: Australia, Commonwealth Bureau of Census and Statistics, *Overseas Trade* (nos. 47, 52, 57, 62, 67); ABS: *Overseas Trade* (1974–75), and *Imports, Australia* and *Exports, Australia* (June 1980, June 1985, June 1986).

[a]Since 1969–70.
[b]Since 1969–70. United Kingdom excluded. From 1974–75 including Denmark and Ireland.
[c]Until 1969–70.
[d]Until 1974–75.

Table 7

Principal Destinations for Australian Exports, 1949/50–1985/86
(Percent of annual totals)

Destination	1949-50	1954-55	1959-60	1964-65	1969-70	1974-75	1979-80	1984-85	1985-86
ASEAN[a]					7.1%	8.3%	7.5%	7.7%	6.5%
Australian territories	4.5%	4.1%	1.9%	2.5%					
Belgium[b]			2.6[d]						
Canada						3.3			
China, People's Republic			1.7	5.1		2.9	4.5	3.4	4.6
EC[c]					10.9	9.9	9.1	9.3	10.6
France[b]	6.6	8.3	6.4	4.2					
Germany, Federal Republic[b]		4.1	4.1	3.2					
India	6.0		1.7						
Italy[b]	3.2	4.6	5.0	3.2					
Japan	4.0	7.6	14.4	16.6	24.7	27.6	26.9	26.3	28.5
Korea, Republic of							2.1	3.6	4.0
Malaya				3.1					
New Zealand	3.5	4.9	5.8	6.0	4.8	6.1	4.6	5.2	4.6
Papua New Guinea					3.6				
Taiwan								2.8	3.2
USSR				2.9		2.8	5.2	2.9	
United Kingdom	38.7	36.9	26.4	19.5	11.8	5.5	5.0	3.3	3.5
United States	8.1	6.9	8.1	10.0	13.5	9.6	10.9	11.7	9.9
Percent of total exports	74.6	77.4	78.1	76.3	76.4	76.0	75.8	76.2	75.4

Sources: Same as Table 6.

[a]Since 1969-70.

[b]Until 1969-70.

[c]Since 1969-70. United Kingdom excluded. From 1974-75 including Denmark and Ireland.

[d]With Luxembourg.

Table 8

Australian Trade Balance with the United States,
1927/28–1985/86

Year	Imports from United States[a]	Exports to United States[a]	Balance	Ratio (U.S.:Australia)
1927–28	35.0	9.0	-26.0	3.8:1
1928–29	35.3	5.8	-29.5	6.1:1
1929–30	30.3	5.2	-25.1	5.8:1
1934–35	11.0	2.8	-8.2	3.9:1
1939–40	20.1	25.7	+5.6	0.8:1
1949–50	52.2	49.6	-2.6	1.1:1
1954–55	102.2	52.4	-49.8	2.0:1
1959–60	149.6	75.9	-73.7	2.0:1
1964–65	692.2	264.4	-428.0	2.6:1
1969–70	965.2	556.4	-408.8	1.7:1
1974–75	1,668.2	831.5	-836.7	2.0:1
1979–80	3,577.3	2,044.1	-1,533.2	1.8:1
1980–81	4,169.0	2,147.0	-2,022.0	1.9:1
1981–82	5,249.3	2,154.5	-3,094.8	2.4:1
1982–83	4,766.4	2,241.1	-2,525.3	2.1:1
1983–84	5,188.5	2,701.5	-2,487.0	1.9:1
1984–85	6,819.3	3,584.1	-3,235.2	1.9:1
1985–86	7,284.8	3,242.7	-4,042.1	2.2:1

Source: Australia, Commonwealth Bureau of Census and Statistics, *Overseas Trade* (various years); ABS: *Overseas Trade* (various years), and *Imports, Australia* and *Exports, Australia* (various years).

[a]1927–60: £; 1964–86: U.S.$.

the last decade. The influence of capital on Australia in the 1980s is less at the bilateral level and more at the structural level of the global markets.

Just as Australia's current economic problems need to be seen in a broader context (of what I have called a new international division of labor), so too does the relationship with the United States need to be seen in a wider context. This context can be characterized broadly as a shift from U.S. hegemony to multipolarity and interdependence in the international economic order—especially the globalization of production and capital mobility and the emergence of a Pacific Basin economy. One aspect of these changes has been the rise of the EC and Japan to major actor status, undermining the United States's ability to set the politico-philosophical agenda. (Paradoxically, however, management of the system is becoming less a collective, multilateral problem and more a problem for resolution among the major industrial powers.) Especially important here is the rise of Japan to a position as the other major actor (along with the United States) in Australia's foreign economic relations in the 1970s and 1980s.

Australia's foreign economic policy in the 1980s and its domestic contingent of structural adjustment have to be conducted in an environment in which the policies of its major economic partners and the world's major economic actors either directly or indirectly enhance or (as is more often the case) detract from the preferred Australian policy option and expectation. This is especially so in the context of the Pacific Basin, in which the United States and Japan are the dominant actors.

The importance of the Pacific Basin economy for an understanding of Australia in the 1980s cannot be overstated. As can be seen from Table 9, by 1986 Australia's imports and exports within the Pacific Basin region accounted for over 60 percent of the total (see Drysdale 1984; Hofheinz and Calder 1982; and Linder 1986).* It has been estimated that the Pacific Basin will by 1990 account for 50 percent of total world GDP. Specifically, as can be seen from Tables 6, 7, and 10 (which shows Australia's balance of payments by region), the United States, Japan, and to a lesser extent the EC are Australia's major economic partners. A collapse of the international trading order precipitated by trading hostilities in which these three actors are the central protagonists would have serious repercussions for Australia.

The current deterioration in the United States's economic relations with Japan and the EC is symptomatic of the structural distortions that

---

*I deliberately use "Pacific Basin" rather than the somewhat pejorative "Pacific Rim."

Table 9

**Australian Trade with Major Pacific Basin Partners,
1980 and 1986**

(Percent of total exports and imports)

Trading Partner	1980 Exports	1980 Imports	1986 Exports	1986 Imports
ASEAN				
Brunei	- -	- -	0.0%	0.1%
Indonesia	1.7%	2.0%	1.7	0.8
Malaysia	2.3	1.1	1.6	1.1
Philippines	0.9	0.5	0.5	0.3
Singapore	2.4	3.0	2.0	2.0
Thailand	0.7	0.3	0.6	0.7
Subtotal	8.0	6.9	6.4	5.0
Asia-Pacific				
China	3.6	1.2	4.7	1.4
Hong Kong	1.5	2.2	2.3	2.1
South Korea	2.2	1.0	4.1	1.9
Japan	26.6	17.1	26.9	22.4
New Zealand	4.7	3.4	4.6	3.8
Fiji	0.8	0.1	0.5	0.1
Papua New Guinea	2.2	0.5	1.7	0.5
Subtotal	49.6	32.4	51.2	37.2
United States	11.7	21.8	10.6	21.9
Canada	2.1	2.7	1.7	2.0
TOTAL	63.4	56.9	63.5	61.1

Source: IMF, *Direction of Trade* (1987).

Table 10

Australia: Balance of Payments by Country or Region—Current Account, 1979/80–1984/85

(Millions of Aus.dollars)

Category of Balance	United States	Country or Region			Total
		Japan	Other OECD	Other Countries	
1979–80					
Balance on merchandise trade	$-1646	$2627	$-1290	$3067	$2758
Net services	-352	-7	-1104	-539	-2002
Balance on goods and services	-1998	2620	-2394	2528	756
1980–81					
Balance on merchandise trade	-2468	1566	-1799	2242	-459
Net services	-457	-111	-1018	-660	-2246
Balance on goods and services	-2925	1455	-2817	1582	-2705
1981–82					
Balance on merchandise trade	-3171	893	-2710	1700	-3288
Net services	-437	-167	-1124	-775	-2503
Balance on goods and services	-3608	726	-3834	925	-5791
1982–83					
Balance on merchandise trade	-2641	1400	-1676	1868	-1049
Net services	-507	-133	-1140	-1004	-2784
Balance on goods and services	-3148	1267	-2816	864	-3833
1983–84					
Balance on merchandise trade	-2483	1250	-1995	3413	185
Net services	-339	-182	-1390	-1018	-2929
Balance on goods and services	-2822	1068	-3385	2395	-2744
1984–85					
Balance on merchandise trade	-3693	1327	-3203	4714	-855
Net services	-455	-232	-1979	-1320	-3986
Balance on goods and services	-4148	1095	-5182	3394	-4841

Source: ABS (1987: 17–22).

exist in the international economic order and that have been in train for a number of years. A major problem with Japanese-American economic relations is that a process of creeping protectionism is under way and is unlikely to stop. This is a particularly acute problem for a state such as Australia which relies excessively on the export of primary commodities and the import of manufactured goods. As a consequence of this standoff between major actors in the international trading regime, the multilateral processes of trade liberalization that Australia and others are pushing for would currently seem an improbable (albeit not impossible) outcome. For agricultural and raw material producers such as Australia this is not of course a recent phenomenon. Indeed Australia's declining share of world trade since the 1950s is in no small part due to the impediments to rural exports in the international trading arena. (See Lougheed 1986; Miller 1986; and National Farmers Federation 1987.)

Australia's structural problems stretch across other sectors of the economy besides agriculture. In any case, as this discussion suggests, Australia is highly sensitive to exogenous developments over which it has little or no control. Moreover, too much store should not be set by international organizations such as the General Agreement on Tariffs and Trade (GATT) as a means of ameliorating problems. In the current international conflict between the United States and its major partners, Australia is at best only a secondary player, as are the major international economic organizations. To understand the effect of the conflict on Australia we need to bear in mind the imperatives of American foreign economic policy, specifically the policy responses to its economic woes of the 1980s. The essence of current U.S. international economic policy, particularly in its relations with the two other major actors in the economic order (Japan and the EC) is a bilateral, activist strategic trade policy pursued in game-theoretic manner. (See Krugman, ed. 1986; Krasner 1987; and Gilpin 1987: chs. 5 and 10.)

As can be seen from Tables 11 and 12, there is an important bilateral relationship between the United States and Japan (they are each other's major trading partners) and an important but asymmetrical relationship between Australia and the United States or Japan. Thus a bilateral U.S. approach to problem-solving is likely to have severe repercussions for third parties such as Australia. Furthermore, as we shall suggest below, the longer term repercussions may be political as well as economic.

Table 11

Japanese Trade with Australia and the United States, 1960–1985

| | | Trading Partner | | | |
| | | Australia | | United States | |
Year		Percent	Position	Percent	Position
1960	Exports	3.6%	4	27.3%	1
	Imports	7.7	2	34.6	1
1965	Exports	3.8	3	29.8	1
	Imports	6.8	2	29.0	1
1970	Exports	3.1	5	31.1	1
	Imports	8.0	2	29.5	1
1975	Exports	3.1	6	20.2	1
	Imports	7.2	4	20.1	1
1980	Exports	2.6	10	24.5	1
	Imports	5.0	5	17.4	1
1985	Exports	3.1	6	37.6	1
	Imports	5.8	5	20.0	1

Source: IMF (various years)

Table 12

U.S. Trade with Australia and Japan, 1960–1985

| | | Trading Partner | | | |
| | | Australia | | Japan | |
Year		Percent	Position	Percent	Position
1960	Exports	1.9%	13	6.5%	3
	Imports	0.9	24	7.6	2
1965	Exports	2.9	9	7.6	2
	Imports	1.5	15	11.3	2
1970	Exports	2.3	8	10.8	2
	Imports	1.5	12	14.7	2
1975	Exports	1.8	15	8.8	2
	Imports	1.2	19	11.7	2
1980	Exports	1.9	14	9.4	2
	Imports	1.1	20	12.8	2
1985	Exports	2.6	9	10.6	2
	Imports	0.8	21	20.0	1

Source: IMF (various years).

AUSTRALIAN-U.S. ECONOMIC RELATIONS IN
THE SECOND HALF OF THE 1980s

In periods of growth and prosperity the element of power in the making of policy is invariably ignored. But as Peter Gourevitch has noted, "In difficult economic times this comfortable illusion [that economic relations are separate from political considerations] disintegrates" (1986: 17). This message is being driven home strongly to Australian foreign policymakers in the country's bilateral relationship with its major ally. The learning process is twofold. In general, the harsh reality of the global financial and trading arenas has highlighted the asymmetry of power relations for a state as exposed as Australia to the vicissitudes of the international economy. In particular, Australia has had to face a declining market share for its exports in its major postwar economic partner, Japan; increased competition from heavily subsidized European and U.S. commodities targeted for markets in which Australia somewhat complacently felt it had regional advantages; and the downgrading of its credit rating and a decline in the value of its stock market greater than any other states (save for Hong Kong and New Zealand) after the October 1987 crash.

As we have noted, Australia's political abilities to formulate its foreign and domestic economic policies are restricted not only by general market conditions, but also by the policy behavior of its major bilateral partners. In particular, the United States during the Reagan administration seems to have relegated international economic relations to a secondary level; indeed according to Feinberg (1983: 131), they have been subordinated more than at any time since World War II. International economic policy, geared to domestic political priorities, has been pursued with "almost total disregard for the outside world" (Cohen 1983: 116).

There is considerable discussion in the United States over priorities and the relationship between domestic and international policy. However, the Reagan administration's "domesticist approach" to foreign economic policy—notwithstanding its impact on partners in bilateral relations (such as Australia) and despite its intentions to the contrary— has not led to an environment of "freer" trade.* This in no small part is because the U.S. government has not practiced what it has preached. Domestic deficits and other (not only economic) problems have caused

*The domesticist approach is discussed in Nau (1982), who defends international Reaganomics. For a contrasting view, see Bergsten (1981).

the administration to respond in a bilateral and often protectionist manner, as even some of its key supporters have acknowledged (Nau 1982: 18ff.). U.S. trade policy has become, even more than in the past, the victim of political expediency in the face of powerful vested interests in the domestic polity.

The inability of the United States to put its economic house in order is only part of the problem for a "dependent ally" such as Australia.* The problem is complicated by the change in the U.S.-Japan relationship. Not only is Japan Australia's other major partner, but it is also the major creditor of the United States and the major perceived cause of the latter's current problems in many quarters of U.S. opinion. It is now axiomatic in Australian policy circles that U.S. pressures on Japan to lessen the U.S.-Japan trade imbalance will inevitably be at the expense of third parties, and Australia will be one of those principally affected. Notwithstanding Japanese assertions that its trading decisions will be made on a commercial basis, circumstantial evidence from the coal and beef industries suggests that judgments are being made on the political criteria of accommodating American anxieties. In this way U.S. policy efforts to open Japanese markets are having a direct impact on Australia.†

It has been estimated that the decision of Japanese steel mills to take more U.S. coking coal—as a way of relieving pressure on the import of Japanese steel into the United States—will be exclusively at the expense of Australian coal exports to Japan and will cost Australia approximately U.S.$100 million in lost revenue.** Furthermore, it has been reported that the steel mills had been asked to do this by the Japanese Ministry of International Trade and Industry as a way of diluting the Omnibus Trade Bill—see below (*Australian Financial Review*, 18 August 1987, p. 1). Similarly U.S. policies of price support and import restrictions on sugar are currently estimated to cost Australian producers Aus$200 million per year in lost revenue. Australian exports of sugar to the United States

---

*In her otherwise excellent study of Australian foreign policy, Coral Bell (1988) uses "dependent ally" to connote a politico-strategic dependence. If there is a shortcoming, it is the author's failure to treat the economic dimensions of the relationship seriously. Had she taken more cognizance of these dimensions, her argument about the "dependence" of the ally would have been strengthened.

†Of course restructuring in the Japanese economy (which cannot be discussed here) has direct implications for Australia as well.

**Above and beyond Australia's lost revenue will be any decline in earnings from Japan's success in devising harder price-setting bargains in a tight marketplace.

declined from 800,000 tons in 1981 to 70,000 tons in 1986 as a direct result of U.S. protectionism. Moreover, the United States is expected to become a net sugar exporter in the near future, thus further depressing world prices. The Australian Bureau of Agricultural Economics (Australia, BAE; 1987: 8) has calculated that the world's seven largest sugar importers paid close to U.S.$800 million less for their sugar than they would have on an open market.

In 1987 Australia was forced to agree to a Voluntary Export Restraint (VER) on its beef imports to the United States rather than have a quota imposed. The VER at 327,500 tons may be higher than what would have been the quota (282,000 tons; *Weekend Australian*, 19–20 September 1987, p. 8); however, a VER policy is one of the most insidious forms of nontariff barrier and quite in conflict with the U.S. administration's rhetoric of freer trade. Subsidies of U.S. wheat exports, although in theory aimed at the EC, have a direct impact on Australia. Recent Australian government estimates put the cost to Australia of U.S. wheat subsidies as high as Aus$1 billion in lost export revenue over a twelve-month period to mid-1987 (*Weekend Australian*, 12–13 September 1987, p. 2). The United States's past and anticipated sales of subsidized wheat to the USSR are in direct contradiction of assurances given to Australia that the U.S. Export Enhancement Program (EEP) would not be used to underwrite exports to so-called "Australian markets" (*Australian Financial Review*, October 1987, p. 13). The Soviet Union is one of Australia's top five grain buyers.

That Australia is not the direct target of such U.S. policies is hardly comforting to the smaller ally—especially given the very favorable U.S. balance in its trading relationship with Australia. As indicated in Table 8, the balance has run in favor of the United States throughout the sixty-year period since 1927–28. Furthermore, as the analysis of the 1980s in Table 10 indicates, this balance is in both merchandise and "invisible" trade.

Current U.S. trade policy and its political implications need to be touched on here. Not only does the policy carry obvious bilateral implications (to be discussed in the next section), but it raises broad questions about the role of the United States in the contemporary international economic order. The policy is evidenced by the domestic debate that took place in the latter half of 1987 and the first half of 1988 over the Omnibus Trade Bill. Various provisions of the bill would have been detrimental to Australia's trade. While these were gradually whittled away and the bill even in a watered-down stage ultimately succumbed to presidential veto, the signals conveyed during the debate remain and are pertinent to our discussion here.

The U.S. policy is seen in many quarters as shortsighted in terms of its leadership role in the world. Conducting international trade along the lines of gunboat diplomacy is grist to the mill of those who like to portray the United States as an international bully—especially given its traditional rhetorical role as the champion of free trade. More important, nations suffering or likely to suffer from U.S. bilateral protectionist and subsidy policies are its close—indeed critical—political allies—e.g., Japan, West Germany, as well as Australia—and a broader, long-term damage to relationships is possible. The popular economist Lester Thurow recently pointed out the following: "Protectionism brings into question the shared interests and good will that give military alliances staying power" (1987: 14).

The vetoing of the Omnibus Trade Bill has not prevented a growth in the EEP, nor has it prevented the *administration* (not Congress) from introducing other protectionist and export-enhancing measures. For example, in May 1988 the Department of Agriculture decided to cut the acreage of wheatland left idle from 27.5 percent in 1987 to 10 percent in 1988. Combined with the EEP, an increase in wheat production of the order of 12–15 million tons will undermine other producers for the world market who do not subsidize production (such as Australia and Argentina) rather than subsidized producers in the EC, the ostensible target of such measures.

A lack of U.S. leadership in the economic sphere and the U.S. preference for a protectionist policy to a policy of domestic macroeconomic reform must inevitably have long-term consequences for U.S. politico-strategic ascendancy in the global political arena as well as the economic one. This is especially so in the wake of the October 1987 stock-market crash. In the long term as a result of this crash cuts will need to be made in traditional instruments of political leverage such as defense procurements and foreign aid. In this context military power in a pluralistic democracy such as the United States clearly depends on economic power.

If the October crash exposed many of the flaws in U.S. economic leadership, it also highlighted an important factor in the bilateral economic relationship—i.e., the degree to which Australia is structurally dependent on financial markets in the United States. The crash demonstrated Australia's limited political sovereignty in the midst of a financial crisis which it did not precipitate and for which it could do little but look to Washington (and to a lesser extent Japan) to control. As noted, Australia's currency declined along with the U.S. dollar, its market declined further than any others, and it became apparent that the future of the Australian economy (along with many others of course) will be determined more by policies in Washington than in Canberra.*

This assertion is borne out by Prime Minister Bob Hawke's offering of "unsolicited" advice to President Reagan that reducing the U.S. budget deficit would be the only way to restore confidence to the world's financial markets (*The Australian,* 10 November 1987, p. 8). The prime minister's advice was a manifestation not only of Australian frustration with the immobilism emanating from Washington, but also the frustration of small states dependent on the actions of larger ones. While blame for the current crisis in the international economic order cannot be attributed solely to the policies of the United States, in the absence of positive fiscal and macroeconomic signals from the United States, no immediate resolution of global economic problems is likely.

The overwhelming characteristic of the contemporary economic relationship between the United States and Australia is *asymmetry.* While such relationships with the world's major power are not unusual, Australia's is made more complex by the pivotal role of Japan. Furthermore, the magnitude of the asymmetry is striking: in 1985 the GDPs of the United States, Japan, and Australia were U.S.$3,262, 1,221, and 223 billion respectively. Thus Australia has become a buffeted bystander as its two major partners attempt to resolve their economic differences in an increasingly bilateral fashion. In the next section we shall consider the political consequences of the U.S.-Australian relationship in the latter half of the 1980s.

CLARIFYING THE POLITICS-ECONOMICS NEXUS
IN THE U.S.-AUSTRALIA RELATIONSHIP

As indicated, the bilateral relationship between the United States and Australia is one of the strongest in the world today. The links have

---

*In the longer run the Australian dollar may become less tied to the U.S. dollar—especially if the yen becomes a more important multi-reserve/trading currency. Already 27 percent of Australia's official foreign debt is denominated in yen, compared to over 7 percent in 1978 (see *Australian Financial Review,* 4 November 1987, p. 12; see also an important study by Australia, Department of Trade 1987).

been underwritten in Canberra by the premise that Australia's national interest—defined as the pursuit of national security in a somewhat hostile international system of states in which the United States has been the major strategic actor—is the primary concern of foreign policy. National economic well-being, in a somewhat more benign international economic order similarly bolstered by the United States as the major actor since World War II, was taken largely for granted and treated as a secondary variable.

In the 1980s—especially the last two or three years—there has been a dramatic change in the thinking of Australian policymakers. National economic well-being is no longer a secondary issue, the international economic order is no longer thought of as a benign but hostile environment for a vulnerable actor such as Australia, and the United States is no longer seen as a hegemon driven by a fortunate combination of liberalism and realism which made it both willing and able to underwrite the post–World War II international economic order (see Winham 1986: esp. 15–57). The United States is preoccupied with its own economic as well as political problems, the resolution of which is pursued in the manner of simply another—albeit still powerful—player rather than hegemon.

It is in this context that Australian policymakers must manage a political and economic relationship with its major ally. The late 1980s are therefore a time of learning and adjustment in Australian foreign policymaking. The extent to which the political and economic aspects of the relationship are now run in tandem seems to bear out a central assertion of this chapter—i.e., the ascendancy of the economic dimension to at least parity with the politico-strategic one.

Given the problems of the current administration in Washington, how Australia is affected by U.S. economic policy is unlikely to be high on the agenda of U.S. policymakers. Events during the second term of the Reagan administration have caused Canberra to ask how the United States could so easily disregard the impact of many of its policies on one of its closest allies—for example, the 1985 Farm Bill, the EEP, the Omnibus Trade Bill, its general protectionist thrust, and its tendency to try and resolve difficulties bilaterally rather than multilaterally.

There is no doubt that Australian policymakers have been hurt and are perplexed by U.S. policy. In August 1986, for example, as U.S. relations with New Zealand in ANZUS were ending, Foreign Minister Bill Hayden noted that while the United States was telling New Zealand it was a friend but no longer an ally, it was effectively telling Australia it was "an ally but not a friend." Moreover, the United States proposed cheap wheat sales to the USSR and sugar sales to China when Hayden was in the United States for ANZUS talks—a gesture seen as a poor return for Australian support of the United States. Addressing a World Affairs Council meeting, Hayden noted the following: "Australians have the problem that their economy is threatened with terrible damage at the hands of their best friend." And damaged it has been, as indicated above, and in such a manner that perhaps for the first time the nexus between the economic and politico-strategic relationships has been raised in many quarters—indeed across the spectrum of Australian foreign policy opinion.

This nexus is currently grossly underconceptualized in the literature. As yet no one has managed to combine all the political and economic variables and come out with a coherent response. Opinion ranges from suggestions that the bilateral defense arrangements generally—or the joint facilities specifically—should or could be used as bargaining chips to improve Australia's economic position with its major ally to a belief that the status of these arrangements should be nonviolable in any circumstances. Who adopts what position is not simply a matter of left-right political ideology. Actors across the political spectrum—politicians and their party factions, interest groups, prominent individuals and newspaper editorials—have adopted different stances. The bilateral defense relationship has been on the agenda of informal debate for several years, and there has been general government and opposition agreement—harmful U.S. economic policies notwithstanding—that it not become a political football. However, the issue has kept reemerging in the Hawke administration, each time with more force and emotion. In September 1987 it cropped up in its most strident form to date.

The United States at that time indicated that as a result of chemically tainted beef shipments, it might suspend all Australian beef imports. The newly appointed Australian Minister for Trade Negotiations Michael Duffy responded that Australia might "at some stage" resort to using the joint defense facilities as a lever in Australia's efforts to halt the protectionist U.S. tendencies (*The Australian*, 15 September 1987, p. 3). This represented the most overt escalation of the conflict to date. Prime Minister Hawke had on the previous day indicated that the bilateral relationship did not have "infinite elasticity," and he studiously failed to contradict or even play down his minister's remarks. Eventually the prime minister did reject Mr. Duffy's assertions, although he did not rebuke him. While he stressed that the facilities were sacrosanct, he suggested that other elements (unspecified) of the politico-security relationship should not be taken for granted. Defense Minister Kim Beazley's and Foreign Minister Hayden's departments issued stronger objections to Mr. Duffy's suggestion. The Opposition distanced itself from the notion that any element of the defense relationship was an issue for negotiation (see *Australian Financial Review*, 15 September 1987, p. 3; *Sydney Morning Herald*, 16 September 1987, p. 3; *The Australian*, 16 September 1987, p. 3).

The above demonstrates the uncertainty in Australian policy circles regarding the politico-economic nexus. The uncertainty is reinforced by secondary actors in the foreign policymaking process. Australia's strategic role in the U.S. relationship is criticized not only in the peace movement and on the political left, but also by the most influential pressure groups in the conservative heartland of Australian politics. For example, the National Farmers Federation (especially its then influential president, Ian McLachlan, who is a much talked about contender for a leadership role in the conservative coalition) and the Australian Wool Corporation (AWC) have suggested that Australia's strategic role might be used to secure a fairer trading deal from the United States. Indeed the AWC has specifically suggested that the joint facilities should be used to dissuade the United States form providing subsidized wheat to China and the USSR (*The Age*, 13 October 1987, p. 3). Australia's major newspapers further reinforce the confused state of opinion. The *Australian Financial Review*, *The Age*, and the *Canberra Times* have come down definitely against the linking of strategic and economic issues in the bilateral relationship. Several others have expressed ambiguity, while *The Australian* has for at least two years been the strongest advocate of "upping the ante" on the United States:

Letters of protest to us from the U.S. Embassy have put the view that you cannot mix trade and strategic interests—wrong. We can and should do this (*Weekend Australian*, 12–13 September 1987, p. 18).

The politics-economics nexus can be more practically and less emotionally located. Foreign Minister Hayden has remarked that at a time of perceived Soviet expansion in the Pacific region Australia's ability to support its major ally in the way the United States would wish is undermined by a deterioration in Australia's economic well-being. The prime minister, the foreign and defense ministers, and the minister for trade have on numerous occasions alluded to the direct link between *security* policy and *economic* policy in the Pacific region. Both American subsidy policies and Japanese protectionist policies have a deleterious effect on Australia's economic well-being. Not only do they impede Australia's economic adjustment, but also revenue lost makes it more difficult for Australia to fulfill its alliance commitments. At the current rate of U.S. $1 billion per year, Australia was second only to Saudi Arabia as a weapons procurer from the United States. Its ability to continue buying at the same rate would invariably be affected by its economic health. We do not know specifically what impact sharp rises in protectionism and trade conflict will have in the Pacific. We do know that historically resentment has grown in states that perceive they are not being treated fairly, and this resentment influences broader politico-security issues negatively. There is a recognition that secondary political consequences will follow from poor economic relationships for the region in which Australia plays an important role in the wider U.S. alliance structure.

Policymakers in Washington can feel fairly confident about the tenure of their facilities in Australia over the short term. The Hawke Labor government has been unstinting in its support for the facilities, notwithstanding some loose rhetoric and the questionable utility to the United States of some of the facilities. (For example, Ball 1987 presents a seminal discussion of the technical limitations of the facility at Nurrungar.) However, they should feel less confident about two arguably equally important aspects of the wider alliance structure—Australia's continued poor economic health and Australian public opinion regarding the bilateral relationship.

To the extent that the poor economic health is seen to be a product of neglect (or worse, deliberate treatment) by Australia's major ally, public support for the security relationship in Australia will almost certainly decline. A certain cynicism already exists in Australian "elite opinion" on the support Australia could expect from the United States if its security were threatened (see Matthews and Ravenhill 1987). Circumstantial evidence that cynicism may be mounting is readily available. For one thing, the media have suggested that Australians across the political spectrum are beginning to question the "specialness" of the relationship (*The Age*, editorial, 17 September 1987). Henry Albinski, a long-standing analyst and advocate of the relationship, recently noted the following:

> It would be imprudent to belittle the corrosive effects on Australian opinion of what, in Australian eyes, is viewed as American callousness and even betrayal of fundamental Australian interests (1987: 56).*

*The point has been made by others. See, for example, Dalrymple (1987: A10). Dalrymple was until 1989 the Australian ambassador to Washington.

At issue is not an overnight rupture of the relationship or even the growth of mildly anti-American policy in Australia in the foreseeable future. Rather it is a decline in alliance commitment to the degree that an "automatic acceptance of the American alliance can no longer be taken for granted" (*Australian Financial Review*, 17 September 1987, p. 12). Some consideration should be given, therefore, to how Australia should respond to U.S. policy.

THE ECONOMIC RELATIONSHIP: WHAT IS TO BE DONE?

The economic relationship would appear to have been treated very casually by both sides for a considerable time. Australian policymakers have thought that their needs and wants were better understood in Washington than might have been the case. The close personal relationships between Hawke and former U.S. Secretary of State George Shultz, between Beazley and former U.S. Secretary of Defense Caspar Weinberger, and the rhetorical hostility to the U.S. administration's protectionist urges have been psychologically comforting, but they do not compensate for the costs to Australia of current U.S. policy.* Despite such "entrée," Washington has been unable or unwilling to divert from courses of action harmful to Australian economic interest. Australia's objections to U.S. protectionist policy may be useful ammunition for the U.S. administration in its battle with Congress, but they are no guarantee of success. Australian policymakers realize this. On a visit to Australia in January 1988 by Clayton Yeutter, the U.S. trade representative, for the inaugural Australia-U.S. bilateral trade talks, there was a clear recognition that Yeutter's assurances were considerably at odds with the mood on Capitol Hill. The half-hearted efforts of the Reagan administration to do battle with Congress and the desire of both Republican and Democratic legislators for the United States to "turn up the wick" is well understood in Canberra (Sargent 1988: 3).

In practical recognition of the potential damage that U.S. protectionist legislation could do to Australia, the Hawke government has established a presence in Washington unprecedented in the history of the bilateral relationship. In March 1987 career diplomat John McCarthy was appointed Australia's "ambassador to Capitol Hill," with the unashamed

*Mr. Hayden (who has since become Governor General) would appear to have been too plain speaking for American sensitivities (see *Times on Sunday*, 6 September 1987, p. 13).

role of lobbyist. Particularly, McCarthy's role is to recruit support for the Australian cause from the American defense industry. Similarly, Australia's ministers for trade and agriculture have adopted a high profile declaratory policy on international trade issues in the hope that U.S. policymakers will take note. In addition to the diplomatic initiatives such as the appointment of McCarthy or confidential letters from "Bob" to "Ron," the government has engaged since early 1986 in a very sophisticated exercise in what might be called "transparency education"—that is, demonstrating to Australia's three major partners the manner and degree to which their protectionist policies cost them money and lead to increased rigidity in the international trading system. There is little doubt that Australian government agencies, such as the BAE, produce some of the most technical and sophisticated research on the costs of protectionist measures in the world today (for example, Australia, BAE 1985 and Miller 1986; Miller was secretary of the Department of Primary Industry).

Government policy toward the United States particularly is geared to suggesting that protectionist U.S. agricultural programs risk becoming entrenched like the Common Agricultural Policy of the EC. This point was hammered strongly by Foreign Minister Hayden, Primary Industries Minister John Kerin, and Trade Minister Duffy at the Canberra meetings with trade representative Yeutter. The EC has been able to withstand the pressure of the EEP. This not only reduces the prospects of the EEP being dismantled, but (as Hayden said) it also undermines the international credibility of the United States by allowing the Europeans to argue "We're all sinners together" (*The Australian*, 13 January 1988, p. 3).

It is not simply in the public sector that transparency education is taking place. From a variety of quarters efforts are being made to "educate" Australia's partners to the self-inflicting costs of their policies. For example, in addressing the U.S. Farm Bureau's annual convention, McLachlan outlined the manner in which subsidies had augmented cost structures (*The Australian*, 13 January 1988, p. 3; see also National Farmers Federation 1987).

The Australian trade community in both its public and private sectors has become a fairly sophisticated critic of the faults in the international trade regime. However, its efforts to reform the policies of its partners will be effective only if the changes have a positive impact on the domestic political process in other countries. In the United States, Congressional ears are more finely tuned to domestic constituents than overseas supplicants. Carter administration trade negotiator Harald Malmgram put it as follows on a recent visit to Australia:

Political leaders in countries like Australia are right to complain that they are being squeezed and discriminated against. However, complaining rarely leads anywhere. Politicians who whine simply join a massive chorus of whiners from 100 odd nations.

In Washington nearly all America's trading partners are complaining. Complaints from depressed Kansas farmers or Michigan unemployed are closer than the whining noises of politicians in other nations (1987: 1–2).

Malmgram's comments provide a perspective on Australia's policy approach and its current chances of success. Not only must a country's domestic situation be considered, but also bilateral relations between a major power and a smaller power must always be considered in the context of the major power's relations with other major allies. (For an interesting general discussion, see C. Bell 1987.) For this reason Australia is also emphasizing initiatives in addition to bilateral agreements—particularly multilateral agreements that would give a fairer deal to its exporters. Australian policymakers have at this stage rejected bilateral free trade agreements, such as the one between Canada and the United States.*

For want of a major alternative, as well as out of principled commitment, Australia is one of the staunchest supporters of multilateral approaches to trade problems. Unlike the major economic actors, especially the United States and Japan, it has nothing to gain by attempting to use national economic power at the bilateral level. Consequently it chooses—through organizations such as the Cairns Group of Fourteen Fair Trader Nations—to act as a facilitator and broker, as in the multilateral trade negotiations (MTN) that got under way in Uruguay in 1986. (For a discussion of the current policy position, see Miller n.d.) Australian policymakers have set great store by the Cairns Group and its role in the reform of GATT. The deputy secretary of the Australian Department of Foreign Affairs and Trade noted the following about GATT:

> Despite its shortcomings the GATT is the *only* rule of law applying to world trade . . . which . . . warts and all . . . represents the best available political commitment . . . in an imperfect world (Field 1987).

GATT may not be able to prevent violations of fair trading principles, but it can provide a forum to raise objections and serve as "a mast against

*Although 1989 is seeing growing support from Australia for the concept of a Pacific OECD.

which governments can tie their hands so as to escape siren-like pressure groups" (Cuthbertson 1987: 2). Australian policymakers consider such a forum particularly important for the United States with its many strong and politically active pressure groups—especially the farm lobby. The reinvigoration of GATT and an active commitment to its principles by major actors is a major aim of Australian policy. It is recognized that the success of the current MTN is contingent on the support and coopera- tion of the major actors—especially the United States.

Here lies a dilemma for Australian policymakers. GATT may well be "the only game in town" (Field 1987: 2), but some shrewd observers, such as influential columnist Max Walsh, think it may not be too good a game. The success of the Cairns Group has therefore been something of a bonus. Its member states—and especially Australia, as leader of the group—are aware of the delicate balancing act that it plays as an "offset- ting coalition" attempting to fill (in part) the void created by U.S. abdication of leadership in the international trading system. The U.S. *Journal of Commerce* noted the role of "the Mighty Cairns" in raising the status of agricultural reform on the GATT agenda. The group "succeeded in embarrassing both the European Community and the United States into serious negotiations on farm talks" (quoted in Dawkins 1987: 18).

Despite the differences among its fourteen members, the Cairns Group has held firm (see Higgott 1988). This solidarity is due in no small part to the guidance and expertise of bureaucrats in the Australian Department of Foreign Affairs and Trade experienced in the workings of GATT. More important, however, is probably the tacit support given to Cairns Group initiatives by a U.S. administration cognizant of the impor- tance that agriculture has come to play in offsetting its massive deficits.

Despite its free trade rhetoric the Reagan administration was as protectionist as many, and a lot more protectionist than most other states in the international political economy or other U.S. administrations. In- deed as I. M. Destler notes (1986: 88) in an important analysis of American trade politics, the Reagan administration was as protective of American industry as any administration since Herbert Hoover's. As much as 25–30 percent of American imports are restrained in some way. Consequently recent indignation at Australian objections to growing U.S. protectionist tendencies was somewhat disingenuous.

The U.S. ambassador and agricultural attaché in Canberra gave Australia a dressing down for making the United States the "whipping boy" for low prices on world markets, and Yeutter criticized Australia's failure to acknowledge that the subsidy battle brought to the EC by the

United States will help Australia in the long run. However, these are smoke screens which hide the importance of agriculture to the United States (see *The Australian*, 13 January 1987, p. 1, and 29 May 1987, p. 5).* Throughout the 1980s agricultural trade has played an important role in limiting the overall U.S. deficit. A decline in surplus in agricultural exports from U.S.$26.6 billion in 1981 to U.S.$6 billion in 1986 is thus a major worry (United States 1986: 38). This decline, as much as any longstanding questions of "fairness" in trading, accounts for the United States's favoring the inclusion of agriculture on the agenda of the MTN. U.S. Secretary of Agriculture Richard Lyng and Senator James Exon, leading a U.S. Senate delegation to Australia in 1987, admitted that U.S. subsidies do hurt Australia but are still necessary; these admissions have been received as cold and cynical comfort (*The Australian*, 19 October 1987, p. 2, and 4 January 1988, p. 2).

It is not unfair to say that Australia trusts the United States less than it did. Rather than just listening, it also watches extremely closely what the United States does. Australian policymakers recognize that U.S. aims and priorities are considerably different from theirs. Furthermore, American ability to do what it wants to do is now weaker than it was. At the risk of cliche, it would appear Australia's "great and powerful friend" is no longer as great and powerful and no longer as friendly either.

CONCLUSIONS

Since the abortive Trade Diversion Act of 1936 to the present, economic factors have caused most friction in what has been in most other ways a model relationship between a major power and a minor ally. It is ironic, not a little troubling, and of direct policy relevance, therefore, that the economic aspects of the relationship have until recently been considered secondary. Most disconcerting has been an overall reluctance to treat the *economic* relationship as a *political* phenomenon. The relationship between politics and markets is axiomatically more precarious than efforts to disaggregate them suggests. It is not surprising, therefore, that an analysis which treats the economic variable in the

*This is not to imply that blame lies only with the United States. There is strong evidence to suggest that EC subsidies under the Common Agricultural Policy were the spark for U.S. protectionism in the agricultural domain.

Australian-U.S. relationship as secondary sees the relationship in less conflictual terms.

This is not to suggest that a fracture in the relationship is imminent. Rather the relationship is more complex to manage than has traditionally been thought in Australia. Australian policymakers now recognize that the debate taking place in the United States over a "realist" foreign *economic* policy has implications for an ally such as Australia as significant as those resulting from U.S. politico-strategic thinking (see Nau 1982; Krasner 1985; Silk 1986).

Australia's problems in international economic relations are not chiefly those of bilateral management, however. The major issues are structural. Not only is Australia in the late 1980s constrained in many areas of policy implementation by what transpires in Washington, but since the deregulation of Australia's financial and banking industries and the deregulation of the Australian dollar, it has also become more vulnerable to the influences of Wall Street through the financial markets and stock exchanges (as the events of October 1987 demonstrated). Even in the most optimistic scenarios for the short to medium term—in which Japan and Germany stimulate domestic demand, the United States makes considerable inroads into its budget deficit and overcomes the protectionist urges of Congress, and commodity markets pick up—many of Australia's structural problems will remain. Yet even were the United States to bring its trading account into balance, it would not solve its deficit problems. By the early 1990s the United States is going to require a $60 billion surplus on its trading account to stem the interest repayments on its overseas (largely Japanese) debt (see Westlake 1987: 16). For this to happen it would have to make major inroads into the global market, and this would be at unacceptable cost to other majors, especially Japan and West Germany.

The magnitude of the U.S. economic problems forms the context in which Australia will have to manage the bilateral relationship. If we consider the management of the economic relationship over time in terms of phases of neglect, conflict, and mutual adjustment, then it is in the second phase. In the first phase, during the heyday of the liberal international economic order, policymakers in Canberra felt the economic relationship needed less looking after than the politico-strategic one. In the current phase we are paying for that neglect. The third phase, the working toward a process of mutual adjustment, is in train, but a successful outcome is not inevitable. Given the asymmetry of the relationship, Australia will perforce be the major adjuster.

The United States would understandably wish to conduct its economic relations with minor but not unimportant allies such as Australia in the wider context of multilateral negotiations—such as the current Uruguay Round. Bilateral wrangling on many fronts is tedious for a superpower and leads to friction in its minor relationships. Such energies are better saved for dealing with other majors.

Unfortunately, an irritant for a major power is an all-consuming issue for a minor ally into which other considerations are factored. In this regard the United States is keen to separate security issues—especially with regard to Australia's support role in the Pacific—from economic issues. If *mutual* adjustment is to be achieved, however, this separation will not hold. There is a growing resentment in Canberra at the efforts of the United States to offset its deficits with other major states at the expense of third parties such as Australia. Such grievances are compounded by Australia's overall feeling of impotence in the face of structural vulnerabilities over which it has little control and for which it must wait on the responses of the major actors.

The United States has clearly been too casual about recognizing the extent to which Australia has resented its treatment in the economic domain while at the same time assuming its automatic support on security questions. The message may have now got across to the major partner, but it is difficult to see how short-term adjustment will come about.

America's relations with Australia, as with many of its other allies, are paradoxical in the post–Guam Doctrine period. As a result of hegemonic decline, the United States asks its allies for more support in regional security—in the Pacific, in Australia's case. However, as a result of the multidimensional nature of American hegemonic decline, U.S. international economic policy is making it more difficult for third parties to take on a greater share of alliance burdens. This is quite clearly the case with Australia in the second half of the 1980s. As things stand, the strong structural components of this paradox appear self-reinforcing.

The test of Australia's maturity in international affairs in the Whitlam era was the distance it could show between its policies and those of the United States. The test in the late 1980s may be the way in which Australia manages the relationship with its major ally. Economic problems may not affect the relationship in a permanently detrimental manner. To the extent that they do not, it will almost certainly be because of Australia's ability to adjust to the new circumstances without growing resentment impeding the effective management of that relationship.

The burden of adjustment will inevitably fall to the minor partner. However, U.S. policymakers should heed the words of that *bête noire* of the early 1970s, Gough Whitlam, who in 1973 indicated that it was "better business for the United States to have cooperative partners rather than resentful allies" (*Australian Foreign Affairs Record* 44, July 1973, p. 532).

REFERENCES

Albinski, H. 1981. *The Australian-American Security Relationship.* New York: St. Martin's Press.

———. 1987. *ANZUS: The United States and Pacific Security.* New York: University Press of America for the Asia Society.

Australia, Bureau of Agricultural Economics (BAE). 1985. *Agricultural Policies in the European Community: Their Origins, Nature and Effects on Production and Trade.* Canberra: AGPS. Policy Monograph no. 2.

Australia, Bureau of Statistics (ABS). 1987. *Balance of Payments—Australia 1984–85.* Canberra: Australian Government Publishing Service (AGPS).

———. Various years. *Imports, Australia* and *Exports, Australia.* Canberra: AGPS.

———. Various years. *Official Year Book of Australia.* Canberra: AGPS.

———. Various years. *Overseas Trade.* Canberra: AGPS.

Australia, Commonwealth Bureau of Census and Statistics. Various years. *Official Year Book of the Commonwealth of Australia.* Canberra: AGPS.

———. Various years. *Overseas Trade.* Canberra: AGPS.

Australia, Department of Trade. 1987. *The Liberalisation of Japanese Financial Markets and Internationalisation of the Yen: Progress, Prospects and Some Trade Implications for Australia.* Canberra. Trade Research and Policy Discussion Paper, no. 3.

Ball, Desmond. 1987. *Nurrungar: A Base for Debate.* Sydney: Allen and Unwin.

Barclay, G. St. J. 1987. *Friends in High Places: Australian-American Diplomatic Relations since 1945.* Melbourne: Oxford University Press.

Bell, Coral. 1984. *Dependent Ally: A Study of Australia's Relations with the United States and the United Kingdom since the Fall of Singapore.* Canberra: Canberra Studies in World Affairs, no. 15.

———. 1987. "The Reagan Administration and the American Alliance Structure." *Australian Outlook* 41, 3.

———. 1988. *Dependent Ally: A Study in Australian Foreign Policy.* Melbourne: Oxford University Press.

Bell, Roger. 1977. *Unequal Allies: Australian-American Relations and the Pacific War.* Sydney: Sydney University Press.

Bergsten. C. F. 1981. "The Cost of Reaganomics." *Foreign Policy*, Fall.

Camilleri, Joseph. 1980. *Australian-American Relations: The Web of Dependence.* Melbourne: Macmillan.

———. 1987. *ANZUS: Australia's Predicament in the Nuclear Age.* Melbourne: Macmillan.

Caves, R., and Krause, L. B., eds. 1984. *The Australian Economy: A View from the North.* Sydney: Allen and Unwin.

Cohen, B. J. 1983. "An Explosion in the Kitchen? Economic Relations with Other Advanced Countries." In Oye, Leiber, and Rothchild, eds.

Cuddy, D. L. 1980. "American Business and Private Investment in Australia." *Australian Journal of Politics and History* 26, 1: 45–56.

Cuthbertson, S. 1987. "Shortcomings in GATT: Origins and Corrections." In *Recent Trends in World Trade.*

Dalrymple, Rawdon, 1987. Speech to the Maine World Affairs Council. *Backgrounder*, March.

Dawkins, J. S. 1987. "Foreign Trade Subsidies: The Case for Agricultural Reform." In *Recent Trends in World Trade.*

Destler, I. M. 1986. *American Trade Politics.* Washington: Institute for International Economics.

Drysdale, P. 1984. "Pacific Growth and Economic Interdependence." Perth: Australian Institute of International Affairs. Mimeo (May).

Esthus, Raymond. 1964. *From Enmity to Alliance: U.S.-Australian Relations 1931–1941.* Seattle: University of Washington Press.

Feinberg, R. 1983. "Reaganomics and the Third World." In Oye, Leiber, and Rothchild, eds.

Field, P. 1987. "Without the GATT Round: What Else?" In *Recent Trends in World Trade.*

Gilpin, R. 1987. *The Political Economy of International Relations.* Princeton: Princeton University Press.

Gourevitch, Peter. 1986. *Politics in Hard Times: Comparative Responses to International Economic Crises.* Ithaca: Cornell University Press.

Harper, N. 1986. *A Great and Powerful Friend: A Study of Australian-American Relations, 1900–1975.* St. Lucia: University of Queensland Press.

Higgott, Richard. 1987a. *The World Economic Order and the Trade Crisis: Implications for Australia.* Canberra: Australian Institute of International Affairs.

———. 1987b. "Australia: Economic Crises and the Politics of Regional Adjustment." In *Southeast Asia in the 1980s: The Politics of Economic Crisis*, eds. R. Robison, K. Hewison, and R. Higgott. Sydney: Allen and Unwin.

————. 1988. "Trans-Regional Coalitions and International Regimes: The Cairns Group, Agricultural Trade and the Uruguay Round." *Australian Quarterly* 60, 4 (Summer).

Hofheinz, R., Jr., and Calder, Kent E. 1982. *The East Asia Edge.* New York: Basic Books.

International Monetary Fund (IMF). Various years. *Direction of Trade Statistics Yearbook.* Washington, D.C.

Katzenstein, Peter. 1983. "Small European States in the International Economy: Economic Dependence and Corporatist Politics." In *The Antinomies of Interdependence: National Welfare and the International Division of Labour,* ed. J. Ruggie. New York: Columbia University Press.

————. 1986. *Small States and World Markets: Industrial Policy in Europe.* Ithaca: Cornell University Press.

Krasner, S. 1985. *Structural Conflict: The Third World against Global Liberation.* Los Angeles: University of California Press.

————. 1987. *Asymmetries in Japanese-American Trade: The Case for Specific Reciprocity.* Berkeley: Institute of International Studies. Policy Papers in International Affairs, no. 32.

Krugman, P. R., ed. 1986. *Strategic Trade Policy and the New International Economics.* Cambridge, Mass.: MIT Press.

Linder, S. B. 1986. *The Pacific Century.* Palo Alto, Calif.: Stanford University Press.

Lougheed, A. 1986. *Trends in International Trade and Australia's Performance.* Canberra: Australian Institute of International Affairs. Occasional Paper no. 2.

Malmgram, Harald. 1987. Address to conference on "Successful Strategies for Australian Trade." Sydney, 23 October. Mimeo.

Matthews, Trevor, and Ravenhill, John. 1987. "ANZUS, the American Alliance and External Threats: Australian Elite Attitudes." *Australian Outlook* 41, 1: 10–21.

Miller, Geoffrey. 1986. *The Political Economy of International Agricultural Policy Reform.* Canberra: Department of Primary Industry.

————. N.d. "Fostering Trade in an Hostile International Environment: An Australian Perspective." Canberra: Department of Foreign Affairs and Trade. Mimeo.

National Farmers Federation. 1987. *The Game Plan: Successful Strategies for Australian Trade.* Canberra: Centre for International Economics.

Nau, Henry. 1982. *International Reaganomics: A Domestic Approach to the World Economy.* Washington, D.C.: Center for Strategic and International Studies, Georgetown University. Significant Issues Series, vol. 6, no. 18.

Oye, K.; Leiber, R. J.; and Rothchild, D., eds. 1983. *Eagle Defiant.* Boston: Little, Brown.

Phillips, D. 1988. *Ambivalent Allies: Myth and Reality in the Australian-American Relationship.* Ringwood, Victoria: Penguin.

Recent Trends in World Trade: Implications for Australia. 1987. Sydney: Australian Institute of International Affairs. Fourteenth National Conference.

Rix, Alan. 1986. *Coming to Terms: The Politics of Australia's Trade with Japan 1945–1957*. Sydney: Allen and Unwin.

Sargent, Sarah. 1988. "Trade: Many in U.S. Want to 'Turn up the Wick.'" *Australian Financial Review*, 13 January.

Silk, L. 1986. "The U.S. Economy and the World." *Foreign Affairs* 65, 3: 458–76.

Thurow, Lester C. 1987. "The Economic Black Hole." *Foreign Policy* 67 (Summer).

United States, Department of Agriculture. 1986. *Agricultural Outlook: Yearbook Issue*. Washington, D.C.: Economic Research Service.

Westlake, M. 1987. "What If the Japanese Want Their Money Back?" *South*, September.

Winham, Gilbert. 1986. *International Trade and the Tokyo Round*. Princeton: Princeton University Press.

World Bank. 1984, 1986. *World Development Report*. New York: Oxford University Press.

———. 1985. *Commodity Trade and Price Trends*. Washington, D.C.

Chapter 6

AUSTRALIAN DEFENSE POLICY AND THE ANZUS ALLIANCE

Andrew Mack

FROM "FORWARD DEFENSE" TO SELF-RELIANCE

In 1987 the governments of Australia, New Zealand, and Canada produced Defence White Papers which stressed the need for increased defense self-reliance. Each country is (or was in the case of New Zealand) a Pacific ally of the United States, and the move toward self-reliance was in each case a response to America's relative decline as a hegemonic power—a decline which first became obvious in the Vietnam debacle.

The most important lesson of the Vietnam experience for Australia—although it was by no means clear to all Australians at the time—was that there were military, economic, and (above all) political limits to the use of American power on behalf of threatened U.S. allies. The implications of the Vietnam experience were underlined by the Nixon Doctrine of 1969, which stated that henceforth America's allies would have increasingly to rely on their own resources in regional conflicts. The Nixon Doctrine, the complete withdrawal of Britain (a former hegemon already in a state of advanced decline) from East of Suez, and the withdrawal of U.S. forces from much of the Pacific effected a change in Australian defense thinking. This change began to crystallize in the late 1960s but did not begin to inform defense decision-making in a major way until much later.*

*In 1959 the annual Strategic Basis paper prepared for Cabinet proposed that Australia's defense forces be developed primarily to defend Australian territory without assistance from allies. The paper was rejected by Cabinet (see Beazley 1987b: 6).

The Nixon Doctrine provided an obvious incentive for Australia to move toward defense self-reliance, and this is precisely what has happened. The need for greater defense self-reliance was hinted at in the 1972 Defence White Paper, and it was signaled clearly in the 1976 White Paper. Since 1976 it has been the defense of Australia itself, not the ability to fight wars in distant theaters, which has increasingly been the determinant of Australia's weapons systems procurements, force posture, and strategy. However, Australia's defense stance was not articulated with any strategic coherence until the publication by Paul Dibb (1986) of what has come to be known as the Dibb Review.* The 1987 Defence White Paper was largely based on the Dibb Review recommendations.

The stress on self-reliance represents a radical shift from the policy of "forward defense," which had involved Australia (and New Zealand) in both the Korean and Vietnam Wars. According to a Department of Foreign Affairs report tabled in the Australian Federal Parliament in 1975, forward defense was predicated on the assumption that threats to Australia would come from the north and that those threats should be met in the north. It was better to fight Communists in Korea and Vietnam than on the beaches of Australia. Such a strategy left Australia highly dependent on its "great and powerful friend," the United States. But the 1975 Foreign Affairs report suggested that such dependence was unavoidable: "Given Australia's military weakness, this policy had to depend for success . . . above all on the presence of the United States in the area" (cited in Bell 1984: 101). Forward defense seemed a logical response to the then prevalent belief that Australia and New Zealand were not only threatened by Communist expansionism, but also had no choice but to rely for their defense on a "great and powerful friend." Britain had played such a protector role until the fall of Singapore in 1942; the United States took over from Britain after World War II.

In the 1950s and 1960s there was not only a broad consensus among allied governments about a Communist threat, but an additional rationale for the commitment of Canberra and Wellington to the foreign policy causes of their protector—i.e., good alliance management required the creation of a "bank" of goodwill which could be drawn on in time of need. Shedding Australian blood in distant theaters was considered a form of insurance premium. Australia would fight for America in the

---

*Dibb was a ministerial consultant under Defence Minister Kim Beazley. He is now director of the Joint Intelligence Organisation.

latter's wars overseas and rely on the United States to come to its aid if it were attacked. As indicated above, the relevance of this approach was undermined by the U.S. failure in Vietnam, the consequent erosion in allied confidence in the United States as a reliable ally, and the Nixon Doctrine.

Other changes in the environment of the 1970s also affected Australian and New Zealand strategic perceptions. First, by the latter half of the 1970s the only cross-border wars of any consequence in the Pacific were being fought between Communist states (China-Vietnam and Vietnam-Kampuchea). Thus—notwithstanding concern about a regional Soviet buildup—previous fears of a Communist monolith had all but disappeared. Forward defense was not only less credible, but it also seemed less necessary. Second, a revolution in surveillance technologies and modern precision-guided weapons systems was making self-reliant defense postures for large, relatively empty island states like Australia far more feasible than they had been even a decade earlier. In other words, just when self-reliance was becoming more necessary, it was also becoming more viable.

Given finite resources, it was impossible for Australia to pursue a forward defense strategy and at the same time focus on the defense of continental Australia. During the 1970s and into the 1980s the latter has taken increasing priority over the former. (Much the same has been true of New Zealand, although at a slightly more relaxed pace. Since the ANZUS rupture New Zealand has had no choice but to emphasize defense self-reliance—as stressed in the government's 1987 Defence White Paper. However, with a much smaller GNP than Australia, New Zealand looks increasingly to Australia for defense cooperation.)

The move toward self-reliance in Australia was frequently contentious. For example, there was a heated debate in the late 1970s and early 1980s over whether Australia should acquire a replacement for HMAS *Melbourne*, the Royal Australian Navy's (RAN) aging aircraft carrier, when it was retired. Opponents argued that the only type of carriers Australia could afford were too vulnerable, that maintaining the long-range, blue-water power projection capability which a carrier offered should not be a high defense priority, and that three carriers rather than one would be needed for an effective continental defense strategy. It was claimed that three carriers would be impossibly expensive, and it would be more cost-effective to replace the carrier's most relevant combat roles (chiefly antisubmarine warfare) with other defense assets. Supporters of the carrier argued that, quite apart from defending Australia, a carrier could make an effective contribution to forward defense. The pro-carrier lobby was finally defeated when Labor came to power in 1983 and decided not to replace the *Melbourne.*

Defense self-reliance has involved a physical shift of defense resources to Australia (and New Zealand), a different approach to strategy and weapons systems procurements, and ultimately a different conception of alliance benefits and obligations. In mid-1973 the government of Gough Whitlam, responding as much to its supporters' entrenched distaste for overseas military entanglements as to the promptings of the Nixon Doctrine, withdrew the Australian battalion which was stationed in Singapore. In 1978 the government of Ian Fraser indicated an intention to withdraw Australia's two squadrons of Mirage IIIs from Butterworth Air Force Base in the north of Malaysia.* The departure of the last of the Mirages in mid-1988 will signal the end of an era of permanent major deployments of Australian military forces in the region. Justifying the military withdrawal from Southeast Asia, the 1987 Defence White Paper notes the following:

> Local defence capabilities have increased over recent decades as regional countries meet the objective of ensuring that threats to their own security can be met from their own resources (Australia 1987: 13).

As Australian forces have been withdrawn from Southeast Asia, the government has laid increasing stress on the importance of its Defence Cooperation Program in discussing its security relationship with the Association of South-East Asian Nations (ASEAN). But the scope of the program needs to be judged in context. Australia's contribution to ASEAN's security via the Defence Cooperation Program amounts to around one third of one percent of total ASEAN defense expenditure, or about two thirds of one percent of Australia's Aus$7.4 billion defense budget (1987–88 figures). By way of contrast, *more than 50 percent* of the U.S. defense budget is allocated to the defense of NATO Europe.

The change in the way various Australian regional security cooperation programs are now described by the government in Canberra is symbolic of changes in the security relationships themselves. Thus Australian forces no longer train the armed forces of regional powers—

---

*The first squadron was not withdrawn until August 1983, and the second was still in Malaysia at the end of 1987. The Royal Australian Air Force (RAAF) is replacing its Mirages with FA-18 tactical fighters, However, none of the three FA-18 squadrons will be stationed in Malaysia.

they train *with* them; Australia does not have a military *aid* program for the region—it has a defense *cooperation* program.

WHAT DEFENSE SELF-RELIANCE MEANS FOR AUSTRALIA

Throughout the forward defense era the task of formulating strategic policy had largely been left to the major alliance partner. Australia and New Zealand were noted for the courage and operational capabilities of their armed forces, but not for their contribution to strategic thought. There has never been a distinctive Australian or New Zealand strategic doctrine, and the relative neglect of independent strategic thinking was reflected in the absence of any serious debate about national defense within either country through most of the postwar period.*

The lack of a specifically Australian strategy for the defense of Australia—which was the hallmark of forward defense—created serious imbalances in Australia's force structure as far as the defense of Australia itself was concerned. As Ross Babbage has pointed out,

> During the forward defence era there was little need to develop a balanced Australian defence force. It did not matter much whether Australian forces were committed to forward theatres with insufficient supporting arms and services—artillery, armour, air support and so on—because allied units were almost always available to fill the gap (1984: 164).

Similarly if allied support could be guaranteed, gaps in Australia's own defenses would not matter; allied forces could be relied on to fill them. Defense Minister Kim Beazley has noted the following:

> Because of the emphasis that forward defence places on possessing forces able to intervene in distant parts of Asia, it causes neglect of essential capabilities for our own security (1986: 9).

Once doubts about allied support became apparent, it became imperative for Australia to have an independent force structure.

---

*This has changed somewhat in the last decade and a half, partly as a response to the imperatives of the Guam Doctrine (which called on America's regional allies to play a greater role in providing for their own defense) and partly as a consequence of the creation of the small but highly influential Strategic and Defence Studies Centre at the Australian National University in Canberra.

Beazley and his ministerial consultant Paul Dibb considered that the most critical defense task was the articulation of a coherent defense strategy for Australia which would determine force structure requirements. The strategy which emerged from the Dibb Review (and which was incorporated with only minor substantive changes into the 1987 Defence White Paper—as noted) was the result of the most intensive process of consultation and debate ever undertaken on Australia's defense needs. (It did not, however, call for submissions from the public as did the New Zealand Defence Committee of Enquiry, which reported to the government in July 1986.)

The Beazley/Dibb strategic approach is described in the 1987 Defence White Paper as involving a "layered defense" or "defense in depth." The primary goal of defense in depth is to stop an attacking force in the sea-air gap which separates Australia from the likely invasion embarkation points to the north. Such a strategy would cause an aggressor "to founder on layers of deployed defence assets through and to our North" (Beazley 1986: 14). According to Beazley, such a strategy required the following:

[the development of] an Australian defence force capable of meeting any hostile force within our area of direct military interest with successive layers of forces capable of detecting, identifying and engaging any hostile approach (1987a: 2).

To achieve this goal Australia requires flexible and long-range capabilities for wide-area maritime surveillance, target acquisition, and damage-assessment. These will be provided by an expanded network of over-the-horizon radars, supplemented by an as yet undetermined airborne early warning and command capability. The new surveillance capabilities will for the first time in Australia's history render a major surprise attack impossible and, together with Australia's extremely capable strike forces, will make the task of armed invasion dauntingly difficult for any potential aggressor.

Australia's strike assets are by far the most capable in the region. The new FA-18 fighters (seventy-five will eventually be deployed), the aging but still highly capable F-111 strike aircraft, and the Orion P3-C long-range maritime patrol (LRMP) aircraft can all carry Harpoon missiles. Harpoon, a precision-guided, sea-skimming missile, can be launched against its target from over-the-horizon and can blow a destroyer in half. Some RAN surface combatants and the Oberon class submarines also carry Harpoon missiles. The operating abilities of the FA-18s will be enhanced by the acquisition of in-flight refueling using the RAAF's existing 707 aircraft as tankers, while the F-111s will be up-dated to keep them operational and reduce operating costs.

The 1987 Defence White Paper announced that eight new light patrol frigates would be built; the cost will be about Aus$3.5 billion. The White Paper's determination was significantly different from the Dibb recommendation, which proposed light frigates of some 2,000 metric tons. The RAN argued that bigger ships were needed to give longer un-refueled combat ranges and better sea-keeping capabilities. The White Paper endorsed the idea of bigger frigates, though the cost per vessel will be much greater.

The RAN's still capable Oberon submarines will be replaced in the 1990s by new submarines specifically tailored to Australian requirements and built in Australia. In addition, the RAN is getting a new mine countermeasures force; six fiberglass minehunters are being built to replace the single minehunter now in commission. Two more FFG frigates are being built to add to the four already in commission; these are the most modern of the RAN's total force of twelve surface com-batants. The FFGs will operate Seahawk helicopters, which will also be able to operate off of the new light patrol frigates.

The central defense-in-depth objective of stopping enemy forces as they cross the sea-air gap between Australia and its neighbors to the north has increased the emphasis on maritime surveillance and strike and meant a change in the role of the Australian army. Most important, the army's mechanized capabilities will be downgraded. A great difficulty in using armor in Australia is getting it swiftly to where it is needed; in some areas of the north, surface transportation is almost impossible in the wet season. The army's mobility will be increased with the purchase of new battlefield helicopters. Mobility is particularly important for handling any low-level threats to Australia's north—an empty, inhospitable region with very poor transportation facilities even in the dry season.

Defense self-reliance has involved a redeployment of defense assets not only from overseas to Australia, but also within the country. Under forward defense, when Australian forces were intended to fight in dis-tant theaters rather than on the home front, it mattered little where the home bases of those forces were located, and locating them near major population centers in the south and east made sense economically. But when the key defense task is defending the Australian continent and when potential threats are seen as coming from the north, strategic logic dictates that defense assets be deployed to the north as well.

Both the recommendations of the Dibb Review and the policy decisions announced in the 1987 White Paper reflect this logic. An FA-18 fighter base is being constructed at Tindal (south of Darwin), and "bare bases" (with minimal facilities but capable of handling the FA-18s) have been or will be constructed at Learmouth and Derby in the northwest and on Cape York in the northeast. There are already major air force bases at Darwin and Townsville. The Orion P3-C LRMP aircraft can operate from the northern mainland airbases and from the Cocos and Christmas Islands. The Second Cavalry Regiment is to be relocated to Darwin, with the prospect of locating a full brigade in the north later. Units of the army's reserves with special responsibilities for surveillance will be allocated to the north. The 1987 White Paper announced that half of the navy would be deployed from the east coast to western Australia, which is closer in terms of steaming time to the critical northern approaches than the navy bases in the east.*

CRITICISMS OF THE DIBB REVIEW

The Dibb Review was received initially with widespread approbation; it subsequently became the focus of considerable criticism from sections of the armed forces, some defense corespondents, and the federal opposition. The approach which Dibb recommended—which he had called the "strategy of denial"—was criticized for being too defense-oriented.

Reviewing the debate between Dibb and his critics is beyond the scope of this chapter. However, we may note that those who urged a more offensive strategy for Australia demonstrated considerable insensitivity to the implications of their approachs. For one thing, offensive force postures provide incentives for regional arms races when political relationships are deteriorating. For another, political constraints may inhibit a resort to offensive operations in low-level conflicts. Most important, such critics failed to *demonstrate* (rather than merely assert) the superiority of offensive strategies. This failure is particularly glaring

---

*One disadvantage of this shift of defense assets to the north is that few defense personnel and still fewer of their dependents welcome a move to areas where the climate is inhospitable and the services are far inferior to those in the south and east. This discontent is likely to exacerbate what is already a worrisomely high level of resignations from the services.

given the acquisition by the Australian Defence Force of highly effective wide-area surveillance and targeting capabilities (i.e., over-the-horizon radar, plus—eventually—airborne early-warning and control). Coupled with the highly capable maritime strike assets currently being deployed, these acquisitions will increase the efficacy of defensive strategies.*

Dibb was also accused of being excessively complacent about the threats which Australia might confront. The Dibb Review was caricatured as "isolationist," reflecting a "Maginot line mentality." Opposition spokesman on defense Ian Sinclair claimed the following:

> The Dibb/Beazley strategic notion of "denial" would mean Australia could be facing an aggressor with all the mobility of a boxer with his hand tied behind his back (1986).

Moreover, according to some critics, Dibb had focused far too much on defending Australia and far too little on contributing to the Western alliance as a whole. As Dibb himself had put it,

> We have an obligation to provide for our own defence, and our own defence forces would not be freely available for other situations that the United States might consider as in the general Western interest (1986: 46).

In a speech to the U.S. Council on Foreign Relations in New York in May 1986, Beazley admitted that there were differences in approach between the Reagan administration and the Labor government. He noted the following:

> Australia wants to focus on activities relevant to our national interest while the U.S. wants to encourage us to do more in support of our common interest in deterrence of the USSR (cited in Summers 1986).

Beazley reminded his audience that it was the Nixon Doctrine that had obliged Australia to pursue a policy of self-reliance. On the need for allies to adopt self-reliant defense postures, he has on a number of occasions quoted former U.S. Defense Secretary Caspar Weinberger, who stated at the Canberra Press Club in April 1986 that "Defense of a country's own borders and own airspace and sea around it . . . has to be one of the first priorities of any country" (cited in Baker 1986).

---

*For a more detailed critique of the arguments of Dibb's critics, see Mack (1987).

AUSTRALIAN/U.S. DIVERGENCES IN DEFENSE POLICY OUTLOOKS

In the current international strategic climate, for a number of reasons Australia is most unlikely to make other than token gestures in the direction of increased defense activity in distant theaters. First, Australia's view of the Soviet threat to the region is more sanguine than that of the Reagan administration. The Soviet military buildup is viewed with concern rather than alarm. Australia deems that deterrence has not eroded significantly. Therefore a forward defense role for Australia is not considered as necessary as it was twenty or thirty years ago.

Second, Australia under Labor is concerned that a number of strategic options which the United States is pursuing in the name of enhanced deterrence may threaten crisis stability and undermine global security. The most obvious example is the Strategic Defense Initiative (SDI), which the Labor government believes has potentially destabilizing effects. In 1987 former foreign minister Bill Hayden (1987) warned about potentially destabilizing aspects of the U.S. Maritime Strategy as it applies to the Pacific. Hayden was particularly concerned about the announced U.S. tactic of attacking Soviet missile-firing submarines in their heavily defended bastions in the Seas of Japan and Okhotsk during the early stages of a conventional conflict between the superpowers. This tactic has been widely criticized as one which would risk nuclear escalation. In addition, there have been sharp differences between Australia and the United States on arms control. One long-standing area of disagreement is the U.S. opposition to negotiating a Comprehensive Test Ban Treaty, for which Australia is a major advocate. A more recent disagreement is over the U.S. refusal to sign the relevant protocols of the South Pacific Nuclear Free Zone Treaty.

From both the reasons above we see that Australia and the United States diverge in terms of threat perception and appropriate security policy. But even if they did not diverge in these areas, Australia would still be constrained from pursuing a policy of forward defense. As noted, in the current economic climate Australia simply does not have the resources to pay for its current defense program *and* to pursue the expensive overseas deployments which a 1980s version of forward defense would require. This is particularly true in the context of today's balance-of-payments crisis. However, Australia has not lost the military capability it once had for overseas operations. This capability still exists and is in some senses superior to that of the past. For example, in-flight refueling will give Australian strike aircraft a far greater radius of action than previously, and the new submarines will be among the most capable in the world. Australia's ability to operate its armed forces effectively at great distances from home is demonstrated regularly in multination exercises such as RIMPAC (Rim of the Pacific).

If Australia's relatively benign assessments of the threat environment radically change in the future, the government may then want to reconsider a forward defense strategy with allies. Australian forces could still participate in such a strategy. Currently, however, such a contingency seems highly improbable.

A final point of controversy involves "U.S. bases" in Australia—that is, joint U.S.-Australian defense facilities at Nurrungar, Pine Gap, and North West Cape. Nurrungar in South Australia is the ground station for the Defense Support Program early-warning satellite, which provides the earliest warning of Soviet missile attack. Pine Gap is a CIA-run ground station near Alice Springs in the Northern Territory. The North West Cape facility in Western Australia is primarily a Very Low Frequency (VLF) communications station.

Both Nurrungar and Pine Gap play an important role in monitoring Soviet compliance with various arms control agreements and have a critical role in U.S. nuclear strategy. This role is more than somewhat controversial. The government admits that in a nuclear war there would be a serious risk that the facilities would be attacked, but it argues that their presence reduces the likelihood of such a war. Critics of Nurrungar argue along the following lines:

The nuclear explosion detectors mounted on the early warning satellite provide targeting information for U.S. war planners which they need to pursue current U.S. nuclear warfighting policies. The Australian government is on record as opposing warfighting policies. The same nuclear explosion detectors also help to verify Soviet compliance with the Partial Test Ban Treaty, which banned nuclear tests in the atmosphere.

The facility is involved, directly or indirectly, with the SDI, to which the Australian government is opposed.

The strategic importance of Nurrungar is sufficient to make it a nuclear target in the event of a superpower war. But there is no reason for the ground station to be in Australia—it could equally well be on the U.S. island of Guam.

The facility's benign arms control role will shortly be taken over by a navigational satellite system popularly known as NAVSTAR; NAVSTAR satellites do not require ground stations in Australia.

The development of a satellite-to-satellite crosslink will soon enable the three U.S. early warning satellites to communicate with each other. This means that the satellite data on Soviet missile launches can in future be routed directly to the United States—thus bypassing Nurrungar.

Pine Gap collects and processes signals intelligence (SIGINT) data. The data are collected by "spy" satellites in geostationary orbit which look down over the Soviet Union and detect electronic emissions emanating (primarily) from the Soviet Union and China. The data are useful for a number of purposes, including the verification of arms control agreements. For the United States they are most important as sources of military intelligence. Critics of Pine Gap have charged the following:

The station is a "spy base" which spies on America's allies (including Australia) as well as on the USSR.

The arms control verification role of the facility—in particular its role in monitoring Soviet missile tests—has decreased in importance dramatically because the Soviets have (a) reduced the power of the telemetric transmissions from their test missiles, (b) increased the degree of encryption of telemetry, and (c) attempted to jam the listening U.S. satellites. All of this has made the verification task far more difficult.

The government has said almost nothing about the role of Pine Gap because its operations are so sensitive, but the critics' case is open to challenge on a number of grounds. First, it is most unlikely that the Pine Gap satellites would be used to spy on Australia. The satellites can cover only a relatively small area when listening on very high frequencies, and there are far more important target areas than Australia to monitor. Moreover, Australian government personnel working on the facility would be able to detect any attempt to spy on Australia. Also, there are other, cheaper ways of clandestinely monitoring Australian radio traffic.

Second, critics have failed to show that collecting military data on the USSR is undesirable. In the past, when such information was not available, "worst case" assumptions about the Soviet threat prevailed— hence the quite false predictions of the late 1950s and early 1960s about "bomber gaps" and "missile gaps."

Third, while it is probably true that Pine Gap is playing a less important role in arms control verification now than in the mid-1970s, it cannot be assumed that the Soviets will continue indefinitely to obstruct U.S. efforts to monitor Soviet missile test telemetry. It is important to point out that for any major strategic arms control agreement to be signed there must be satisfactory verification procedures. Pine Gap's role in such procedures is both indispensable and insubstitutable. Moreover, unlike Nurrungar, the Pine Gap facilities cannot be moved elsewhere.

North West Cape is the least important U.S. facility today. Once one of the two most important VLF communications stations in the world for U.S. submarines, North West Cape's strategic importance has been downgraded over the past decade. The station no longer communicates with U.S. missile submarines in the Pacific at all (because the new Trident submarines are now deployed off the western seaboard of the continental United States). Nor does it play a critical role in communicating with U.S. hunter-killer submarines. The North West Cape's most important VLF function today is communicating with Australian submarines. North West Cape is also a relay station for high frequency and satellite communications.

The government of Bob Hawke believes that in hosting the controversial U.S. facilities it is making a more important contribution to global deterrence than it would by returning to a policy of forward defense. Dibb noted that hosting the facilities (together with permitting U.S. warship visits and B-52 training missions) "is a *sufficient* tangible contribution to the [ANZUS] Alliance from the perspective of both parties" (1986: 47; emphasis added).

DEFENSE POLICY SHIFTS, THE DIBB REVIEW, AND THE 1987 DEFENCE WHITE PAPER: EFFECTS ON THE ANZUS ALLIANCE

The shift toward defense self-reliance, the perception that the United States is less able to help its allies than it was thirty or forty years ago, and the now fairly stable perception that Australia's strategic environment is relatively benign have changed the way many Australians feel about ANZUS. Thirty years ago, when Australia believed it was threatened and defenseless and critically needed the physical support of the United States for its security, Australian governments were concerned to do nothing which might upset the alliance relationship. Today the argument for the ANZUS alliance is very different and is no longer based on an expectation that direct U.S. military assistance would necessarily be forthcoming should Australia be involved in a regional conflict. In short, the government does not think Australia can (or should) rely on U.S. combat support in any such conflict, nor does it believe that it needs that support. As Beazley has noted, "It would be irresponsible to depend on direct American combat support for our security" (1987a: 9). Moreover, in the 1950s the United States had no vital security interest in Australia, but in the past thirty years the U.S.-Australia relationship has changed dramatically. The United States now needs Australia—as host to the vital U.S. defense facilities—more than an increasingly confident and self-reliant Australia needs the United States.

In the late 1980s Labor's support for ANZUS is based on pragmatic and unsentimental considerations. There is growing confidence in Australia's ability to defend itself. The key alliance benefits for Australia are considered to be access to state-of-the-art U.S. military technology (including resupply in time of war) and to high-level intelligence. Moreover, it is true, as Beazley has frequently pointed out, that the very existence of the alliance relationship may act as a deterrent to aggression. Australia might not be certain that the United States would come to its aid if it were attacked, but a potential aggressor cannot be certain that the United States would *not*. This uncertainty contributes a deterrent effect which would be absent if there were no alliance.

Notwithstanding the changes in the U.S.-Australia relationship, Australian governments—particularly Labor governments—will still feel constrained from challenging the United States on alliance issues because most Australians continue to believe their country is essentially defenseless and must therefore rely on the United States for its security. They would consider such challenges as challenges to the alliance itself, and the opposition parties would certainly so present them. Since the alliance has massive popular support, Labor will continue to feel it politically necessary to be circumspect. It is in this context that the differences between the Dibb Review and the 1987 Defence White Paper should be understood.

A number of commentators seem to believe that the 1987 Defence White Paper differs fundamentally from the Dibb Review. Thus Peter Samuel (1987) claims that the White Paper "rejects most of the isolationist proposals of an earlier advisory report." In fact, the differences in substance between the Dibb Review and the White Paper are minimal. Nearly all of the former's force acquisition and deployment recommendations are endorsed by the latter. This should not be surprising. Beazley chose Dibb to undertake the review not simply because Dibb was a highly competent, experienced, and respected strategic analyst, but also because his strategic outlook was similar to Beazley's own. Moreover, Dibb himself authored much of the White Paper.

The differences between the Dibb Review and the White Paper arise in part because the latter is broader in scope than the former. Dibb was asked to report on the content, priorities, and rationale of defense forward planning and the capabilities appropriate for Australia's present and future defense requirements. He was not asked to report on the ramifications of alliance relationships or the Soviet buildup in the North Pacific or the potential for instability in the South Pacific. Some of Dibb's critics took him to task for failing to discuss issues on which he had no mandate to report.

The major difference between the Dibb Review and the White Paper is rhetorical: it lies in changes in language and emphasis. Apart from the increase in the size of the light patrol frigates noted above, there are no significant changes in force structure recommendations or in overall strategy. Indeed there is no difference between Dibb's strategy of denial, to which the critics objected, and the White Paper's strategy of defense in depth, which they applauded. However, much of the language and emphasis which critics found objectionable in the Dibb Review—a stress on defensiveness, for example—does not appear in the White Paper. In its place considerable emphasis is placed on Australia's long-range strike, interdiction, and offensive capabilities. Dibb acknowledged but did not stress the offensive capabilities and the possible need to use them in high-level conflicts; the White Paper stresses both offensive capabilities and tactics.

As should be clear, the impact of these largely rhetorical changes on the critics was remarkable. Addressing the National Press Club shortly after the White Paper was published, Beazley announced that it had been welcomed across the political spectrum, from the hawkish Australian Defence Association to the dovish Democrats. In addition, the White Paper received the seal of approval from the United States when Weinberger announced the following:

> Defence self-reliance . . . based on broad concepts of strategic responsibility and regional commitment, constitutes a strong foundation for the defence of Australia and for Australia's execution of alliance responsibilities (cited in Buckley 1987).

With the publication of the White Paper, Beazley achieved a major political victory. He kept the major recommendations of the Dibb Review intact while at the same time completely disarming his critics.

There is no doubt that Beazley has won the intellectual and political battles over the future direction of Australia's defense policy. The major difficulty he confronts is to get the necessary funding in a period of extraordinary fiscal stringency. The May 1987 mini-budget slashed the defense budget by one percent in real terms for 1987–88. However, Beazley is optimistic that the major capital expenditure programs—e.g., the light patrol frigates and submarines—will not be cut back, though their implementation may well be delayed. Nonetheless, funding constraints make it difficult to deal adequately with growing dissatisfaction among service personnel over pay and conditions; as indicated, such dissatisfaction is leading to unacceptably high levels of resignation.

CONCLUSION

The past two decades have witnessed an extraordinary change in official Australian thinking about security. As argued above, the move toward defense self-reliance was a response in part to changing external circumstances and in part to a growing realization that technology could compensate for a lack of forces and make Australia's geography a defense asset rather than a liability.

Some Australians favor radically different defense alternatives, such as nonalignment and/or armed neutrality. The level of popular support for such options is small because—unlike the government—most Australians do not believe that their country can be defended without the aid of a "great and powerful friend." Just after the Dibb Review was published, a public opinion poll showed that no less than 68 percent of the population believed Australia's defenses were inadequate to defend the national interest and 40 percent believed that Australia would face a military threat within the next ten years (Young 1986).*

From the U.S. point of view Australia's move toward defense self-reliance is not unproblematic. On the one hand, the policy is very much in line with U.S. concern that its allies take a greater responsibility for their own defense and rely less on the United States. On the other hand,

*For a complete review of public opinion on security issues from World War II to 1985, see Campbell (1986). For a detailed argument as to why Australia is unlikely to follow New Zealand's example, see Mack (1986).

Australia cannot make the sort of material commitment to U.S. global strategic policy that it made in the past (and which many in the United States would wish it to make again today). The United States confronts the classic dilemma of a hegemonic power in relative decline. It needs to persuade its allies to share the burden of common defense but when they do, the alliance becomes more a relationship between equals, and the former hegemon's leadership role is undermined. The United States needs its allies more than it did thirty years ago, but it is able to influence them less. The implications of this change are increasingly understood by the Australian government but are as yet barely comprehended by the Australian public.

REFERENCES

Australia, Department of Defence. 1987. *The Defence of Australia*. Canberra: Australian Government Printing Service.

Babbage, Ross. 1984. "Australian Defence Planning, Force Structure and Equipment: The American Effect." *Australian Outlook* 38, 3 (December).

Baker, Mark. 1986. "Meet the 'Doctrine of Self-Reliance.'" *The Age*, 4 June.

Beazley, Kim C. 1986. "Australia's Defence Policies: Present and Future." Paper presented to seminar on Reviewing Australia's Defence Needs, Australian National University, Canberra, 18 October.

———. 1987a. "Defence Policy Information Paper. "Canberra: Office of the Minister of Defence, 19 March.

———. 1987b. "Thinking Defence: Key Concepts in Australian Defence Planning." Roy Milne Memorial Lecture, 6 November.

Bell, Coral. 1984. *Dependent Ally*. Canberra: Australian National University, Department of International Relations. Canberra Studies in World Affairs no. 15.

Buckley, Amanda. 1987. "Critics Fail to Stop Switch to New Strategy." *Australian Financial Review*, 13 October.

Campbell, David. 1986. *Australian Public Opinion on Security Issues*. Canberra: Australian National University, Peace Research Centre. Working Paper No. 1 (April).

Dibb, Paul. 1986. *Review of Australia's Defence Capabilities*. Canberra: Australian Government Publishing Service.

Hayden, Bill. 1987. "Security and Arms Control in the North Pacific." Paper presented at conference on Security and Arms Control in the North Pacific, Australian National University, Canberra (August).

Mack, Andrew. 1986. "Crisis in the 'Other Alliance': ANZUS in the 1980s." *World Policy Journal*, April.

———. 1987. "Offence Versus Defence: The Dibb Report and Its Critics." *Australian Outlook* 41, 1 (April).

Samuel, Peter. 1987. "Australian Turnaround: Out with Isolationism." *Wall Street Journal*, 6 April.

Sinclair, Ian. 1986. Media release, Canberra, 1 June.

Summers, Anne. 1986. "Defence White Paper Will Lock Govt. into the Dibb Revolution." *Australian Financial Review*, 27 May.

Young, Peter. 1986. "Majority Believe Our Defences Inadequate." *Australian*, 6 June.

Chapter 7

AMERICAN PERSPECTIVES AND POLICY OPTIONS ON ANZUS

Henry S. Albinski

The detailed circumstances that led to the reshaping of the ANZUS alliance have been covered by other contributors to this volume; so only the essentials need to be recounted here. The New Zealand Labour Party, led by David Langeange, David, entered office in July 1984 committed to a nuclear-free New Zealand. A key provision of that program was the denial of entry into the country of nuclear-powered vessels (NPVs) and nuclear-armed vessels and aircraft. The declaratory policy that the government followed was enshrined in legislation in 1987, shortly before Labour's reelection to a second term. Taking umbrage at Labour's policy, the United States unilaterally suspended its ANZUS-based security obligations toward New Zealand and withdrew nearly all intelligence-sharing, military cooperation, and defense consultations with it. While American links with Australia have remained intact, New Zealand's "chair" in ANZUS has been declared indefinitely vacant, and New Zealand's status and political access in Washington have been reduced from "ally" to ordinary "friend."

The analysis in this chapter, cast in a U.S. perspective, undertakes to fit these developments into wider context. We will examine the place of ANZUS collectively and of New Zealand and Australia individually against the setting of American security assumptions and objectives. We will weigh the consequences flowing from the alliance discord and how they impact on U.S. relations with the two partners, as well as on other nations and regions. We will consider the implications of various options available to the United States under changed alliance circumstances. In sum, the dominant themes will focus on "Why worry?" and "What is to be done?"

THE WIDER FRAMEWORK: AMERICAN SECURITY ASSUMPTIONS
AND OBJECTIVES IN THE PACIFIC

American perceptions of ANZUS and its members inevitably relate to strategic conceptions that reach well beyond the confines of the Southwest Pacific. From its vantage point as a superpower, the United States focuses on the transregional linkages that inform the global scene. It consistently calculates the aspirations, behavior, and influence of the Soviet Union and its cohorts and of those who (like Iran and Libya), while not attached to the Soviet Union, can hinder the West's capacity to advance order and stability.

The Asia-Pacific region offers some special challenges for American security interests. The region has produced some of the fastest growing economies anywhere. It is America's foremost trading partner, with Japan as the keystone. Yet while Europe has remained reasonably stable since the close of World War II, the Asia-Pacific region has been torn by conflict: wars in Korea and Vietnam; Sino-Soviet, Sino-Vietnamese (and other) intraregional rivalries; and Communist insurgencies and other forms of civil strife. The postwar decolonization process has often been violent. With respect to New Caledonia, the process of decolonization remains incomplete and contentious.

The Pacific basin is an immense maritime environment, with the United States geographically on one side and the Asian land mass and its extensions on the other. American efforts to achieve desired outcomes are therefore conducted at great range and necessarily by complex and politically and materially expensive means. American security concerns have been aggravated by steadily improving Soviet military assets, based in or projected from Soviet territory and more recently from Vietnamese bases. Moreover, in a number of countries, including some of America's friends and allies, the Reagan administration was perceived as alarmist about Soviet ambitions, too reliant on military responses to many-sided problems, and (through most of its tenure) unenthusiastic about serious arms control. These impressions have been coupled with a generally receding sense of an impending Soviet military threat, favorable evaluations of Soviet reasonableness in the search for accommodation under General Secretary Mikhail Gorbachev, and—specifically—a more subtle Soviet approach to Pacific basin nations. As the U.S.–New Zealand dispute festered, in 1986 the Soviets tried to capitalize, predicting a chain reaction for New Zealand's antinuclear choice and censure of the United States for its bullying of a small yet principled country. Gorbachev outlined a broad Soviet plan for tension-reduction and gradual denuclearization in the Pacific, in which (among other things) he championed nuclear-free regional zones. The Soviets made conciliatory gestures toward a number of Asian-Pacific states. They began to establish a commercial foothold in the South Pacific, where their political and economic presence and reception had been minimal and the writ of the ANZUS powers had de facto occupied pride of place.

In the South Pacific the United States has pursued and continues to pursue interlocked security strategies. One is to uphold the economic viability and political stability of the region, as well as to foster regional friendships. A second is to ensure the integrity of the extended and often convoluted lines of communication and transport across the Pacific and into the Indian Ocean. A third is to warn antagonists and reassure friendly regional nations that the United States is sound and reliable, able and willing to fulfill defense obligations and offer strategic cover for deterrence—and if required for riposte—in a manner that will not confuse strength with provocation.

The United States is keenly mindful that its influence is finite. It is also aware that many tasks relative to the above objectives can be more effectively implemented in tandem with other nations, or indeed that others are by reason of their location, reputation, or mix of resources much better able to make complementary contributions. Friends and allies are in this sense indispensable—for their neighborhood, as well as for supporting America's version of regional and transregional strategic interests. Nations in formal alliance or other security arrangements might in principle be construed as among the most compatible and helpful associates (not of course to the exclusion of others) and among the best role models for onlookers.

It is in the perspective of the indispensability of friends and allies that we examine ANZUS, in particular the real or perceived degradation of American security interests following the recent turmoil within the alliance. We will search first for any costs that have been incurred within the alliance and vis-à-vis its New Zealand and Australian members. We will then consider extra-alliance costs and consequences for the United States.

INTRA-ANZUS CONSEQUENCES OF ALLIANCE STRAIN

Though not impervious to differences among its signatories, ANZUS came to stand as virtually a paragon among alliances. Its original tripartite membership never varied. The economic ties and cultural, linguistic, political, and in many respects geostrategic values of the three partners contributed to a commonality of purpose, as well as camaraderie, even intimacy. Without any changes in its printed language the alliance proved flexible in shifting its attention to originally unanticipated sectors of interest in the Pacific basin and—especially after the Soviet occupation of Afghanistan—to the eastern littoral of the Indian Ocean, which abuts on the western Australian coastline. The alliance also was beneficial for the United States because Australia and New Zealand were not mendicants and demanded no handouts. They were donors of civil and defense aid to others and paid out of pocket for their American military equipment. Moreover, their insular and relatively remote geographic position meant that unlike other U.S. allies (such as Japan, Korea, Thailand, or NATO's European members), they were not exposed to potential international conflict flashpoints and thereby did not impose onerous burdens on American diplomatic currency or security resources.

It is nevertheless arguable that whatever the recent stresses within ANZUS mean beyond the relationship among the three signatories, the intramural, corporate alliance effects on American security interests are marginal. Unlike NATO or the erstwhile SEATO, ANZUS did not evolve a secretariat. Unlike NATO, it did not evolve standing forces. Hence the breakup of ANZUS did not impinge on the viability of any major institutionalized administrative or military arrangements. The ANZUS council of foreign ministers or their deputies is no longer convened, replaced now by bilateral U.S.-Australian ministerial consultations. Moreover (as will be discussed), this does not preclude regular Australian–New Zealand consultations, or even American consultations with New Zealand as far as Washington wishes to carry them; the same applies to various forms of defense cooperation. The essential point is that a great deal of the defense-related cooperation that emerged within the ANZUS compass was *bilateral*, not bound to trilateralism, even if the three partners de facto frequently harmonized their efforts. For example, in New Zealand, Labour's predecessor government, the National Party, explicitly denied that New Zealand's contribution to combined exercises in the Indian Ocean was a collective ANZUS endeavor. Instead it was pictured as a convenient way for New Zealand to enhance its capabilities in a region where its own extended lines of communication ran.

Perhaps a distinction between combined exercises and ANZUS exercises is more semantic than substantive, but there are more substantial examples of informal cooperation inspired by the formal alliance. The

Australian and New Zealand combat participation in the Vietnam conflict was not formally mounted under ANZUS aegis. It reflected not only Canberra's and Wellington's rationales to defend against a regional threat, but also their wish to sustain the will and repute of a valued great power ally who otherwise would have stood nearly alone; thereby they wished to store up good will for themselves in Washington from which they might collect on issues especially pressing for them. While their participation was not a direct obligation of the alliance, it was no less welcomed by the United States.

Has the distortion of ANZUS precluded such informal alliancemanship undertakings in the future? In the first place, another conflict in the Pacific on the scale of Vietnam is not foreseeable. In part because of its traumatic experience in Vietnam, the United States is unlikely to involve itself in something similar. In the second place, New Zealand and Australian policies have changed. New Zealand (the nuclear aspects of its differences with the United States aside) is strongly opposed to such a forward defense venture just to support the United States or to take out insurance for itself in Washington.* Such motives have dissipated with Vietnam. New Zealand had been less enthusiastic than Australia about pitching in with the United States even when ANZUS was originally framed. Even before Labour came to office in 1984, New Zealand was leaning toward a more circumscribed, South Pacific–oriented defense focus. While the Lange government announced that the New Zealand battalion would be withdrawn from its forward position in Singapore, the move had been presaged long before, under the National Party. Arguably though perhaps less definitively, traditional Australian motives for forward defense also expired with Vietnam. A Defence White Paper issued in 1987 by the government of Bob Hawke, while not altogether eschewing some capacity for force projection, is a prescription mostly for the defense of Australia and its immediate strategic environment, not a doctrine supportive of sustained, remote operations with a major ally. Its tenets had de facto been evolving for some time.

In sum, Vietnam was a watershed for both New Zealand and Australia, though the full implications were not immediately apparent. The legacy of Vietnam did not emasculate tripartite cooperation under ANZUS, but it curtailed and possibly ended a commitment to forward defense—essentially meaning combat deployments to bolster far-flung American strategic objectives. In the future, should Australia elect to

*For a discussion of forward defense, see the contribution by Andrew Mack.

operate with the United States in a regional conflict, it will not need to invoke ANZUS to justify or cloak its actions. Its decision under such a scenario, while complementary to American objectives, would be independently reached, regardless of whether there was a functioning tripartite ANZUS.

While the ANZUS dispute matters little to alliance performance, it may result in probative losses to U.S. security objectives from New Zealand or Australia. Because of Washington's unwillingness to break or bend its no confirmation/no disconfirmation (NC/ND) rule on nuclear armaments aboard its ships, the U.S. Navy no longer enters New Zealand ports. This carries very little direct significance for American security interests. U.S. ship visits in the past had been infrequent and sporadic, mostly for good will, crew rest and recreation, and refueling and replenishment; they were usually in conjunction with exercises carried out with New Zealand (and Australia). The new situation has meant some loss of American tactical experience, especially in light of the high level of performance usually displayed by the New Zealanders. The United States continues to benefit from training and exercising with the much larger and more elaborately equipped Australian forces.

During the tenure of the ANZUS alliance the United States never possessed military communication, tracking, stores, or basing facilities in New Zealand. Therefore nothing of this sort has been jeopardized. Moreover, hypothetically New Zealand's ban on NPVs and nuclear-armed ships and aircraft does not preclude combined exercises with such units outside the country's territorial waters or airspace. The government has allowed a blanket waiver of its policy respecting military transport flights servicing an American civil Antarctic operation in Christchurch. In addition, by the Labour government's own choice, certain privileges continue to be available to the United States. Although nearly all American intelligence is now denied to New Zealand, New Zealand intelligence continues to be available to the United States, including data on Soviet ship movements in the Pacific monitored by New Zealand's own installation.

New Zealand's willingness and capacity to perform tasks congruent with American security interests—again quite apart from how it now defines its ANZUS responsibilities—is of issue as well. The South Pacific is a region of increasing political volatility and Soviet attention. The United States has to date been militarily paramount in the region. With friends such as Australia and New Zealand, it has been able to sustain a doctrine of strategic denial vis-à-vis the Soviets. While ANZUS efforts may no longer be upholding Western interests in the South Pacific, in important respects current New Zealand and Australian contributions have not diminished. With added determination, New Zealand has focused its diplomatic and defense attention on its natural, South Pacific neighborhood. Its access and influence in the region cannot be matched by the nonresident American superpower. Its representation in the region is widespread and of high caliber—for example, it is a member in the region's premier body, the South Pacific Forum (SPF), from which the United States is absent—and its political intelligence is arguably more sophisticated than anyone else's. New Zealand remains anxious about Soviet and Libyan (among other) interpositions and shares these concerns with other island country governments. The bulk of its foreign aid effort is concentrated in the South Pacific, where small but well-conceived assistance goes a long way. The Lange government plans to double foreign aid as a proportion of GNP between 1985–86 and 1990–91. New Zealand's defense cooperation programs among the island countries are likewise carefully crafted and well received.

Washington's suspension of defense links has harmed New Zealand's capabilities. Adverse domestic reactions to New Zealand's position in the ANZUS dispute have caused resignations among key service personnel. Loss of American intelligence has hurt. The suspension has affected the ability of a total standing force of only 13,000 to hone its skills by training and exercising with Americans and receiving preferential logistical support. New Zealand is compensating for some of these losses through intensified defense cooperation with Australia (though Australia has promised not to transmit its American-sourced intelligence). The overall New Zealand defense effort, though representing only about 2 percent of GNP, is not being allowed to slip. The Lange government has undertaken a modernization of existing equipment and has projected the acquisition of more capable naval assets. The ANZUS imbroglio has spurred New Zealand to raise and diversify its patrol and readiness efforts within the South Pacific. Any foreseeable commotions in the island community could be handled with minimal and conventional Western assets, by New Zealand or Australia acting alone or jointly.

Australia is the centerpiece American ally in the region. Its value to the United States in terms of defense has always been far greater than New Zealand's. The elaborate U.S.-Australian network of political and military interchanges remains unimpaired by what has happened to ANZUS and by Washington's ostracism of New Zealand. These relationships continue to enhance the capabilities of both nations. Hence while

Australia understandably gains much from its access to American intelligence, the Australian Defence Signals Directorate's regional intercept and cipher capabilities are an exceptional asset to the United States and to the National Security Agency particularly. The Australian defense forces—numbering 70,000, highly trained, and well equipped—are impressive in their regional setting and useful for potential operations in coordination with American forces in sealane protection and other roles. Despite financial austerities, Australia is proceeding with major equipment enhancement programs that include F-18 fighter bombers, Black Hawk helicopters, a new generation of conventionally powered attack submarines, mine countermeasure vessels, and lift capabilities.

Australia's location, size, and resources allow it to be considerably more ambitious than New Zealand in sustaining diplomatic, aid, and defense coverage in the Indian Ocean, Southeast Asia, and North Asia. Its material resources enable it to underwrite nearly 30 percent of the recurrent budgetary outlays of Papua New Guinea, by far the largest nation in the South Pacific and the geostrategic link between that region and Southeast Asia. Australia's outlays for Papua New Guinea are larger than all of New Zealand's civil aid expenditures combined. Australia's traditional access has enabled it to represent its American ally in mainland Southeast Asia, notably through its participation in the Five Power Defense Agreement. It retains a key role in the Integrated Air Defense System centered on the Malaysian base at Butterworth. Australian P-3s stage out of Butterworth for reconnaissance flights in the Indian Ocean's northeast quadrant and the South China Sea, supplementing regional patrol coverage deployed from Australia.

The Australian Labor Party government's disagreement with the Lange government's policies, as well as Australia's constancy on American ship visits, joint facilities, and a host of other arrangements, has been immensely gratifying to Washington. Australia does not deny access to NPVs and does not enquire into the armament of visiting ships. Most U.S. navy ships put into ports in Western Australia, which is most accessible to the strategic choke points that connect the Pacific and Indian Oceans and where the Australian government is in process of basing fully half of its naval assets, but American ship visits are made to every Australian state and to Darwin in the Northern Territory. In 1986 American units visiting Australian ports included a nuclear-powered attack submarine, the nuclear-powered carrier *Carl Vinson*, and the battleship *Missouri*. The U.S. Air Force enjoys transit rights through Darwin for B-52 training and navigational flights. It has access to Australia's

Cocos Islands (in the Indian Ocean) for deployments that include passage to and from Diego Garcia. The joint naval communication station at Exmouth Gulf, Western Australia, is part of a global communication network. Australia and the United States jointly operate critical satellite tracking and data transmission facilities in central Australia; the sites are ideal for their geography, terrain, and isolation and benefit from the political hospitality extended by the host government.

What the United States has done, or should and can do, to preserve the numerous advantages of its relationship with Australia has a close bearing on what has happened in New Zealand. At bottom, American interests dictate that Australia not emulate New Zealand and that Washington not be faced with wrenching decisions should Australia begin to drift. Before we discuss the U.S.-Australia relationship in depth, we need to examine American perceptions of alliance strain beyond the ANZUS perimeter, considering appropriate responses for American security interests and the problems associated with them.

EXTRA-ANZUS CONSEQUENCES OF ALLIANCE STRAIN

Above we emphasized the interlocking, transregional nature of America's strategic reasoning and touched on its appreciation of ANZUS alliance developments in relation to other security arrangements and alliances. Hence Washington's rebuttals to New Zealand's underlying logic as well as its policy measures have been directed as much to outsiders as they have been to New Zealand itself.

The Lange government argued that it did not wish to remove New Zealand from ANZUS and the various defense relationships that had evolved with the United States. It in fact stood ready to upgrade its conventional force capabilities. It insisted only on the exclusion of any nuclear presence from its territory. It claimed that nothing in the ANZUS treaty mandated New Zealand to host NPVs or nuclear-armed vessels and that, moreover, the alliance had only gradually (not at time of founding) acquired nuclear characteristics. It further pointed to New Zealand's unique position in the Pacific, far removed from conceivable Pacific basin sites where American naval or air combat operations could be foreseen. Since U.S. ship visits in the past had been sporadic and mainly intended for nonoperational purposes, there would be no visible diminution of America's operational capabilities or of its governing security interests even if no U.S. ships were to call at New Zealand ports.

In effect, Labour contended that the alliance and Western and U.S. strategic aims would be unaffected. As a kind of tradeoff for denying entry to American NPVs and nuclear-armed vessels, New Zealand did not expect to be sheltered under an American nuclear canopy. It saw itself as uncommonly unsusceptible to direct threat and did not wish to be part of an international strategic system which would needlessly expose its territory to interdiction.

Addressing a much wider audience than New Zealand, the United States was eager to publicize its view that nuclear weapons as part of a global allied strategy were not new or surreptitious. When ANZUS was formed, a global strategy that included nuclear weapons was already being pursued. Washington was even more determined to expose what it regarded as the folly of an ally's pick-and-choose approach to alliancemanship, especially in its nuclear aspects. Alliancemanship implies responsibilities as well as benefits. Thus America's ANZUS partners (as well as allies elsewhere) should sustain rather than undermine the American strategic mission. The United States stressed that the ANZUS treaty obligated all members, singly and collectively, to contribute actively to regional security. Through an assortment of weapons systems and munitions, the United States is the preeminent Western deterrent source. If nuclear blackmail or war could be averted, America's allies (as much as anyone else) would be the beneficiaries, even though the multiple costs and risks of upholding international security are far more burdensome for the United States than for its alliance partners. The United States rejected New Zealand's argument that nuclear disengagement brought safety, responding that in today's troubled world a direct and literal view of "national threat" as a yardstick for measuring security was blinkered and wrongheaded.

Emphatically the United States underscored that global security is essentially indivisible, and collaterally so is the ability of American forces to operate freely and effectively. It is impractical and operationally unsound de facto to announce to antagonists which ships are nuclearly armed and which are not or to divide the navy artificially into nuclear and non-nuclear elements or to load and offload weapons from ships to accommodate the idiosyncratic sensibilities of host governments. American reasoning reversed the New Zealand argument. Since few American ships visited New Zealand, why was Wellington so exercised? The United States conceded that ship visits to New Zealand were not strategically vital but stressed that the *principle* of access was inherently important.

The United States agrees that New Zealand is not an exposed, frontline state, but the strategic lines of communication do not bypass it. Moreover, while the South and Southwest Pacific is not an area of head-on, Soviet-American military competition, this is in part because of reasonable solidarity among friends and allies. The pivotal doctrine of strategic denial aimed at the Soviets has over time worked well. Washington has urged that strategic denial continue to be pursued, not to invite developments that could unravel the advantages. If it works, don't fix it.

Because ANZUS had been such a model, cohesive alliance for so long and because New Zealand's action was precedent-setting among American allies, untoward reactions among other U.S. friends and allies could compound already sensitive relationships. The preoccupying American fear has been that doubts would spread about the efficacy of the security system underwritten by the United States and about Washington's competence at alliance management. Doubts could create disincentives for others to shoulder their fair share of responsibilities and raise incentives to follow New Zealand down an antinuclear path. Those who would wish the United States ill would exploit the disarray and reap a generous harvest.

New Zealand insists that it has made a choice based on its own circumstances. It avers that other countries face different circumstances and will need to decide their nuclear policies accordingly. Nevertheless, the United States fears a widespread contamination of the "Kiwi disease"—i.e., other countries could welcome or emulate New Zealand's action even though the latter adheres to its promise that its position is not for deliberate export. Moreover, American critics feel that on various occasions New Zealand has not abided by its pledge and that it would not at all mind if others followed its lead. Lest others failed to notice its resolve, the United States concluded that it had to express its displeasure with New Zealand vigorously and concretely.

Before the recently successful Soviet-American arms control negotiations, Washington feared that the European peace movement, invigorated by New Zealand's example, could hamper political decisions in Belgium and the Netherlands to allow the installation of intermediate range systems. It is also uneasy over the Canadian New Democratic Party's promise to abandon NATO and to disengage from established forms of military cooperation, including NPV and nuclear-armed ship calls. Japan has long cultivated a deliberately ambiguous approach toward American ship visits. Antinuclear sentiment there is gaining force, and various localities have indicated their opposition to hosting a nuclear-related American naval presence. Such feelings could compound Tokyo's political problems and endanger access to Japanese ports by U.S. vessels, whose armament is currently not questioned. In seemingly extraneous context, the U.S. Navy's ships have on several occasions been excluded from friendly ports because they were unable to certify conclusively that crews were free from the AIDS virus. The United States is anxious that various nations, masking a wish to slow or halt potentially nuclear-armed American ship visits, will be tempted to ban U.S. ships under the guise of avoiding health risks.

Lest U.S. apprehensions be discounted as too speculative, American officials point to existing problems and embarrassments. We shall consider two of these. First, within the United States when the Navy wished to establish a fleet base on Staten Island after the U.S.–New Zealand argument had surfaced, the request elicited a strong antinuclear protest campaign. A lawsuit ensued, and the courts held that local communities could not overturn the defense prerogatives of the national executive by such means as public referenda. It is instructive that the campaigns of both supporters and opponents of the Navy's proposal included references to New Zealand and to the merits or demerits of its case.

Second, a U.S. Navy visit to China scheduled for early 1985 was postponed. While the episode was rather confused, the Chinese seemed to be endorsing the recently established New Zealand position and apparently thought that the United States might waive its NC/ND policy. Washington was very upset that its contretemps with New Zealand had somehow played into China's hands as China at the time appeared to be distancing itself from the United States and courting opinion in the South Pacific island community, where antinuclear sentiment was widespread. The United States could not afford to leave an impression that it was in complicity with China and was prepared selectively to dilute its otherwise inflexible position. Not until late 1986 did the United States undertake another ship visit to China, apparently without a breach of U.S. policy.

The Association of South East Asian Nations generally favors a continuing American security presence in the Western Pacific; its members were disturbed that New Zealand's nuclear outlook could affect Japan and ultimately reshape the regional balance. America's foreseeably most acute security problem in Southeast Asia is the future of its Philippine bases. The fall of President Ferdinand Marcos in 1986 released a new political climate as well as a new political order. The

Filipinos have become more politicized and nationalistically outspoken. Antinuclear sentiment has surfaced. The Philippines faces no direct outside military threat. There is noticeable feeling—with considerably more justification than in New Zealand—that in the event of Soviet-American conflict the bases would be a magnet for attack and are thus a serious threat. There is some question whether American nuclear weapons are permanently stored at the Philippine bases or are housed on Guam and can be transferred as needed to standby Philippine facilities. But many Philippine political elites wish to go beyond a ban on nuclear warhead storage. They would happily follow New Zealand's lead in demanding American confirmation that even visiting vessels and aircraft are nuclearly disarmed. The present Philippine base agreement lapses in 1991. A renegotiation of American base rights is constitutionally subject to two-thirds approval of the Philippine Senate and possibly to a public referendum. The Philippine constitution already declares that the nation pursues a policy of freedom from nuclear weapons. Washington worries that the Philippines might wish to strike an especially hard bargain for base renewal, much stiffer than the already generous American financial concessions agreed to in 1988. If continued American use of the bases becomes untenable—perhaps because of Philippine insistence that a New Zealand-styled antinuclear formula on ship and aircraft visits be honored—the United States would need to reconsider relocating its existing base structure.

A decision on base relocations would be traumatic, requiring a fallback to Micronesian sites. It would be colossally expensive to effect the transfer, and bases in Micronesia would be more expensive to maintain than are those in the Philippines. More important, strategically it would be a second-best solution to the security requirements of the United States and its regional friends and allies. It would deprive the United States of forward-basing advantages in the Western Pacific, where the Soviet naval and air buildup at Vietnamese bases has in recent years become increasingly troubling to American planners. Micronesian basing could not replicate the operational and logistical benefits now available in the Philippines. Moreover, should the United States feel compelled to organize alternative basing in Micronesia, it could encounter indigenous obstacles. Such obstacles could in turn relate to political developments in the greater South Pacific–Oceania region and indeed to the radiating influence of New Zealand's nuclear decision.

The South Pacific has been viewed as an ANZUS lake, composed of small and frail entities. Indigenous leadership has tended to be conservative (even traditional), sentimentally and economically tied to the West, and especially to Australia and New Zealand. However, the original postcolonial leadership is passing into new hands. As a wider sense of community has evolved, regional countries have become more alarmed about being caught up in great power rivalries. They feel especially antagonistic toward the French. France has persisted in its nuclear testing program in French Polynesia, offending the region's deeply seated antinuclear disposition. In addition, despite the recent fashioning of a political formula that is acceptable to much nationalist opinion in New Caledonia, the legacy of colonialism in the territory has left suspicious feeling toward France in a region whose experience with decolonization from Anglophone nations was uncommonly smooth. Because the United States has not been perceived as sympathetic to island country feelings directed at France, it has suffered political damage in the region.

American strategic interests in the South Pacific revolve more around keeping the Soviets at a distance and preserving a friendly environment than on directly enlisting security cooperation from countries in the region. However, the de facto disintegration of ANZUS has been disturbing to the island countries. They found old and reliable friends in deep disagreement—not only the United States and New Zealand, but also Australia and New Zealand. Most disagreed with New Zealand's step, but antinuclear feeling in the islands was invigorated by New Zealand's action and there was visible sympathy for how tiny New Zealand was standing up to a superpower with whose global strategic imperatives they did not empathize.

There has not been a consistent island country policy on NPVs or potentially nuclearly armed vessels. When a left-of-center government was elected in Fiji in 1987, its spokesmen foreshadowed a nuclear-free policy that referred to the New Zealand model. Fiji's ethnic animosities prompted a military coup against the government, whereupon the deposed prime minister complained that a security-obsessed America was very likely implicated in destabilizing his government—i.e., the coup was a more extreme variation of what the United States had done to punish New Zealand for its apostasy. Earlier, apprehension had been voiced in the South Pacific that the American military strike against a troublesome regime in Grenada indicated that no small nations were immune from *force majeure* U.S. intervention.

Vanuatu—the former New Hebrides, where France and Britain had held a condominium—has been the most politically strident of the island nations and the only one to join the nonaligned movement. It has thrown a blanket ban on great power naval visits, has been cited for its friendship with Cuba and dalliance with Libya, and has been a vocal supporter of the indigenous Kanak independence movement in neighboring New Caledonia. Following Kiribati's one-year fishing rights arrangement with the Soviet Union, Vanuatu struck a deal allowing the Soviets fishing rights within its exclusive economic zone (EEZ), as well as fishing fleet porting and other privileges that the Kiribati agreement had lacked.

Vanuatu's behavior has not been entirely congenial to most other regional states, and it has been unsettling to Australia and New Zealand, as well as to the United States. Nonetheless, in key respects Vanuatu has struck a responsive chord among island community members by championing issues on which the United States has been virtually singled out as obdurate and unsympathetic. Now other regional countries are giving serious consideration to fishing arrangements with the Soviet Union. Washington has denounced such steps most explicitly, characterizing them as footholds that could become Soviet strategic bonuses. However, it was the predatory activity of American tuna boats in island country EEZs and the reluctance of the U.S. government to intervene that made arrangements with the Soviets seem attractive. Alarmed by the Kiribati agreement, pressed by Australia and New Zealand to do something constructive, the United States in late 1986 agreed to restrict American tuna catches and to compensate island countries inordinately dependent on tuna revenues. In the meantime, America's reputation in the region had suffered a serious setback, as had the credibility of its admonitions about Soviet intrusiveness.

As noted, America's standing in the region has also been harmed by Washington's approach to French-related issues. On one issue which unites island opinion—the continuing French presence in New Caledonia—the region perceives that the United States has been reluctant to take a forthright anticolonial position. Even more derogatory to America's regional reputation has been the handling of France's nuclear testing. This issue has brought into sharp relief a range of American security interests, the New Zealand factor, and dilemmas of policy choice. In 1983 the Australian Labor Party government proposed a nuclear-free zone (NFZ) scheme for the South and Southwest Pacific. The eventual product was a regional treaty binding island countries, Australia, and New Zealand to renounce the manufacture, acquisition, testing, or storage by any party of nuclear weapons on its territory or in the area and the dumping of nuclear waste materials in the environment. The Australian initiative was carefully crafted to leave the question of visits by NPVs or nuclear-armed vessels to the discretion of individual signatories. (While New Zealand was committed to barring such visits, in deference to its American alliance Australia was not.)

All nuclear powers were invited to adhere to the NFZ treaty's protocols—in essence to pledge their adherence to its terms. Although accession to the protocols would not impair the right of American passage in international waters and airspace or prohibit entry into willing countries, Washington refused to adhere to the treaty on the grounds that American benediction could be misperceived as endorsement of NFZs elsewhere or could tempt critical American friends and allies unilaterally to tinker with their existing nuclear policies. The Reagan administration averred that NFZs would not erase the dangers of nuclear war and that only a stable and interlocked deterrence structure would. As in the case of New Zealand and ANZUS, the United States felt that acceptance of the NFZ protocols could lead to a problem of contagion. In consequence, it felt that it should act promptly to show its displeasure; in the interest of consistency it needed to foster deterrence structure strategies across the board.

The newly emerging entities in Micronesia have been construed as one area of potential contagion. The Micronesian territories lie north of the equator and are thereby technically outside the South Pacific zone, although the Republic of the Marshall Islands and the Federated States of Micronesia have sought and been granted membership in the SPF. Balau (Palau) could follow. Parts of the former American Trust Territory of the Pacific Islands are undergoing a change of status under special terms. In exchange for "freely associated" sovereignty and very generous continuing American economic support, their defense effectively remains an American prerogative. The United States maintains key defense-related facilities (such as the unarmed missile testing range at Kwajalein) which hypothetically would serve as the fallback location should the Philippine bases need to be evacuated. If any of the nominally sovereign Micronesian entities were tempted to adhere to the South Pacific NFZ, American strategic interests would be impaired. Even if no formal steps were taken by Micronesian governments toward some form of denuclearization, restive, antinuclear, land-conscious public opinion could seriously complicate efforts of the American military to operate there. Such public opinion has already been manifested, with favorable reference to New Zealand's example. It has provided another rationale for the American policy of steadfastness against the deviant ally New Zealand and the South Pacific NFZ protocols.

The reception of the NFZ protocols by nuclear powers has not been uniform. Following the American example, the British demurred. China adhered. So did the Soviet Union. Despite the gratuitous reservations it attached to adhesion (which it later rescinded), the Soviet Union nevertheless emerged as the reasonable, regionally sensitive superpower, while the United States carried the onus of being rigid, mesmerized by global geopolitical imperatives that South Pacific islanders could neither grasp nor empathize with, and unmoved by regional sensibilities or strong advice from a stalwart ally, Australia.

While sensitive to nuclear weapons and strategies generally, the South Pacific island countries rivet in particular on France and its testing program in the neighborhood. Feelings against France were exacerbated in 1985, when French agents in Auckland harbor blew up the Greenpeace vessel *Rainbow Warrior*, which was to steam on a voyage of protest toward France's testing site. France has thumbed its nose at the South Pacific NFZ protocols. The United States could have acceded to the protocols without being obligated to pressure France to abandon its testing in the region. But the United States values its French connection, especially in Europe, and the French nuclear capability that goes with it. Washington's decision not to embrace the protocols was on balance only marginally predicated on its wish to avoid a slight to France, although U.S. administration spokesmen nevertheless asserted such a wish as a governing American rationale: since French nuclear testing helps to deter a nuclearly capable Soviet Union, the United States cannot appear to condemn it. The ripples in the South Pacific, Australia, and New Zealand were predictable, ranging from sadness to incredulity to condemnation of the American position.

FUTURE U.S. DEALINGS WITH NEW ZEALAND AND AUSTRALIA

Given New Zealand's antinuclear stand and the debilitation of ANZUS as a tripartite alliance, we shall now consider the constraints and opportunities facing the United States in the handling of its New Zealand and Australian relationships.

It is arguable that New Zealand's position is neither surprising nor reversible. New Zealanders constitute a small, compact, and geographically isolated society. They do not feel themselves to be at or near the

center of great and combustible events. Unlike the Australians in World
War II, they did not experience imminent threat and did not regard the
United States as their redeemer. After the war their enthusiasm for forg-
ing links with the United States and supporting it diplomatically and
militarily was consistently less marked than Australia's. New Zealand is
characterized by a sense of openness, social achievement, public civility,
and attention to humanistic and life quality concerns. Relative to
Australia, it does not convey a spirit of bustle and imposing visions. In
recent years it has been undergoing economic renovation and a breeze
of nationalist feeling but in the context of protecting and improving on
what it uniquely is.

Hence while one might think of New Zealand's aversion to nuclear
associations as arising from an insular mentality, many New Zealanders
prefer to see it as a natural outgrowth of who they are and what they
wish to be—i.e., a people arranging a progressive and qualitatively special society where nuclear weapons disconcert rather than fit, a Western
and internationally active nation prepared to make contributions on
terms other than those set by much more powerful and in some respects
overbearing nations. The voluble David Lange has tapped this sentiment.
New Zealand opinion has continued to support the principle of alliance
links with the United States, but it has also remained unmistakably antinuclear. Technically Lange has been able to claim that de facto it was
the United States who determined that these two choices could not
coexist in the ANZUS framework.

The National Party opposition in New Zealand has been sharply
critical of Labour's behavior. However, in the 1987 electoral campaign it
too was impelled to acknowledge the country's temper. While it pledged
to rescind the offending provisions of the antinuclear legislation, it
would delay the admission of NPVs pending further examination of
nuclear reactor safety standards. It confirmed that New Zealand neither
wanted nor needed nuclear weapons carried by visiting ships. It would
trust the United States to respect this position without facing a test of the
NC/ND rule. Only through such respect could a proper and smooth
defense relationship with America be restored, and with it the integrity
of the ANZUS alliance.

For Washington, the National Party's position does not seem an
attractive alternative to Labour's. It approximates the ambiguous
Japanese approach (noted above) but moves beyond. Equivocation
would be politically untenable in New Zealand. Especially in the
aftermath of its argument with the Labour government, the United

States could not publicly endorse or be expected to abide by New Zealand's "trust" that no nuclear weapons would be found aboard entering vessels. This was a sticking point in Washington's dealings with the Labour government. Secretary of State George Shultz told Lange that if American visits were to be resumed, sooner or later nuclear-armed vessels would be included. Since New Zealand's nuclear policies even under the National Party would remain unsatisfactory to the United States, a restoration of normal defense relations could not be expected.

There is little reason to believe that the bilateral problem will be resolved under a Labour government. Within his party Lange is a moderate on foreign and defense policy issues. His government's striking, market-driven economic reforms, resented by influential elements on Labour's left, virtually nullify prospects that any "capitulation" on the nuclear issue could be carried off by the prime minister. It is also well to bear in mind that much of the U.S.-Labour dialogue over the nuclear/ANZUS issue has been conducted in an unpleasant atmosphere since 1985. Early that year the United States had proposed a visit by the U.S.S. *Buchanan*, an old, conventionally powered destroyer with an antisubmarine nuclear weapon capability. The United States thought that an informal deal had been struck to allow the *Buchanan* to visit. New Zealand refused to accept it, claiming it could not unreservedly determine that the ship was nuclearly disarmed. After this incident, suspicion, mistrust, accusation, and even personal invective between the United States and New Zealand found a breeding ground. The tensions and ill will are unlikely to be dissipated soon, and therefore the climate for rapprochement is unsuitable.

Efforts by an American administration to needle New Zealand or to go beyond the present level of riposte—for instance, through overt commercial discrimination—would almost surely prove self-defeating. Such efforts would be resented by New Zealanders at large and would further diminish any prospect of accommodation. They could also serve to strengthen elements in and outside the Labour Party that wish to march beyond present policy—for instance, to renounce ANZUS altogether and/or to fit the country into something akin to nonalignment. These elements are already upset that Lange has been too lenient or orthodox in his approach to a defense policy that continues to sustain Western—indeed American—regional security interests. Moreover, it is plain that a further American war of verbal or material attrition against New Zealand would adversely affect U.S. security interests elsewhere, further tarnishing America's reputation and fueling antinuclear and anti-American sentiment. It would be highly ironic if to bring New Zealand back to ANZUS or to demonstrate its resolve to others, the United States pushed New Zealand farther away and antagonized other friends and allies. Legislation was adopted by the House of Representatives to censure New Zealand but had failed to pass Congress when the Senate adjourned prior to the 1988 elections. While its effect would have mostly been hortatory, confirming New Zealand's removal as a privileged American ally, a subsequent U.S. administration could have found its hands more tightly bound while seeking to find a way out of the current impasse.

In Australia there is a vocal and not negligible body of opinion that decries the consequences of the American alliance, citing the incontestable fact that Australia has become more absorbed into American security planning and strategies (including the nuclear features) than New Zealand ever had, yet that Australia is closer to Asian impact points than New Zealand. The risks of unwanted and avoidable entanglement and of being targeted by the Soviets are deemed patently unwarranted. Moreover, while the United States is often portrayed as alarmist, clumsy, and diplomatically accident-prone—for instance, in its approach to South Pacific issues—the Soviets are not construed as directly threatening to Australia (or for that matter others). If Australia faces potential conflict, it would likely arise out of differences with Indonesia. Thus the vaunted American security guarantee under ANZUS is not needed against the Soviets. Indeed ANZUS does not explicitly obligate U.S. support for Australia. The Americans could well elect to remain neutral, or side with an Indonesia at odds with Australia if Washington's cost-benefit calculations so dictate.

The Australian government has addressed such criticisms. It considers that the defense cooperation, planning, and regional security advantages of the ANZUS alliance well outweigh incurred or apprehended costs. Nevertheless, out of both political realism and conviction the Hawke government has not been sanguine about its American connections. It must outmaneuver or conciliate those who press for a more autonomous and allegedly risk-reduced Australian foreign and defense policy. While the Labor Party has its own share of such objectors, the Australian Democrats, who control the balance of power in the federal Senate, would renounce ANZUS in its present form.

Labor's approach to following both its programmatic and its political instincts has varied. At times it has taken a pronounced pro-alliance stance. Hawke, who personally is a considerable asset to his party, has bluntly declared that he would resign as prime minister rather than lead a government committed to shutting down American defense facilities in Australia. His government not only opposed New Zealand's nuclear stand, but also encouraged a forthright American demonstration that allies could not casually sift and sort their contributions and still expect alliance benefits. In effect Canberra agreed with the United States that unless Washington responded vigorously and Australia backed it up, the Kiwi disease would more easily leap the Tasman Sea and infect Australia itself.

The Hawke government has taken a number of initiatives designed not only to advance Australian interests, but also to neutralize critical domestic opinion. While distinguishable from American policies or preferences, these initiatives fall well short of courting estrangement with the United States. Many of them concern international arms control deliberations. Some entail Labor's wish to demystify ANZUS—to present it as a highly desirable relationship, but only one of Australia's bonds and not a sheet anchor of the nation's security. As we noted above, some initiatives entail a more consciously systematic emphasis on the defense of Australia and its approaches rather than major, forward-deployed operations with a great ally. In part this has meant a more sustained attention to Australia's strategic environment, such as the South Pacific, of which the regional NFZ scheme has been a prime example.

In recent years the United States has for the most part been sensitive in its dealings with Australia and mindful of the political difficulties with which Hawke needs to contend. Earlier American tendencies to take the ANZUS alliance somewhat for granted, to be less than scrupulous about advising and consulting with partners on U.S. intentions, have been corrected. Benign neglect has been rectified with the shock of New Zealand's wayward policies and fresh appreciation of Australia's strategic value. The United States also knows that outright abuse of New Zealand would be very badly received in Australia, carrying severe political costs for America's standing and that of the alliance.

There are two main areas in which the United States has not been able or willing to allay Australian fears and criticisms, however. First, it has not been able to avoid substantial, cross-party criticisms in Australia that U.S. agricultural subsidy policies, mainly designed to offset protectionist European practices, have been highly injurious to Australia's ability to market its commodities overseas at a fair price. It has been remarked—to invert a reference to New Zealand—that the United States is treating Australia as an ally but not a friend. The American administration has tried to contain protectionist sentiment, and the secretaries of state and defense have warned that U.S. interests would suffer if Australia were victimized in this manner. Nevertheless, the political exigencies of protectionism, centered in Congress, have tended to prevail, and many Australians have blamed the United States at large. To Washington's relief, the Australian government has not proposed the American satellite tracking and transmission facilities or other basic alliance features as bargaining chips in exchange for more satisfactory American commercial policies.

Second, while a complex, institutionally divided American political system can seldom assure economic relief even for close allies, foreign and defense policies can be more responsive to their circumstances. The United States has slipped in promoting its Australian reputation, and that of the alliance, in some of its actions outside the perimeter of ANZUS membership. On globally substantive issues the foremost drawback has been the U.S. image as a reluctant arms control negotiator. This has made it more awkward for the Australian government to defend against criticisms of the joint satellite tracking and transmission facilities, to which critics have ascribed capabilities such as battle management. American refusal to adhere to the South Pacific NFZ protocols and attendant expressions of sympathy for France's nuclear testing program have further disturbed Australia. As we have noted, the NFZ treaty was an Australian initiative, carefully fashioned to avoid prejudice to U.S. strategic interests, and the Hawke government poured considerable political capital into it. Australia not only failed to persuade the United States to sign the protocols, but also found that much moderate domestic opinion was distressed by what appeared to be a singularly misguided American judgment, counterproductive to Western interests generally.

The United States obviously cannot be expected to accept Australian advice simply because a solid ally deserves to be cultivated. But it can give greater weight to such advice when the stakes are especially high (and include a favorable Australian, as well as regional, reception) and an American-serving rationale is adduced.

Sometimes support from Australian sources can be deceptive, as was the case in the campaign leading up to the July 1987 elections in Australia. The Liberal and National Party opposition, long the standard-bearer of the American alliance, promised to exert economic pressure on New Zealand to force it back into ANZUS and to negotiate a new bilateral treaty with the United States if ANZUS could not be reestablished on a viable tripartite basis. Such economic pressures would not work, however. They would stiffen the New Zealanders against a nation they feel has historically patronized them and would diminish Australia's—and the West's—capacity for influence through much of the region.

Efforts at negotiating a new, exclusively U.S.-Australian security treaty are neither necessary nor desirable. The ANZUS status quo is clumsy but manageable, in large measure because (as noted) much of what traditionally passed as ANZUS cooperation hinged on bilateral arrangements. The United States can therefore maintain a full working relationship with Australia while ostracizing New Zealand. Australia and New Zealand can independently carry out and even enhance their defense cooperation, whether or not they choose to regard this as falling under an ANZUS rubric. If New Zealand were completely bypassed as the result of a newly drawn U.S.-Australian pact, its Labour Party leadership would likely be even less interested in sustaining a reasonable defense effort or in respecting its self-imposed pledge not to proselytize on behalf of its antinuclear policies. The terms and obligations of a new alliance would be especially difficult to negotiate. The U.S. Senate would probably be reluctant to ratify a treaty with provisions at least as strong as those adopted for ANZUS in the quite different climate of 1951. Australia would almost surely face a furious, divisive, and far-ranging debate about the alliance and its implications for the country. In any case the United States and its Australian alliance would have suffered.

CONCLUSIONS

Viewed purely in terms of American security interests, which animated a tripartite ANZUS during earlier years, the recent discord within the alliance has had few tangibly negative effects. We have suggested that while the nominal loss of New Zealand has been inconsequential for the United States, the resulting realization of the importance of Australia and the need to nurture and protect it have strengthened the foundations of that relationship. In light of controlling American strategic assumptions and objectives, disquieting reverberations have or could far exceed the problems of an intramural relationship among three alliance partners, and we have thus analyzed a number of these. Inevitably a superpower's span of interests is matched by the complexity of the substantive and stylistic options available to it to deal with developments.

Some inferences can be extracted from our study for alliance management. In general, preventive or proactive approaches to alliance management are sound policy. With the exceptions noted, this is the approach that the United States is now following with Australia. Arguably the United States could have done little to prevent New Zealand's Labour policies from being adopted. Perhaps even a more attractive, less ominously grounded New Zealand public image of the United States would not have sufficed. In theory, the United States could be harshly punitive against those who threaten to or do displease it. However, as our assessment suggests, practicalities and prudence often outweigh theory. A heavy-handed American treatment of Pacific island countries would very likely be seriously counterproductive—not because these nations are strong and able to resist, but for the opposite reason. From another angle, New Zealand's position in the American strategic equation is minor. That of Australia—or for that matter Japan, Germany, Canada, or others—is quite different. One lesson that can be read from what was done to New Zealand is therefore not that there was a suspension of treaty obligations, defense obligations, and defense cooperation, but that the suspension was directed at a nation so clearly *unrepresentative* of American allies who intrinsically matter and who could thus not realistically be treated in like manner. So that the dilemma of either doing nothing or overreacting is kept to a minimum, good alliance management is essential, and its skills are at a premium.

Chapter 8

POLICY IMPLICATIONS: AN ANTIPODEAN PERSPECTIVE

John Ravenhill

Despite its vast geographical expanse, the South Pacific is but a minor part of the global geopolitical jigsaw: to claim that the region is central to U.S. strategic interests would indeed be far-fetched. An illustration of how peripheral the South Pacific is to global politics is that New Zealand's ban on nuclear ships and the U.S. response to the ban failed to gain even a mention in the annual survey articles on U.S. foreign policy published in *Foreign Affairs*, despite the tremendous controversy they generated within the region itself. The United States does have significant strategic interests in the South Pacific, however. Besides the vital intelligence stations in Australia, there are important missile-testing facilities in Micronesia. If political upheavals should force the removal of U.S. bases from the Philippines, islands such as Palau may have much enlarged military roles. In addition, it would be a great advantage to the United States if the policy of strategic denial that has excluded the Soviet Union from playing a significant role in the region could be sustained.

The contributors to this book have highlighted the increasingly rapid rate of political change in the South Pacific. The resulting instability and rise in anti-American sentiment might easily spill over into Micronesia—especially now that the Marshall Islands and the Federated States of Micronesia are members of the South Pacific Forum. In this chapter I shall explore how the United States might best respond to the new instability in the region.

THE DEMISE OF ANZUS

De Gaulle is reputed to have said that alliances "are like pretty girls and flowers: they last as long as they last." Quantitative studies of alliance formation and disintegration have not yielded much beyond this pithy formulation: the findings are diverse and even conflicting. It is clear, however, that the parties' perceptions of the benefits and costs of continued membership are the crucial factor in determining the duration of an alliance. In the ANZUS case, the junior partners have seen a significant shift in the balance of costs and benefits of alliance membership since the early 1970s. For many New Zealanders, the benefits of the U.S. security shield no longer outweigh the costs of membership in a nuclear alliance. Opinion in Australia has not moved as far, but the calculus has changed sufficiently that the benefits of alliance membership are increasingly being questioned.

As a tripartite arrangement, ANZUS—for all intents and purposes—is dead. The anti-nuclear stance of the New Zealand Labour Party is unlikely to be reversed in the foreseeable future. Even if a National Party government were to repeal the New Zealand Nuclear Free Zone Arms Control and Disarmament Act, the uncertainty created by the current Labour government's policies and the prospect that they would be reinstated by a future Labour government have eroded the foundations of New Zealand's participation in the alliance. Rather than a narrowly defined treaty arrangement, ANZUS has always been what the parties have made of it, which has been both its strength and its weakness. Questions of the legality of New Zealand's actions or of the U.S. response to them are now of historical interest only. The key question is what comes next? Fashioning a response will be a significant diplomatic challenge for the new administration of George Bush.

Washington's decision to maintain the ANZUS treaty while suspending its guarantee of New Zealand's security was judicious. Any attempt to negotiate a bilateral treaty with Australia or a wider Pacific defense pact would be fraught with problems, and Congressional approval would be difficult to obtain for either one.

One great advantage of the ANZUS treaty is its vagueness. Any negotiations for a bilateral treaty with Australia would open a number of Pandora's boxes in that country and offer a field day to groups opposed to the alliance. What obligations would the Australian government have to host visits by nuclear vessels or aircraft? Would it be obliged to accept the continued presence of the joint facilities as part of its treaty responsibilities?

Proposals for a wider alliance of Pacific states to embrace not only the South Pacific but also the Association of South East Asian Nations (ASEAN), South Korea, Japan, and possibly China have little appeal.* Any

*One such proposal put forward by Lt. Commander James Stavridis, U.S. Naval Academy, is reproduced in *Pacific Islands Monthly*, September 1987, pp. 34–37.

such treaty would inevitably be viewed as provocative by the Soviet Union, and it would link countries of very diverse backgrounds, ethnic composition, and ideologies, in contrast to the homogeneity and shared democratic values that help to sustain ANZUS. Also, other states in the Pacific region are acutely sensitive to the implications of Japan's potential military might, and U.S. moves to encourage Japanese rearmament have already met with hostility.* Finally, both Australia and New Zealand believe that their security is more likely to be threatened from countries *within* the region than from the Soviet Union.

ANZUS, then, continues to serve a useful purpose by symbolizing the close relations between Australia and the United States, but the thorny problem of New Zealand remains. Washington's uncompromising response to New Zealand's anti-nuclear policy has succeeded in deterring other allies from following the same path, but there is now a need to reach a new *modus vivendi* with Wellington. A question raised by David Lange in a recent article is pertinent here: "Who is shooting whom in the foot?" New Zealand has been a very effective representative of Western interests in the South Pacific, and its contribution to the Western alliance—both historically and at the present time—should be measured not by the strength of New Zealand's armed forces but rather by the intelligence it gathers in the Pacific islands and the financial assistance it provides to them. This contribution has been acknowledged and appreciated both by Canberra and by Washington.†

New Zealand has not dramatically changed its foreign policy alignment. It has taken decisions that have led to its exclusion from the ANZUS pact, but it has not pursued nonalignment or neutrality. Neither of these alternatives would be acceptable to the New Zealand population; only 16 percent of the group polled by the government's Defence Review Committee wanted New Zealand to withdraw from ANZUS. New Zealand remains firmly within the Western camp with no loss of its determination to prevent the Soviet Union from establishing a

---

*Sir Wallace Rowling, New Zealand's former Labour Party leader and recent ambassador to the United States, insisted that such U.S. encouragement was contrary to the spirit of ANZUS.

†Before the election of the Lange government, John C. Dorrance, a State Department specialist on the region and current U.S. consul in Sydney, asserted that "the United States takes the view that Australia's and New Zealand's close relationships and particular interests in the South Pacific—including defence cooperation—suggest that these two countries play the lead role in that area to the extent that island states seek external cooperation" (quoted in Siracusa and Barclay 1984: 157).

strategic presence in the region. As in Australia, New Zealand's commitment to defense self-reliance includes plans to increase expenditures on
defense.

Washington's response to the nuclear ship ban galvanized popular
opinion behind the government's stance, and continued antagonism
toward Wellington and a refusal to enter into any form of defense
cooperation is likely to increase anti-American sentiment in New
Zealand and strengthen those left-wing elements of the Labour Party that
favor a policy of neutrality.* Continued U.S. hostility toward New
Zealand will also be seized upon by those political forces in the island
states that wish to see the policy of strategic denial extended to exclude
the United States from the region.

Withdrawal of the American security guarantee under ANZUS is
sufficient penalty for New Zealand's non-nuclear stance; further measures
and continuing antagonism between Washington and Wellington will be
counter-productive to Western interests in the South Pacific. Reconstruction of cooperation in the defense field is now needed. Albinski points the
way in ch. 7 above: Since ANZUS security guarantees were not institutionalized, their suspension does not preclude New Zealand–U.S.
cooperation in economic relations and other elements of foreign affairs
and defense. Despite the U.S. suspension of defense cooperation, New
Zealand has continued to supply intelligence to the United States and
provide staging facilities for U.S. flights to Antarctica. At the very least, the
United States should reciprocate by reinstating New Zealand's access to
U.S. intelligence and to military training and equipment.†

Washington will have to come to terms in the future with a South
Pacific region that is more nationalistic in outlook than ever before.
Australia and New Zealand as well as the Pacific island states desire to
become self-reliant and establish their own identities in foreign and

---

*At times Washington's policies toward the Lange government have come
dangerously close to interference in New Zealand's internal affairs. In March
1988, for instance, Secretary of Defense Frank Carlucci met with the leader of
the New Zealand's Opposition (Jim Bolger) but refused to meet with New
Zealand's new ambassador to Washington (Sydney Morning Herald, 11 March
1988). Washington apparently decided that the Lange government should be
denied access to top-level decision-makers as part of the punishment for its anti-
nuclear stance. For earlier examples, see McMillan 1987: 22–23.

†In this context the passage by Congress of the "Broomfield Act" (HR85) in
August 1987, which excludes New Zealand from the preference clauses of the
Arms Export Control Act and the Foreign Assistance Act, was not helpful.

defense policies. Neither Australia nor New Zealand believes that ANZUS is significantly relevant to the types of threats they face in the foreseeable future. In this environment there is likely to be much less deference to Washington than in the past. Unlike the United States, Australia and New Zealand do not have the responsibility of playing a global role, and therefore believe they are better placed to assume moral leadership, and on some issues to play the honest broker between the superpowers—as Australia has attempted to do on disarmament. Washington's failure to accommodate the new nationalism of the region will only be counter-productive to U.S. long-term interests.*

Ideally, Washington should seek to increase the benefits of the ANZUS alliance to its partners and decrease the costs; minimally, it should refrain from actions that would decrease the benefits or increase the costs. Many observers believe that some policies of the Reagan administration—in the agricultural sphere, for instance—have had the unfortunate effect of reducing the benefits of the alliance to Australia and New Zealand.

In Australia there has been increasing concern about the use made by Washington of the joint facilities. It is assumed that the facilities will have a major role in the Strategic Defense Initiative if it is implemented. Pressure to remove the facilities from Australian soil may intensify if they are perceived to contribute to the nuclear war-fighting capability of the United States. A more informed attitude toward the facilities is emerging in the Australian public, and distinctions are made between them according to the different roles they play. The leading Australian analyst in this field, Des Ball, has recently proposed that the Defence Support Program ground station at Nurrungar be closed because (a) the data it collects about Soviet missile silos contributes to U.S. war-fighting capability, and (b) there is no need for it to be located in Australia (1987).† In contrast, he and most other analysts believe that the Pine Gap facility should be maintained because it plays a critical role in arms control verification and cannot be located elsewhere.

---

*Perhaps it is too much to expect that right-wing elements in Congress will accept the new realities, but they should be advised of the damage done to America's image and American interests when Australians learn that access to the U.S. market for their most important exports is threatened by congressional proposals to penalize Australia for refusing to cooperate in monitoring MX-missile tests (see *The Australian*, 18–19 April 1987).

†Ball had earlier advocated closure of the North West Cape communications facility because Australia does not have access to the message traffic that passes through it, which (he argues) is incompatible with Australian sovereignty.

Nurrungar is becoming increasingly redundant to the Defence Support Program as new communications technology is introduced, and the United States should give serious consideration to closing it if only to forestall general public pressure for removal of all the facilities, which are seen as the only certain targets in Australia in a nuclear exchange between the superpowers.

In the short term, a more important area of concern in Australia is the U.S. policy of subsidizing its agricultural exports, which is now the principal source of public discontent in Australia with the American relationship. Canberra appreciates the Reagan administration's efforts to stem the protectionist tide in Congress, but it has been angered by the administration's implementation of the Export Enhancement Program in a manner which has adversely affected Australia's agricultural exports to its traditional markets. Promises of consultation and consideration of Australian interests in implementing the program have not been fulfilled.

The Australian government has few weapons except bluster in this dispute. Defense purchases can be delayed, but Australia has no alternative supplier for the advanced weapons it is acquiring, and substantial delays will impede the government's defense force plans. Attempts to use the joint facilities as a bargaining chip are not likely to succeed, but pressure from Australia's agricultural lobby to try to exploit their location on Australian soil will intensify if the trade dispute deteriorates. All alliance relationships need a foundation in favorable public opinion; continuation of the current disregard of Australian interests will cause a further loss of support for the relationship and risk long-term damage.

If Labor/Labour governments remain in office in Canberra and Wellington, there will be continuing disagreements with the United States over the nature of the Soviet threat. For the current governments of Australia and New Zealand, the Soviet presence in the South Pacific is more a political than a military problem. Indeed they perceive that the United States bears as much the responsibility for the escalating arms buildup in the Pacific as the Soviet Union (over which the United States is still seen to enjoy a substantial strategic advantage). To many commentators in Australia and New Zealand, the major opportunities Moscow has exploited in the South Pacific are largely of Washington's own making.*

*Even a staunchly anti-Soviet commentator in the United States has acknowledged that America has conceded the moral high ground in the South Pacific to the Soviet Union, and must "be more sensitive and responsive to the experiences, needs, and desires of the islanders" (Tanham 1988: 94).

Three principal policy shifts are necessary if the United States is to combat growing Soviet influence: (1) greater attention must be paid to the sensitivities of states in the region, (2) stronger pressure must be exerted on France to halt its nuclear testing in the South Pacific and to expedite decolonization of New Caledonia, and (3) more economic assistance must be provided to the islands.

The long overdue signing of an agreement between the United States and the Forum Fisheries Agency should remove the tuna fishing problem from the agenda for at least four years. To ensure that the problem does not recur, an early and generous offer from the United States for access to the EEZs of the Pacific island states will be essential.

Just as one problematic issue was resolved, another emerged: the U.S. refusal to be a party to the South Pacific Nuclear Free Zone Treaty, which has unnecessarily handed the Soviet Union a significant propaganda bonus. The possible adverse effects of the Treaty of Rarotonga on U.S. interests are minimal. The prohibition of nuclear weapons storage within the region might conceivably prevent the United States from opening a base in Australia should future access to the Philippines be denied, but it is doubtful that such a base would be acceptable to Australian public opinion.* Washington may be concerned that its signing of the South Pacific Nuclear Free Zone Treaty would encourage the establishment of other such zones in regions which are more central to its strategic interests, but that did not prevent its signing of the Treaty of Tlatelolco in 1971, making Latin America a nuclear-free region. The newly installed Bush administration should take note of the Congressional resolution urging reconsideration of the U.S. decision not to sign the protocols to the Treaty of Rarotonga.

Pacific sensitivities are particularly acute over the current French role in the region. France's decision to continue to test nuclear weapons at Mururoa displays a colonial arrogance that is deeply resented. U.S. refusal to sign the South Pacific Nuclear Free Zone Treaty was perceived as implicit support for the French tests—a perception confirmed at the June 1987 ASEAN conference when Secretary of State Shultz reportedly endorsed the French testing (*Australian Financial Review*, 22 June 1987). On this issue the United States has placed loyalty to its European ally above that to the Pacific states. Washington's support for France's modernization of its *force de frappe* need not be at the expense of its relations with

---

*In a radio interview on 7 June 1988, Australia's former Foreign Minister Hayden stated bluntly that Australia was unsuitable as an alternative location for sites in the Philippines.

the Pacific, however. The United States can continue its support for France's nuclear program and at the same time attempt to convince the French to test elsewhere. Its reported offer to host French underground tests in Nevada should be publicly announced, and if the French decline it (as they almost certainly will), Washington can remind them of the damage their testing is doing to Western interests in the Pacific. This may not bring about a change of heart in Paris, but it will clearly dissociate the United States from the French position. Washington should not let concern over French reaction deter it from signing the Treaty of Rarotonga.

Washington's economic assistance to the Pacific islands is extremely modest; in fiscal 1987 U.S. official aid to the region totalled only $9 million. For Canberra and Wellington the costs of financing the policy of strategic denial are becoming unsustainable—especially now that the Pacific islands have the opportunity to play the Soviet card. A former U.S. ambassador to Papua New Guinea and the Solomon Islands recently observed:

> Many islanders believe the United States has taken more from them than it has given. They feel it has harvested regional fisheries, benefited from anchorages for its naval vessels, and enjoyed Pacific island nations' support in international bodies without contributing significantly to the area's economic development. Many are also bothered that the world's most technologically advanced nation does so little to help those who so closely share its political, economic, and religious values (Gardner 1988: 26).

He suggests that a $10 million boost to the U.S. aid program would go a long way toward improving America's image in the region.

In the economic realm, Japan could usefully take the lead in promoting "Western" interests. Over the last decade Japan's assistance to the South Pacific islands has grown fivefold to over $25 million annually, but this is only one percent of its total overseas aid. Japan already provides significantly more assistance to the region than the United States does. To date it has shown a marked preference for bilateral diplomacy rather than working through regional institutions such as the South Pacific Forum (Herr 1986: 176), and it is the second largest bilateral donor to Fiji, Kiribati, and Papua New Guinea (OECD 1987). The Japanese lack the expertise and knowledge of the region possessed by Australians and New Zealanders, and there is some resentment at their lack of empathy with local cultures. (Somewhat ironically, Japan has expressed concern at the growth of anti-nuclear sentiment in the region.)

In the future Japanese financial assistance coupled with Australian and New Zealand expertise in regional programs may be the most effective means of sustaining strategic denial.*

CONCLUSION

In an era of budgetary restraint when the United States is contemplating a reduction of its global commitments, the South Pacific will not be high on Washington's foreign policy agenda. The loss of one of the island states to the Soviet Union would not be a vital blow to U.S. security interests, but there are obvious benefits to the United States in maintaining political stability in the region and its general pro-Western orientation.

As long as the Soviet Union is intent on establishing a global presence to substantiate its claim to superpower status, it is unrealistic and probably counter-productive to attempt to exclude it completely from the South Pacific. The best hope of containing Soviet influence is to minimize the opportunities for them to exploit. The fact that the major openings exploited by Moscow to date have resulted from U.S. blunders is a sad reflection on Washington's policies. Greater awareness of regional sensitivities and a (very) modest financial investment offer the greatest potential for preserving Western interests in the region.

REFERENCES

Ball, Des. 1987. *A Base for Debate*. Sydney: Allen & Unwin Australia.

Gardner, Paul F. 1988. "Tuna Poaching and Nuclear Testing in the South Pacific." *Orbis* 32, 2 (Spring).

Herr, R. A. 1986. "Regionalism, Strategic Denial and South Pacific Security." *Journal of Pacific History* 21, 4.

McMillan, Stuart. 1987. *Neither Confirm Nor Deny*. Sydney: Allen & Unwin.

*In August 1987 Japan reportedly rebuffed a French proposal that Japanese finance be coupled with French expertise in the South Pacific (*Sydney Morning Herald*, 8 August 1987).

OECD [Organization for Economic Cooperation and Development]. 1987. *Geographical Distribution of Financial Flows to Developing Countries.* Paris.

Siracusa, Joseph M., and Barclay, Glen St. J. 1984. "The Historical Influence of the United States on Australian Strategic Thinking." *Australian Outlook* 38, 3 (December).

Tanham, George K. 1988. "Subverting the South Pacific." *The National Interest,* Spring.

INSTITUTE OF INTERNATIONAL STUDIES
UNIVERSITY OF CALIFORNIA, BERKELEY

215 Moses Hall   Berkeley, California 94720

CARL G. ROSBERG, Director

Monographs published by the Institute include:

RESEARCH SERIES

POLICY PAPERS IN INTERNATIONAL AFFAIRS